DATE DUE		
OCT 1 2 1994		
2/24/09		

DEMCO

The Space Between

The Space Between
Literary Epiphany
in the Work of Annie Dillard

Sandra Humble Johnson

THE KENT STATE UNIVERSITY PRESS
Kent, Ohio, and London, England

©1992 by The Kent State University Press, Kent, Ohio 44242

All rights reserved

Library of Congress Catalog Card Number 91-11437

ISBN 0-87338-446-6

Manufactured in the United States of America

Library of Congress Cataloging-in-Publication Data

Johnson, Sandra Humble, 1943–

The space between : literary epiphany in the work of Annie Dillard / Sandra Humble Johnson.

p. cm.

Includes bibliographical references and index.

ISBN 0-87338-446-6 (alk. paper) ∞

1. Dillard, Annie—Criticism and interpretation. 2. Epiphanies in literature. I. Title.

PS3554.I398Z72 1992

818'.5409—dc20   91-11437

British Library Cataloging-in-Publication data are available.

For Dan and Brooke

Contents

Preface

Long before I came to the writing of Annie Dillard, I was fascinated by a moment in language I had perceived as glowing. Wordsworth had talked about it and called it a "spot of time"; but what intrigued me most was his achievement of that moment when he provided no explanation for its power. So when I first read *Pilgrim at Tinker Creek,* a work suggested as part of a wilderness study, I was astounded by its condensed, gemlike language that not only considered the phenomenon of illumination as a central theme, but offered up these fiery moments page after page with poetic power and biting energy. Dillard's writing seemed at once ancient and contemporary. With its metaphysical elasticity and glittering words, it echoed the poetry of Gerard Manley Hopkins. *Pilgrim,* I realized then, is not a "wilderness" study or an environmental casebook, unless it is the wilderness of the spirit, which in one sense is its subject. And the redeeming force throughout is Dillard's epiphanic moment.

I later discovered that all of Annie Dillard's writing was a perusal of illumination and, thus, I set out to discover the dynamic of this language phenomenon. But I wanted to understand its meaning as something more than the bloodless operations of a literary device; I wanted to verify what I had sensed as the intuitive patterns of epiphanists as they poured their most personal spiritual events into words—Wordsworth's childhood "spot" refracting the image of a woman with wind-whipped garments, Hopkins's "inscape" reflected from the wing of a falcon, T. S. Eliot's agonized "still point" whispered in a deserted English garden, and Dillard's ecstatic "dot" of self reacting to a cedar tree filled with doves. Most of all, I wanted to discover why these moments became my moments; why I felt a mysterious ownership of certain words, particular passages.

This book is the culmination of that search; it reveals that the organic energy of literary epiphany springs as much from the absence of language as from its presence. Along the way I have corroborated my initial reactions to epiphany by uncovering the study of others, whom I have come to regard as my "epiphanic family," although they are no doubt unaware of our relationship. Robert Langbaum, Morris Beja, Ashton Nichols, and Martin Bidney have all thought long on the subject, evidenced by their scholarly and what seems to me joyous appraisal of a particularly rarified topic. I now offer back to them, and to all readers who have come to value the magnificent prose-poetry of Annie Dillard, my own findings on the dynamics of language when it approaches the glowing event known as literary epiphany.

I want to thank those teachers, colleagues, and friends at Bowling Green State University who first read my manuscript and encouraged me in the completion of this project. Dr. Ralph Wolfe's enthusiastic intelligence and spirited knowledge of Wordsworth has sustained me since the beginning. Dr. James Harner graciously offered to continue his careful reading and commenting on the manuscript, even after a move to Texas A&M University. Both Dr. Howard McCord and Dr. Ruth Schneider participated in the joy of the subject matter. In addition, I want to acknowledge the assistance of the Department of English, particularly Dr. Alice Philbin, who provided me with two doctoral fellowships in 1988 and 1989 so that I could continue to write.

Several other occasions and persons have helped my progress toward this publication. First, Dr. August Nigro and the National Endowment for the Humanities allowed me to increase my knowledge of the literary epiphany in an especially significant setting when I received a grant for study at Manchester College, Oxford, England, in the summer of 1988. Also, Barbara Korn at Wittenberg University gave me invaluable assistance with the mechanical aspects of the manuscript.

I am extremely grateful to the editors at Kent State University Press for their sensitive and intelligent handling of this work: John Hubbell, Julia Morton, and Linda Cuckovich have been consistently encouraging.

To my parents, Dorothy and Tracy Humble, I owe the foundation on which the concept of epiphany rests: their dreams, energy, and unconditional love have been the models for my life.

My daughter Brooke has helped me in that she continued to be an understanding child in the midst of piles of books, legions of notes, and long writing hours. Finally, Dan my friend and husband, gave me the emotional luxury of writing in an environment where I received only support and love. Without him I could not have written this book.

1

The Same Old Vision

The Appearance of Epiphany

Annie Dillard, in the concluding pages of *An American Childhood,* writes:

> What is important is anyone's coming awake and discovering a
> place, finding in full orbit a spinning globe one can lean over,
> catch, and jump on. What is important is the moment of opening
> a life and feeling it touch—with an electric hiss and cry—this
> speckled mineral sphere, our present world. (248–49)

The moment of "coming awake," which is the central concern of *An
American Childhood,* has been Dillard's literary preoccupation since the
publication in 1974 of her Pulitzer Prize–winning *Pilgrim at Tinker
Creek.* Admitting that she presents essentially the same message in all of
her work, Dillard said in a 1981 interview that "given half a chance, the
same old palaver comes inching out—molecule by molecule. It is visionary in content, if not in quality. It is the same old vision that I keep writing about over and over again" ("Drawing the Curtains" 35). This vision,
a moment which sizzles with an "electric hiss and cry," is not only the
philosophical tenet, the raison d'être which supports her work, but also
the literary device with which she steadies and centers the massive range
of material she scrutinizes. "Virtually all of Dillard's narrative," according to James Aton, "concerns itself with epistemology: how to see the
world and the implications of that vision at a particular moment in
time" (80). Language theory, ecology, art, literary criticism, religion, and
history, among other matters, are brilliantly woven into a soft, mystically
intriguing collage, which, in one sense, defies genre definition, but in a
more important sense announces the emergence of a new genre that
uses illumination at its core.

Although Dillard has published a volume of poetry, *Tickets for a Prayer
Wheel* (1974), the bulk of her writing is prose, a nonfiction that can be

loosely designated as romantic in tone and essaylike in structure. But in general her language is experienced like poetry, rather than read like prose. This simplistic and superficial comparison, however, severely limits an accurate categorization of Dillard's work, which in many respects hies back to nineteenth-century British romanticism, more specifically to Wordsworth. Elements of Dillard's style and content can also be linked to a later romantic, Gerard Manley Hopkins. Dillard's romanticism is "high" romanticism in that she touches upon the deepest concerns of these nineteenth-century artists, particularly nature's revelation of a divine spirit. However, Dillard, a very conscious twentieth-century technician, is romantic with a twist; she brings almost two centuries of scientific thought to bear upon the concerns of the romantic's quest if she is to avoid being an anachronism in the literary art-philosophy world. This is a paradox central to an understanding of her work. Undeniably a twentieth-century thinker, Dillard is nonetheless an outright, bold romantic in the tradition of a nineteenth-century poet, grappling with images of birds and mountains, seeking unity in her natural environment, questioning the purpose or reality of beauty, dismissing institutional strictures, and most significantly, finding solace in the moment which strains toward antidefinition, a moment which by its very nature defies rationality, an illumination of human essence and its relationship with a greater being. This is the epiphanic moment.

The twist, however, is that Dillard introduces within these ephemeral journeys the most minute and excruciatingly factual detail from the arenas of contemporary science and history and uses them to scrutinize the very fabric of life. This scrutiny commences in a seemingly heartless manner, particularly through *Pilgrim,* with the painful minutiae of existence brought full to the reader's attention; then when the detail has been paraded out and duly catalogued, Dillard with a bold, dramatic sweep of her favorite literary device—the epiphanic moment—scatters the logic of science and diachronic time to the corners of the page. In fact, she eventually brings the world of science and physics to affirm her own philosophically romantic conclusions, noting that physicists themselves have become "wild-eyed, raving mystics" in that they have "perfected their instruments and methods just enough to whisk away the crucial veil, and what stands revealed is the Cheshire cat's grin" (*Pilgrim* 202). When Dillard can place the wild-eyed physicists in her philosophic camp, the epiphany becomes at the very least an epistemological tool, if not the central structure of her neoromantic epistemology.

Critics and book reviewers have often been at a loss when they have attempted to place Dillard in a literary tradition. Margaret Reimer notes the disparity of responses at the publication of *Pilgrim* when she writes of its "peculiar power, for reviewers were either rhapsodic in their praise or passionate in their indignation" (182). The confusion centered on the genre of Dillard's book. What is it? Eudora Welty, in reviewing *Pilgrim,* was alarmed by Dillard's style and mystical prose; she accused Dillard of being "a voice that is trying to speak to me out of a cloud instead of from a sociable, even answerable, distance on our same earth . . . . What's going on here?" (8). Dillard's prose, very much like poetry, skims across the page in *Pilgrim* with a fresh, contemporary power, but, on the other hand, is obviously dealing with a traditional romantic message. *Pilgrim* crosses boundaries: prose and poetry, literary art and ecological treatise, religion and philosophy, science and art. It is mysterious, which is exactly where Dillard's genius would have it; *Pilgrim* is a mystery resulting from its insistent employment of the most abstract of literary structures—the illuminated moment. "What's going on here," in answer to Welty, is the emergence of a skilled neoromantic craftswoman who can handle language and subject matter with the unleashed imagination of Wordsworth, Shelley, and Blake, and the polish and control of Pope. One might say, with Pope, that Dillard can both "guide" and "spur the Muse's steed" ("Essay on Criticism" Part I, line 84).

With her insistence on the importance of the moment Dillard has revealed a propensity for extreme romanticism. She has ultimately gone beyond nineteenth-century romanticism with her epiphanic moments. Wordsworth, who realized the importance and nourishing power of his own moments or "spots of time," which are scattered throughout *The Prelude,* wrote in book 11 that his mind is "nourished and invisibly repaired" by these moments which have a "distinct preeminence" in his life (264, 258).[1] For Hopkins the moment is startling and gemlike and provides brilliant clashes of language in a Christian setting, illustrated by "God's Grandeur": "The world is charged with the grandeur of God. / It will flame out, like shining from shook foil" (1–2). But for Dillard the illuminated moment is more central than it is for Wordsworth and Hopkins; it is the focus of her thought and art and consistently provides the pillars on which her writing rests.

Annie Dillard was 31 years old when she received the Pulitzer Prize for *Pilgrim at Tinker Creek* (1974). This prose nonfiction work is structured around her year's sojourn near Tinker Creek in Virginia, where through the meticulous observation of her environment, she involves herself, much like Thoreau at Walden, with elemental questions of life. Here Dillard provides for the reader her first important illumination, the moment of seeing a cedar tree filled with mourning doves and light: "I saw the tree with the lights in it. I saw the backyard cedar where the mourning doves roost charged and transfigured, each cell buzzing with flame. I stood on the grass with the lights in it, grass that was wholly fire, utterly focused and utterly dreamed" (*Pilgrim* 33). The narrator continues her observation by the creek throughout the book, but it is for the renewal of this moment she waits: "I have since only very rarely seen the tree with the lights in it. The vision comes and goes, mostly goes, but I live for it, for the moment when the mountains open and a new light roars in spate through the crack, and the mountains slam" (34). The moment for which she lives appears again in several forms in *Pilgrim*. In the chapter titled "The Present" the narrator experiences a moment which she feels is the locking in of the exact present. She has stopped along a Virginia highway at a gas station which is attended by a young boy who has his new beagle puppy "skidding around the office" (77). The sun is changing the color of the mountains with "brilliant blown lights" and "yellow brome," "purple pigment," and "rumpled rock in gilt" (78). The narrator bends to pet the puppy and feels a "wildly scrawling oscillograph on the present moment. The air cools; the puppy's skin is hot. I am more alive than all the world" (78). The "puppy epiphany," which emphasizes the relationship of time with the illumination, a relationship which will be considered here in chapter 3, further enunciates Dillard's specialized treatment of the moment.

A variation of the illumination occurs in *Pilgrim* in chapter 12, "Nightwatch." At the deserted Lucas farm, a "garden in the wilderness" near Tinker Creek (213), the narrator watches through the framed window a goldfinch perch on a thistle. Downy seed erupts from the dried plant and scatters into the wind. This, like the tree with lights and the puppy, is highly significant for the narrator: "I was holding my breath. Is this where we live, I thought, in this place at this moment, with the air so light and wild?" (216). Once again the narrator emphasizes a moment's sensations with its seemingly altered environment, and although the goldfinch spot will be discussed later as distinct from the tree with lights and the puppy, its high relief in the text marks it as another Dillard illumination.

Finally, a very quiet epiphany, the falling maple key, concludes *Pilgrim*. Although many other illuminations occur throughout the narrative of *Pilgrim*, the maple key reiterates Dillard's peculiar reliance on this device if only because it appears as a conclusive episode. By the final chapter, "The Waters of Separation," the narrator has been humbled and emptied; she can no longer apply effort to her search for meaning in a parasitic world. It is the winter solstice. She stands alone, "lost, sunk . . . gazing toward Tinker Mountain and feeling the earth reel down," when suddenly she sees a winged seed spiral in the wind to the ground: "It flashed borrowed light like a propellor. Its forward motion gently outran its fall. As I watched, transfixed, it rose, just before it would have touched a thistle, and hovered pirouetting in one spot, then twirled on and finally came to rest; it was a maple key, a single winged seed from a pair" (267). The narrator picks the maple key from the ground, tosses it into the air, and it is carried off:

> I threw it into the wind and it flew off again, bristling with
> animate purpose, not like a thing dropped or windblown, pushed
> by the witless winds of convection currents hauling round the
> world's rondure where they must, but like a creature muscled and
> vigorous, or a creature spread thin to that other wind, the wind of
> the spirit which bloweth where it listeth, lighting, and raising up,
> and easing down. O maple key, I thought, I must confess I
> thought, o welcome, cheers. (267–68)

The fall of this single seed creates in the narrator an elaborate response, a kind of resonance; "the bell under my ribs rang a true note, a flourish as of blended horns, clarion, sweet" (268). Like the other illuminations, its reverberations create meaning, a "true note," for the narrator.

Dillard has indicated that the 15 chapters of *Pilgrim* parallel the *via positiva* and *via negativa* of the medieval mystic. The first half is "keyed by [the] Seeing chapter" which "builds up [the] Via Positiva, the journey to God through action & will & materials" while the "apex of structure" occurs with "Intricacy" and the book changes movement to the Via Negativa, "the spirit's revulsion at time and death" (personal correspondence to William Reyer). Throughout the first chapters, the narrator seeks the Spirit with an increasingly arabesque stratification of description applied to earth's materials. In the central chapter, "Flood," the exquisite cataloguing of insect, plant, and mineral life makes an abrupt turnabout and descends into the way of "nothingness," the *via negativa,* where the Spirit cannot be sought or considered symbolically through any earthly medium. The narrator says she has "glutted on richness and welcome[s] hyssop. . . . [she] stand[s] under the wiped skies directly, naked without intercessors" (259). The ascent and descent of the mystic's way are redeemed by the individual moment wherein lies the only evidence humankind can assume as proof for a divine plan or creator.

This overview of *Pilgrim at Tinker Creek* characterizes Dillard as an artist of the literary phenomenon which has been variously referred to as the epiphany, illumination, or significant moment. It is useful, first of all, to clarify the variation which can occur within the development of this moment in order to place Dillard's manipulation of these forms within a historical framework and to specify her peculiar use of the device.

Morris Beja, in *Epiphany in the Modern Novel,* working with Joyce's comments on epiphany in *Stephen Hero,* defines the literary epiphany as a "sudden spiritual manifestation, whether from some object, scene, event, or memorable phase of the mind—the manifestation being out of proportion to the significance or strictly logical relevance of whatever produces it" (18). Beja indicates that the event or object marking the moment must be seemingly unimportant and not logically connected with the reaction it produces in the recipient. This definition specifically connects epiphany with its verbal construct and points toward its uses in modern literature, including the works of James Joyce, Virginia Woolf, and Thomas Wolfe. But the highlighting of a moment is not a modern device, although Joyce was the first to denote this kind of psychological and literary mode of perception with the theological term "epiphany" (Langbaum 336). The illuminated moment is as old as Paul's conversion on the road to Damascus and Augustine's interest in time, which Beja connects with the tradition because time for Augustine was "measured within the minds and souls of men" (Beja 24, 27). French philosopher Henri Bergson is also a precursor to the modern concept of epiphany when he writes that "one places oneself within an object in order to co-incide with what is unique in it and consequently inexpressible. . . . To analyze, therefore, is to express a thing as a function of something other than itself" (Beja 55). Arthur Schopenhauer, the German philosopher, rejects empiricism and idealism and believes in a "faculty beyond the senses" which can illuminate the "will," or the thing itself (Beja 30). In addition, Kant, Sterne, Locke, and Proust, the latter of whom Beja considers to be the "most thorough literary exponent" of an epiphanic theory, are ancestors of the tradition (28). Emerson may be added to this list when he writes that epiphany rises out of "vulgar fact": "Day creeps after day, each full of facts, dull, strange, despised things . . . presently the aroused intellect finds gold and gems in one of these scorned facts, then finds . . . that a fact is an Epiphany of God" (quoted in Langbaum 339). Wordsworth coins his own epiphanic term when he speaks of the "renovating virtue" of his "spots of time" (*Prelude* 11.208–11), while Walter Pater comments on epiphany when he writes that "success in life" is to "burn always with this hard, gemlike flame," to "be present always at the focus where the greatest number of vital forces unite in their purest energy" (*Renaissance* 222).

While the epiphanic experience may display some commonality among various writers, the illuminated moment itself can be subdivided into five types: the experience of the "sublime," the mystical experience, the conversion, the vision, and the epiphany. The "sublime" is "characterized by nobility and grandeur, impressive, exalted, raised above ordinary human qualities" and is, according to Longinus, writing in the first century A.D., a "thing of spirit, a spark leaping from writer to reader, rather than a product of technique" (*Handbook to Literature* 489). Although this early appraisal of illumination does not recognize "technique" as the transmitter of the moment, Longinus does insightfully identify the essential character of the moment by labeling it as a "spark leaping from writer to reader." The literary epiphany, on the other hand, is highly involved with technique and devices which result in the transmitted "spark." One critic has, in fact, called epiphany the "modern sublime" (Langbaum 351).

Journeying as it does along the path the way of the *via positiva* and *via negativa*, Dillard's structure for *Pilgrim* results in the illuminated moment, which can be called the mystical experience. The elements of this experience share similarities, as Beja points out, with some elements of the epiphany (25). First, the mystical moment is sudden and intense with an exhilaration or pain that brings a new awareness. This moment is irrational in nature but brings an intuitive insight. Further, this illumination is authoritative and cannot be refuted by logical argument. It is fleeting and momentary. The mystical experience is an affirmation of God or a divine spirit and a denial of self (Beja 25). In addition, it is marked by an impersonal tone. The epiphany, on the other hand, is not necessarily a revelation of divinity but could as easily be a revelation of the self and, in this way, is entirely personal. The epiphany is, however, like the mystic's moment, fleeting, intuitive, and irrational.

The third subcategory of illuminated moment includes the experience of conversion. The great religious conversions of literary history can be linked in ways more reminiscent of epiphany than mysticism in that a conversion appears to illuminate the self rather than highlight a divinity. The seventeenth-century Puritan John Bunyan, with his tinker's pots and pans, is changed by a moment when he hears a voice instruct him to give up his sinful habits of drinking, bell-ringing, and gaming (Bunyan 11–13). This moment reveals the godhead but more significantly illumines Bunyan's self as he recognizes his "ungodly" pursuits. Bunyan, the recipient of illumination, has been identified and changed, rather than made selfless, by the moment. This constitutes conversion and, in some respects, echoes epiphany in that it emphasizes the self.

Finally, the vision must be distinguished from the epiphany, the latter being a relatively modern concept ushered into practice by Wordsworth through his notion of "spots of time." The major difference between the epiphany and the vision in post-Wordsworthian terms is the engagement of the reader: the literary epiphany works upon the reader, forcing him into an experienced moment, while the vision is a literary moment experienced or "read" by the reader from what could be deemed the "outside" of the moment. The writer describes his vision; the reader recognizes the description but does not physically experience the vision. It is this "outside" reading that sets Blake apart from Wordsworth or Coleridge, according to Robert Langbaum (341); Wordsworth and Coleridge construct the epiphany while Blake builds the vision. When Blake says he sees "a World in a Grain of Sand" and holds "Infinity in the palm of [his] hand" (*Auguries of Innocence* 1, 3), he describes for the reader his own experience, but he does not force the reader into the mysterious psychological operations of the epiphany. Wordsworth, however, leaves the reader to forage his own way through the powerful moments the poet himself cannot explain. When he recalls in book 11 of *The Prelude* the "spot" when, as a child, he sees a "naked pool," a "girl who bore a pitcher on her head," and a "beacon on the summit," he writes that he "should need / Colours and words that are unknown to man / To paint" or describe the tenor of this remembered scene (11.303–10). When the poet says he has no adequate language to identify this inexplicable moment, readers, having been supplied with few clues about the logical connections between the girl, the beacon, and the pool, are allowed to make their own connections and are consequently drawn into the subjectivity of the moment. What Wordsworth could not paint with words he has transmitted in another manner, a manner far deeper in psychological import for the reader, a manner which prefigures modern techniques that eliminate transitions and congruent juxtapositions.

This sense of epiphany, as it will subsequently be referred to here, is the critical marking place between illuminated moments as they were conceived before and after Wordsworth's "spots of time." Before Wordsworth structured his "spots" in *The Prelude*, illuminations were predominantly visionary. The distinction here is the emphasis upon external and internal forces acting within the moment; the concept as it appears in Wordsworth's work places emphasis on the artist's mind. Wordsworth, in the preface to *Lyrical Ballads*, emphasizes the role of the artist rather than the role of divine presence in the epiphany in his statement that a poet is "endowed with more lively sensibility" and "has a greater knowledge of human nature, and a more comprehensive soul, than are supposed to be common among mankind" (*Prose Works* 138). In addition, the poet can express what he "thinks and feels, and especially those thoughts and feelings which, by his own choice, or from the structure of his own mind, arise in him without immediate external excitement" (138). The poet's mind reacts with emotion and creates without "immediate external excitement"; for Wordsworth the human mind, rather than some divine spirit, is the shaping presence of experience. It can be said then that Wordsworth "exemplifies a transition between the emphasis of previous ages on an eternal force and the modern concentration on the subjective elements of experience" (Beja 32). Generally, the vision, then, is pre-Wordsworthian and the epiphany post-Wordsworth; the former experience is seemingly initiated and controlled by divine sources outside the writer, while the latter issues from the individual mind which molds the moment.

Other elements in the epiphany can be identified as separate from the vision; some will be discussed in chapter 4. It should be noted here, however, that the major difference between epiphany and vision is the use of allegory and metaphor. Epiphany is, according to Langbaum, the "opposite of allegory, conceit, metaphor; it really happens" (342). When Henry Vaughan "sees eternity the other night" he tells his reader in metaphoric language his experience of seeing eternity as a "ring" ("The World" 1–2). When Blake holds eternity in his hand it is metaphorically represented by a small sphere or grain of sand. But when Wordsworth describes the three elements of his moment—the girl, the pool, and the beacon—he cites no parallel or relationship between these elements and any philosophical or religious corollary.

Variations of the illumination appear throughout Dillard's work, but generally her moments can be identified as either a combination of the mystical experience and the vision, which can be described as the mystic-vision, or the epiphany, which is characteristically romantic and related to Wordsworth's imaginative, perhaps unintended, design in the "spots of time." When Dillard sees a cedar tree with mourning doves fill with a light that knocks her "breathless by a powerful glance" (*Pilgrim* 33), she is in command of the epiphanic mode. But when she watches the goldfinch light "weightlessly on the head of a bankside purple thistle," where the down is erupted and sown to the wind (*Pilgrim* 215), she is visionary, for here she sets up an allegorical equation for the goldfinch (beauty), the thistle (the Fall; Adam's curse), and the sown seed (the action of beauty). Here is a comment on the "fortunate Fall" (*felix culpa*) in that Dillard suggests that beauty must feed on death to become what it is; the "real" is the product of beauty and death: "If this furling air is fallen, then the fall was happy indeed. If this creekside garden [of Eden?] is sorrow, then

I seek martyrdom. . . . Creation itself was the fall, a burst into the thorny beauty of the real" (*Pilgrim* 216). The natural event at the Lucas farm takes on allegorical significance for Dillard as the bird, the thistle, and the fall of the thistledown come to symbolize all of the evil and beauty of human history. The moment is visionary rather than epiphanic because the writer suggests a meaning for each object and action in the scene. It lacks the necessary ambiguity and psychological depth of the epiphany.

Dillard punctuates narration and stabilizes meaning by introducing these various types of illumination into many of her works. For example, *Holy the Firm* (1977), a tiny jewel of poetic prose, is constructed around an illumination, though this one is more mystical or visionary than epiphanic. The moment is based upon the description of a burned moth, a metaphor which continues as the dominant motif throughout the three parts of the work. Dillard writes that she consciously makes a decision to construct a narrative, an "artistic structure," from the events of three days spent alone in a small cabin on Puget Sound: "I decided to write about whatever happened in the next three days. The literary possibilities of that structure intrigued me" ("A Face Aflame" 15–16). One event is an airplane crash which disfigures the face of a young girl, Julie Norwich, whom Dillard knows. This horrifying event echoes the moth's burning as both child and insect represent delicate lives with the potential to create beauty from sacrifice.

The writer has the memory of a moth she saw caught in the wax of a burning candle; its hollowed, burned, golden body becomes a wick for the candle and continues to burn for several hours. This scene provides a metaphor for the artist or the nun, Dillard's frequent substitute figure for the artist; both represent "holy" persons dedicated to an austere life. The artist "burns out" her life to flame the world with art just as the nun sacrifices her life for God. This sacrifice is one the artist must make, caught in the "wax" of materials and forms. The nun, mirroring the artist, "burns out" her life in praise and thought. Because Dillard uses the moth to set up a metaphor representing the dedicated individual, this particular illumination is essentially visionary. The insight is within the artist, an insight shared with rather than created within the reader as an epiphany might be.

Teaching a Stone to Talk: Expeditions and Encounters (1982) is another work that approaches the illuminated moment from various angles. The content of this collection of essays is extremely diverse, ranging from the narrator's stylized encounter in the woods with a weasel ("Living Like Weasels") to a surrealistic composition which unites nineteenth-century polar explorers, guitar-playing Catholics, and characters dressed like the Keystone Cops floating on an ice floe ("An Expedition to the Pole"). But the ultimate concern of these illuminations remains the same: the narrator lives for the vaporous moment of contact with divinity or the Absolute.

Dillard's continual preoccupation with the moment is clearly evident in "An Expedition," which provides a kind of "slow epiphany." The significant illumination occurs in the final scene, when the heterogeneous group on the floe rejoice as they near the North Pole. The tone is surreal and the narrative object laden, the objects themselves incongruently appearing out of place and out of time. This surrealistic scene lends the same air as the Donald Barthelme short story "The Balloon" or, even more graphic, a Dali painting. With this tendency toward surrealism the narrative generates a sense of artifice. Even the narrator's attitude is disarming and playful as she assumes the part of a Keystone Cop, wearing a "black cardboard constable's hat with a white felt star stapled to the band" and a tin badge; she carries a popgun and glides about the ice with bare feet, bumping into people and saying "I beg your pardon woops there" (34). Clowns slide on the ice and Christ poses for snapshots, all of which give the effect of a Charlie Chaplin film or a mime show. But even while this absurdity denotes a contemporary literary stylization, Dillard is moving toward the traditional moment when the people will see God, who is the Absolute at the "Pole of Relative Inaccessibility."

Dillard's point in this essay, which is organized under the subtitles "The Land," "The People," and "The Technology," is that "the people," the masses of ordinary individuals, will try to reach God with every manner or "technology" available to them. Dillard portrays the people as unskilled, inappropriate in their praise of God, ignorant, and unattractive, but always attending to the expedition toward the "land" wherein lies the dwelling place of the spirit:

> The Absolute is the Pole of Relative Inaccessibility located in
> metaphysics. After all, one of the few things we know about the
> Absolute is that it is relatively inaccessible. It is that point of spirit
> farthest from every accessible point of spirit in all directions. Like
> the others, it is a Pole of the Most Trouble. It is also—I take this as
> given—the pole of great price. (19)

"All the people," Dillard writes, "in all the ludicrous churches—have access to the land" (*Teaching* 8) and, as the nineteenth-century polar explorers did not give up their determination to reach their goal, so will the ungainly people of the earth with all their "ludicrous" traditions not cease their search for the spirit. Thus, Dillard groups together on an ice floe unlikely characters representing a broad cross-section that shares the same determination and desire: to reach the epiphany. She ends this essay by announcing the sighting of the Pole:

> Ahead as far as the brittle horizon, I see icebergs among the floes. I see tabular bergs and floebergs and dark cracks in the water between them. Low overhead on the underside of the thickening cloud cover are dark colorless stripes reflecting pools of open water in the distance. I am banging on the tambourine, and singing whatever the piano player plays; now it is "On Top of Old Smokey." I am banging the tambourine and belting the song so loudly that people are edging away. But how can any of us tone it down? For we are nearing the Pole. (52)

Thus the entire essay, in concerning itself with the movement toward this moment, moves in a similar manner toward a slow epiphany.

"Total Eclipse" is, on the other hand, a *tour de force* of epiphany; it provides a moment within a moment. Dillard with her husband goes to view a solar eclipse from a hillside but finds another unexpected moment within the moment she sought; this internal or secondary moment is the true epiphany and is as fleeting as the eclipse that provokes it. In this flash of insight she "learns" something beyond human expertise; no theorizing or rationalizing could have prepared her for this kind of knowing, which goes beyond factual data doled out by human education systems. On that hillside Dillard sees into the deep level "where are the violence and terror of which psychology has warned us" (94). "This is a given. It is not learned" but must be experienced (95). This moment cannot be captured by cameras or language; the camera could no more catch the eclipse than "language can cover the breath and simultaneity of internal experience" (95).

But as Eliot in the rose garden illumination of "Burnt Norton" observes, "human kind / Cannot bear very much reality" (*Four Quartets* 42–43) and hurries back to human time and habit. So Dillard's narrator cannot endure for long the intensity of such a moment derived from the solar eclipse. She "turns at last even from glory itself with a sigh of relief" (103) and seeks the mundane comforts of a restaurant where the people exclaim over the eclipse and laugh and eat eggs. They have returned to the level at which they predominantly dwell. But Dillard has witnessed something which took her to a level without words. When a boy remarks in the restaurant that the eclipse looked like a "Life Saver up in the sky" (98), Dillard's narrator seizes the phrase, for these words, a part of a human lexicon, are something to save her from what is essentially an ineffable moment. Through the vehicle of the "word" she can return to a world where there are manageable moments, ordinary moments among people who can describe ordinary events:

> It was good to be back among people so clever; it was good to
> have all the world's words at the mind's disposal, so the mind
> could begin its task. All those things for which we have no words
> are lost. The mind—the culture—has two little tools, grammar and
> lexicon; a decorated sand bucket and a matching shovel. With
> these we bluster about the continents and do all the world's work.
> With these we try to save our very lives. (99)

The world's lexicon, its language and grammar, are insufficient for the magnitude of meaning she has witnessed in the eclipse. Words will, however, have to do, she proposes, for this is what is left to the writer. The paradox here is that in her narrative stance of not being able to verbalize the moment, she has, indeed, verbalized with the only techniques left to the epiphanist; abrupt transitions and disjointed images, among other devices, re-create a moment she claims cannot be re-created, that moment in which a "loping god in the sky had reached down and slapped the earth's face" (101). The reader, too, feels the force of the blow.

In another essay in this collection, "A Field of Silence," Dillard offers a moment both visionary and epiphanic in character; in addition, it wears a Swedenborgian or Blakean cast. In a farmyard "as old as earth" stillness encompasses the narrator (133). She is filled with fear and has a strong desire to turn away from this intimidating silence but cannot. Mesmerized by the still scene where the "roosters [have] stopped" and "the fields and the fencing, the road, a parked orange truck—were stricken and self-conscious," the narrator hears a "human whistling" (135, 136). A woman in a pink dress pushing a wheelbarrow drifts into view. Reminiscent of Wordsworth's woman bearing a pitcher on her head, this woman spreads out in silence with the rest of the moment; "the distant woman and her wheelbarrow were flat and detached, like mechanized and pink-painted properties for a stage" (136). This "object sense" in the initial part of the moment can be compared to Wordsworth's nonrepresentational gathering of material; it is neither symbolic nor allegoric and consequently resonates with the epiphanic mode of signification.

This moment is not comfortable for the narrator: "I was not ready for a life of sorrow . . . deriving from knowledge" (137). But with a fear similar to the terror she feels when she sees the total eclipse of the sun, the narrator gains a knowledge which she finds difficult to bear because the moment amplifies silence and loneliness (137). Dillard develops a mystic's vision reminiscent of Swedenborg when she writes that she has seen angels on the silent field: "From that time I began to think of angels. I considered that sights such as I had seen of the silence must have been shared by the people who said they saw angels. I began to review the thing I had seen that morning" (137). What appeared to her at first as a silent, still tableau was actually moving, vibrating; it is the whirl of angel wings, "thousands of spirits, angels in fact, almost discernible to the eye, and whirling" (137). This acknowledgment of holy entities gives the moment its visionary, mystical character. The whistling woman in pink, however, is not metaphorically connected with additional meanings and helps develop the sense of epiphany.

Published two years after *Teaching a Stone to Talk, Encounters with Chinese Writers* (1984) continues this pattern of the illuminating moment. In her introduction to this work, Dillard mentions three times that she is writing about "moments" rather than the "truth" of China. Dillard, who in 1982 visited China with a "six-person delegation of U.S. scholars, writers, and publishers," records "mostly anecdotes—moments—from which few generalizations may be drawn except perhaps about Chinese—and human—complexity" (*Encounters* 3). This paradoxical, faintly ironic statement about the insignificance of dealing merely with "Chinese and human complexity" appears to be the obligatory statement a writer makes about the inability to convey all of reality or the "big picture" in a literary work. Thus, Dillard, following her established pattern, brings only "anecdotes" or "moments" to the page. These, of course, do reveal elements of a very major subject—human complexity, a revelation accomplished by the organically developed epiphany which engages the reader in its process.

Dillard speaks of her predilection a second time in the introduction: "The truth about China I leave to the experts. I intend only to tell some small stories, and to depict precise moments precisely, in the hope that a collection of such moments might give an impression of many sharp points going in different directions—might give a vivid sense of complexity" (4). Dillard's description of "many sharp points" clearly defines one aspect of literary epiphany, as the grouping of unrelated objects, places, and emotions is a key element in epiphanic development. Dillard further suggests the nature of epiphany when she disclaims she is writing "truth"; simply recording "precise moments" allows readers their own truth-finding, or illuminating, experience. When the writer's role is simply that of conveyor of diverse information faithfully recorded, readers are forced into making their own "deep" connections; this is the essence of the process of epiphany.

Dillard's last comment in the introduction of *Encounters* concerning her use of "moments" is not only significant for *Encounters* but also becomes a definitive statement about the use of illumination in the Dillard canon:

> These are only glimpses, not portraits; their subject is not China, and not even entirely Chinese writers, but a few vivid, equivocal moments in the days of some of earth's people in the twentieth century. What interests me here, and elsewhere, is the possibility for a purified nonfiction narration—a kind of Chekhovian storytelling which might illuminate the actual world with a delicate light—coupled with humor in the American tradition and no comment. (7)

Dillard had been working toward these "few, equivocal moments" which "illuminate the actual world with a delicate light" since *Pilgrim at Tinker Creek*. She suggests here her technical approach to composing the epiphany with the phrases "purified nonfiction narration," "illuminate the actual world," and "no comment." While this does not reveal in totality the artificially stylized components which finally produce the brilliant and fiery illumination, Dillard's remarks imply the self-initiating power of language when it is offered to the reader without authorial closure. Her "actual world" includes suffering and violence, but if the narration can be purified from extraneous observation, language might provide the peculiar, delicate lighting of epiphany.

The moments of *Encounters* are Joycean in effect as they reveal more about human nature than about a godhead. In "A Man of the World" the illuminating occurs when Wu Fusan, an elderly, "smooth" man who has lived through many revolutions (11), tries, Dillard writes, to size up the depth of her spirit: "He is going into my soul with calipers. He is entering my eyes as if they were a mineshaft; he is testing my spirit with a plumb line" (13). Later, her intuition about this moment is confirmed by an Italian woman who had lived in China many years. Wu Fusan had suffered and knew how to distinguish the breadth of soul in others; could they suffer for a cause? "He was sizing up my spirit, my heart and strength, my capacity for commitment" (14). This "sizing up" is brief, lasting "less than a minute," a momentary occurrence that left an "odd unverifiable impression" on Dillard (13, 14), an impression that is personal yet nonetheless verified by an outside individual, in this case, the Italian woman. This outside affirmation of an ephemeral event lends even more power to the epiphany.

In "The Meeting" the U.S. delegation meets with a group of literary people, the "literary workers," of China. The Americans are appalled by what they perceive as the unsophisticated "Jack and Jill" (*Encounters* 29) predilection of these Chinese publishers, editors, scholars, writers, and translators. When the Chinese ask for reading recommendations, the Americans do not know where to begin the list, for the Chinese are missing a century of literary tradition. But Dillard realizes that she in turn is ignorant of past and contemporary Chinese literature.

At the end of this essay is the usual Dillardian moment with its attendant twist. As the "head man" gives final goodbyes to the American group, he defends the Chinese practice of writing not for art's sake but for the good of the state. " 'Our writers are free to write about the darker side of life,' " he says. " 'But all our writers want to write what the people need. For they love their homeland, and they love socialism' " (32). Instead of rejecting an artistic stance that places a group mind above individual thought, Dillard weeps for this "son of a gun, this hack" because of his great love for China (32). The twist occurs when Dillard admits, even in the face of the Chinese literary deficiency, that she would give over personal causes for this same love of homeland, where people have suffered to maintain the earth's oldest civilization. She would give up sophistication, knowledge, and individual priorities, she writes; she would adopt any political system which aided the cause, and "if necessary lie through my teeth all day long, and cry all night, because we are trying to make it work with bicycles and bamboo" (33). By setting up literary correctness, the sophisticated canon of her delegation, as the foil for the human passion of the Chinese spokesman, Dillard echoes the tension of the epiphany: language taste may be decorous but it does not live unless it is sparked by the spirit of intense commitment and emotion, which will in turn create the alogical experience.

Dillard's more recent offering, *An American Childhood* (1987), intensifies her previous literary commitment to the illuminated moment. This autobiography, covering her earliest childhood remembered consciousness to her rebellious teenage years in a Pittsburgh girls' school, develops the theme of the child's increasing awareness. Noel Perrin describes *American Childhood* as Dillard's "equivalent of Wordsworth's *Prelude*," calling it "an autobiography in semimystical prose about the growth of her own mind" (7). Although Perrin is correct in citing similarities between the two works, Dillard's prose, rather than "semimystical," is, like Wordsworth's poetry, characteristically epiphanic in development; Dillard's emphasis is illumination of the interior self. As the narrator in *Pilgrim* desires to see God, whom she perceives as a "hoop of flame" rolling along "the mountain ridges like a fireball" (76), in *American Childhood* she is driven to a "life of concentration" in order that she might surface to the "exhilaration" of consciousness, the "breakthrough shift between seeing and knowing you see, between being and knowing you be":

> Who could ever tire of this radiant transition, this surfacing to
> awareness and this deliberate plunging to oblivion—the theatre
> curtain rising and falling? Who could tire of it when the sum of
> those moments at the edge—the conscious life we so dread
> losing—is all we have, the gift at the moment of opening it? (17)

The image of surfacing in the stream of time to the moment of "radiant transition" threads its way through the narration, while the motifs of "topology" and "skin" unite with "surfaces" to create a metaphysical intensity akin to Donne's. "Topology" and "skin," which Dillard draws variously as a geography lesson, a child's sensitive epidermis and a Pittsburgh neighborhood, are top layers of physical, psychological, and spiritual worlds whose surfaces are penetrated by the writer.

Dillard's analysis of epiphany is so predominant in *American Childhood* that the work offers a virtual catalogue of information concerning variations on the moment. In *Teaching a Stone to Talk* she has created "moments within moments"; in *American Childhood* she draws and dissects a single moment of consciousness to prodigious lengths. First, an awakening elemental consciousness transforms the infant's oblivion to the awakened observation of the older child. Dillard says that "children ten years old wake up and find themselves here, discover themselves to have been here all along" (11). As a child she awakened "piecemeal" to this consciousness until finally the "intervals of waking tipped the scales" and she was "more often awake than not" (11).

This baseline consciousness appears to be a kind of sporadic backdrop to a more intense consciousness which is epiphanic. An illustration of the more intense moment is Dillard's memory of an ice-skating scene in her native Pittsburgh. After a severe winter storm in 1950, the roads are still and cold, emptied of traffic. With her parents and sister, Dillard watches a strange and beautiful sight under the light. Jo Ann Sheehy, a neighborhood girl, ice skates on the frozen streets, the light illuminating her movement. Dillard's family moves to the window, mesmerized by the transfiguration of the scene into a cold, silent tableau:

> She was turning on ice skates inside the streetlight's yellow cone
> of light—illumined and silent. She tilted and spun. She wore a
> short skirt, as if Edgerton Avenue's asphalt had been the ice of an

Olympic arena. She wore mittens and a red knitted cap below
which her black hair lifted when she turned. Under her skates the
street's packed snow shone; it illumined her from below, the cold
light striking her under the chin. (30)

This strange scene, this "still, frozen evening inside, the family's watching through the glass," Jo Ann skating in the moonlight under "cold
stars," is a moment of "beauty and mystery," a moment tinted with reck-
lessness and danger to the child. The Sheehy family is Catholic, a forbid-
ding enigma to Annie, whose family is Presbyterian. In addition, the
child has heard Tommy, Jo Ann's brother, call the Dillards' black maid,
Margaret Butler, a "nigger" (31). For the young Dillard, the unacceptable nature of the Sheehy family and the beauty of Jo Ann skating are
mysteriously coupled. The paradox plants a seed of consciousness that
builds later into the concept of beauty linked with pain as it appears in
the goldfinch-thistle illumination in *Pilgrim*. The greater intensity of this
consciousness—which juxtaposes beauty, danger, and mystery—over the
general awakening of the infant mind characterizes this illumination as
epiphanic.

   Dillard's narrative, which plays with variations of consciousness, can
be confusing in the early chapters of *American Childhood*, yet it is in
many ways a mirror of the chaos of the child's mind, full of unsorted im-
pressions and ideas. As the child's consciousness begins to make connections, as when it identifies the rolling motion of car headlights as they
flash "monsters" upon her bedroom wall (21), the young Dillard becomes increasingly aware of her own life. She fears that she will become
wholly awakened, too fully aware; she predicts "with terrifying logic
that one of these years not far away" she would be "awake continuously
and never slip back; and never be free" of herself again (11). One distinction here appears to be that when an innocent is "awakened" to the
knowledge of living, experiences that distinct time when "consciousness converges with the child as a landing tern touches the outspread
feet of its shadow on the sand" (11), that child enters the initial awareness of the mind. This occurs at age 10 for Dillard. The infant gains consciousness sporadically, awakening to dim mysteries, such as the
"monster" headlights on the bedroom wall; but true awareness eventually came to the 10-year-old Dillard when she "slid into [herself] perfectly fitted, as a diver meets her reflection in a pool" (11). The
epiphanic moment, although this is a hairline distinction for Dillard, is
more intense than the baseline awakening of the infant and is usually
filled with beauty and mystery akin to the sensations elicited by the ice
skating tableau.

While *American Childhood* presents many moments of true epiphany, it also describes the visionary moment. In one such incident Dillard flees through the snow from a "sainted, skinny, furious red-headed man" who is angered by the child's snowball throwing (47). A chase in which the man will not give up his pursuit of the delinquent snowball thrower becomes allegoric when Dillard writes that the man, who chased her "silently, block after block . . . over picket fences, around garbage cans, and across streets," obviously recognized that "you have to point yourself, forget yourself, aim" (47). The realization is a reiteration of the romantic's credo of excess; performance is based on an all-or-nothing principle, on sacrificial dedication, already a major theme in Dillard's previous work. It is the weasel who will not let go its hold from the eagle's throat, even in death, and is carried high "over field and woods, lightly, thoughtless" in *Teaching a Stone to Talk,* and the moth (or artist) who will burn out its life for beauty in *Holy the Firm.* In this Pittsburgh snow scene, then, the chase is allegorical, a furious, unrelenting pursuit of the perfect artistic movement; the man, who is "sainted" by the holiness of his single-mindedness, had chased the child "passionately without giving up," and so, just as the dedicated artist catches the "moment," he catches the child (48).

This powerful allegory notwithstanding, the epiphany rather than the vision is predominant in *American Childhood.* In the epilogue Dillard gathers together all of these moments by means of the topology motif which she has been developing throughout the book. Reminiscent of Wordsworth's explanation of his "spots of time" as "renovating" moments which "nourished and invisibly repaired" his spirit (*Prelude* 11.257–59, 264), she sees the epiphanic moments she had described as "dots" of self scattered across the landscape of her life: "You may then wonder where they have gone, those other dim dots that were you" (*American Childhood* 248). These "dots" strongly suggest Wordsworth's "spots" in their reference to encircled moments of extreme consciousness where, as the poet writes in *The Prelude,* the "efficacious spirit chiefly lurks / Among these passages of life in which / We have the deepest feeling that the mind / Is lord and master" (11.268–71). Dillard's geography of consciousness allows the dots to appear and fade like Wordsworth's spots, the "hiding places of [his] power," which in like manner materialize and dim (11.335). Awakening in flashes to find herself in a new location, both the figurative mental landscape and the literal earth, Dillard articulates her sensations: "You notice unbidden that you are afoot on this particular mountain on this particular day in the company of these particular changing fragments of clouds," and when you "pause in your daze to connect your own skull-locked and interior

mumble with the skin of your senses and sense, and notice you are living," you are astonished (248). Although Dillard offers in this passage
from the epilogue an explication of her illuminations, the sense of
epiphany rather than vision prevails because she is linking otherwise insignificant childhood occurrences with flashes of insight: "swinging a
bat on the first pitch, opening a footlocker with a screwdriver, inking
and painting clowns on a celluloid" (248). These insights, however,
should not be characterized as formulaic lessons on morality; each is instead the experiencer's sensation that she is fully comprehending life.
These events, like Wordsworth's spots, are not symbolically significant
but are unexplained, lighted scenes of consciousness. Thus, in *American
Childhood* Dillard weaves together a sophisticated metaphor with the
concepts of topology and surface and her own epiphanic sensations
which defy metaphor.

Dillard's contribution to literary theory, *Living by Fiction* (1982), begins as an explication of modern and contemporary fictive techniques
but concludes with a philosophical treatise on the contribution and
meaning of art in a shattered and fragmented world, a world which had
been without context since World War I (25–26). Dillard's search for a
unity in art forms and, thereby, syllogistically, the world, is the same
quest she has set for herself in all her other work; it is answered by the
same sequential pattern which culminates in the antithesis of logic, the
illuminated moment.

In this treatise Dillard sets out via many avenues to reveal the validity
of art as proof for meaning in the world. But one avenue is particularly
significant to her development as a neoromantic and her application of
illumination. Just as Wordsworth laments the deafened ear which cannot "Hear old Triton blow his wreathed horn," Dillard laments her own
historical position, for Christianity and science have killed the ability to
interpret natural phenomena or the physical environment directly:
"They razed the sacred groves, killed the priests, and drained the flow of
meaning right off the planet" (136). For Dillard, then, the only possible
link back to meaning is the reappearance of God in nature. This reappearance is a valid possibility in Dillard's world, for even rational science
no longer holds that it can explain or has answers for the curiosities of
natural phenomena. Everything slips and slides; yet for Dillard the illuminated moment has the potential to steady a wobbling universe.

In *Living by Fiction* Dillard happily and frequently invokes the scientist's admission of the existence of mystery in the universe, a line of reasoning she first introduced in *Pilgrim* when she noted that with Werner
Heisenberg's Law of Indeterminacy in 1927 certainty was pulled out

from under the feet of quantum physicists. These physicists have lost the comfort of certainty because they cannot know "both a particle's velocity and position" simultaneously. This admission, of course, delights Dillard, who will call up illumination and intuition as the only method to catch a glimpse of what lies behind the final "veil." Einstein had worked on theory and supposition and found, thereby, something that did indeed exist. Yet the final mystery for Einstein, according to Dillard, was that the world is "comprehensible" (*Living* 138); the truth of Einstein's theory of relativity, she writes, shocked even him (133). If physical theory can thus be hypothesized and proved, our abstractions, our theories and suppositions concerning things of the spirit, may likewise actually prove accurate. This becomes Dillard's affirmation for epiphany or vision. If Einstein could theorize and intuit and afterwards discover his intuition verified by physical data, then certainly the poet-writer can rely on intuition. The writer's frequent grasp of the unknowable but felt moment is a point in favor of *true* knowing. Further, according to Dillard, intuition is always more accurate than culturally accumulated raw data or knowledge. Like Wordsworth in the preface to *Lyrical Ballads,* Dillard in *Living by Fiction* justifies and interprets what she has already achieved in her earlier narratives.

The Writing Life (1989) presents short, loosely connected narratives concerning Dillard's thoughts on the writing process and, once again, she structures the work around significant, illuminating moments. These illuminations seem to arise out of a paradox that confronts the fundamental operation of creation: each artist attempts to find a form to place about the vastness of all possibilities; a writer strains to capture in language a concept that outruns language. Dillard characterizes words as tools which mine for thought, or probes which pick out a form. But when the tool, which at first was handled and controlled by the artist, begins to uncover knowledge, that same tool gains an organic momentum; words become entities that take on a life outside of the writer: "The line of words is a miner's pick, a woodcarver's gouge, a surgeon's probe. You wield it, and it digs a path you follow. Soon you find yourself deep in new territory" (3). Language sails into space finding its destination, the single planet in a universe with no walls. Dillard suggests that the writer watches untethered language on the monitor of a word processor just as individuals at NASA Space Center watch their own screens to track a rocket: "You are in Houston, Texas, watching the monitor. You saw a simulation: the line of words waited, still, hushed, pointed with longing. The big yellow planet spun toward it like a pitched ball and passed beside it, low and outside" (21). The writer, like the NASA controller, waits for signals that might be interpreted later; the words will take their own course and reveal to the screen-watcher new ideas, perhaps undiscovered worlds.

Within the notion that words can achieve life outside the writer lies the concept of epiphany, a literary device that reverberates with its own tensions. One example of these tensions occurs in a narrative about a large June bug that flops its heavy body against the window of Dillard's study, a small library carrel at Hollins College where she wrote portions of *Pilgrim at Tinker Creek* (27). A single light illuminates the dark room where the writer works alone in the evening: "The horizon of my consciousness was the contracted circle of yellow light inside my study—the lone lamp in the enormous, dark library" (30). Her mind, like the light, is an isolated, focused entity in the dark; she shuffles index cards, reworks sentences, and is generally oblivious for half an hour to the heavy thud of the beetle's "hollow, bonking sound" against the glass (31). On the blind Dillard has taped a drawing of the horizon beyond so that she can avoid distractions from the real life below (29); enclosed entirely by man-made structures, even the artifice of a sketch rather than a natural panorama, Dillard has prepared the way for epiphany. The phenomenon is unexpected, just as the tree with lights and the woman pushing a wheelbarrow are unanticipated; Dillard "unthinkingly. . . parted the venetian blind slats" to see the insect, but instead she is bombarded with a sky of lights, a Fourth of July celebration below with "far sprays of color widening and raining down" (31). The single light of the mind in the study carrel explodes into the other-worldly illumination of the moment; as with all epiphanies, this event comes unannounced and is activated by a commonplace event, here the inspection of an insect. Dillard implies, however, that the lowly June bug's tapping is a message intended for the isolated writer. She questions the beetle's ability to fly to the second story of a building, the study carrel's position, and in addition, she notices the insect's persistent knocking, wondering "what monster of a fat, brown June bug could fly up to a second story and thump so insistently at my window as though it wanted admittance" (31). The continuous tapping suggests a spiritual power that seeks to communicate with the writer. Creating a sensory crescendo, Dillard orchestrates the insect's thump into the muffled explosions of the distant, "out of sync" fireworks, and the narrow beam of her study light into the startling colors, "red and yellow, blue and green and white. . . blossoming light in the black sky" (31). Dillard, the actor in this narration, receives the illumination, suddenly realizing that she had "forgotten all of a wide space and all of historical time" and "it all came exploding in on me at once—oh yes, the world" (31). But Dillard, the creator-writer of the scene, has fashioned the words, language that possibly "mined" its own knowledge, into an epiphanic moment for the reader.

Dillard continues in *The Writing Life* to link the seemingly insignificant events of daily life with illuminations that often resonate with supernaturalism; an old green Smith-Corona typewriter generates its own volcanic eruption when the writer leaves the room (63), another sign of language's self-engendering power; and in the college library a phantom chess player sometime during the night moves pieces on a board which Dillard finds when she returns to write each evening (35–36), a scenario emphasizing the eerie block of light which leads her into the rare-book room. A "strange chunk of light on the floor between the stacks" draws her attention and, holding her breath, she approaches the room (36). Here she discovers a blonde baby in diapers standing near the chessboard and the writer immediately assumes a connection between the infant and the phantom game, but the baby, Dillard learns, is the librarian's child who is accompanying his parents who have come to "pick something up" (36). The reader, however, is left to wonder, along with the writer, about the identity of the "lunatic opponent" who finally "scrambled the board so violently the game was over" (37). This late-night illumination in the library constitutes epiphany because Dillard allows the objects to stand alone—the baby, the chessboard, and finally the unknown mover of pieces in a game which the writer plays but does not fully understand, just as Dillard does not comprehend the source of her astonishing spiritual moments.

Dillard concludes *The Writing Life* with the narrative of Dave Rahm, a stunt pilot whose skills were so daring and poetic that he was called on by Jordan's King Hussein for special performances. After flying with Rahm on a hair-raising, exhilarating ride, Dillard understands the discomfort of such tossing and straining against gravity, the force flinging her against the plane's side, piling up her blood "between my skull and skin," causing her eyeballs to feel "spherical and full of heartbeats" (104). But the painful intensity Dillard experiences suggests the anguish of any artistic venture, and Dillard, indeed, paints Rahm, who eventually loses his life during a spectacular performance for Hussein, as an artist of the skies. Repeating the concerns of her earlier books, Dillard describes an illuminating moment when she watched the pilot maneuver his plane fearlessly above her home. Rahm, she writes, had become a Mozart, moving "his body through his notes" (108). Suggesting his alliance with her own craft, Dillard writes that the pilot "furled line in a thousand new ways, as if he were inventing a script and writing it in one infinitely recurring utterance until I thought the bounds of beauty must break" (109). The stunt pilot had gone inside his art, becoming a vehicle for beauty linked with the plane which flung him in the endless spirals and loops of a "ribbon whose end unraveled in memory while its beginning unfurled as surprise" (111). Dillard concentrates the effect of the illumination's extended length—she watches the plane for forty minutes—by suggesting she stands looking upward, "lost" in the vining paths of the plane: "I lost my direction and reeled. My neck and spine rose and turned, so I followed the plane's line kinesthetically" (108). In this way, her body repeating this twining motion, the narrator becomes the recipient of the plane's rolling beauty and therefore the receiver of the epiphany's power. Although this moment suggests a metaphor—Dave Rahm, the stunt pilot, representing all artists in single-minded pursuit of the creative moment, the open-ended nature of the pilot's creation implies the enigma, the unknowability of epiphany. Rahm's plane "trailed a line like a very long mathematical proof you could follow only so far, and then it lost you in its complexity" (108). The artist, the writer, or the reader may begin with the known but will eventually be confronted with the unknowable, that which trails off into mystery when the creation is spiritually bound up with beauty. The complex spiraling of Dave Rahm's plane represents for Dillard the comfort, the solace, of that entity which cannot be defined.

From *Pilgrim at Tinker Creek* to *The Writing Life*, Dillard's writing is a full-blown presentation of the illuminated moment. At times the moment occurs as a part of the narration, as in the cedar tree with lights and the goldfinch of *Pilgrim*, the moth of *Holy the Firm*, and the woman in pink in "A Field of Silence" (*Teaching*); the remainder of Dillard's work is exposition on those key moments. The sum total of her work—the moments combined with the narrative supporting and leading up to them—is a treatise on illumination. In *Holy the Firm* the narrator addresses Julie Norwich, the maimed girl, and tells her if she leads a nun's life of dedication she will experience the moment which Dillard describes as "Mornings, when light spreads over the pastures like wings, and fans a secret color into everything, and beats the trees senseless with beauty" (75). This moment, suggestive of her original epiphany in *Pilgrim*, the tree with lights, measures the worth of existence and illustrates Dillard's central quest in all of her work.

2

The Cheshire Cat's Grin

The Need for Epiphany

Annie Dillard's concentration on the illuminated moment in her work is apparent, but why she relies so heavily on this literary device is less obvious. The reasons for its appearance in this writer's works, its relationship to traditional romantic thought, its connection with ecological literature, and its development in spite of postmodern literary predilections are all significant aspects of an understanding of Dillard, whom Mary McConahay calls "at once a contemporary oracle and a literary anachronism" (107–08).

While there is some basis to McConahay's pronouncement of anachronism—Dillard is, after all, fond of nineteenth-century romantic conventions—Dillard is nonetheless brilliantly contemporary, taking elemental questions of existence and giving them intellectual buoyancy through language structures which seem to sweep the reader down into psychologically paradoxical depths, and, in turn, to fling the reader into an ethereal world of thought, much as Joyce, Woolf, or Faulkner do. William Scheick calls Dillard's work "translucent," a term he uses to describe those instances when "surface details in her account are brought to the edge of visibility, and momentarily they lose their revealed and verbalized temporal surface opacity (their 'thingness,' their conventional meaning) and seem—to author and reader—to become translucent" (55). This translucency stems from the poetic and epiphanic nature of her prose.

Nineteenth-Century Romanticism

As previously mentioned, this Dillardian translucence has its roots in Wordsworth's "spots of time," but connections can also be found with

Coleridge's "secondary imagination." The organicism of the nineteenth-century romantic imagination working upon the mind and object of contemplation and creating an original product of thought bears strong similarities to Dillard's epiphanic organicism. But Dillard's interest in the organic quality of art, specifically the literary piece, is more pervasive than even that of nineteenth-century poets.

To understand Dillard's translucence completely, it is important to trace the roots of her epiphanic tradition back to her romantic forebears. A key work here, of course, is Wordsworth's *Prelude,* which is loosely arranged around his "spots of time"; the poet recognizes that from there he "drink[s] the visionary power" (2.330), a power whose failing he laments in the "Intimations Ode": "Whither is fled the visionary gleam?" (*Poetical Works* 4.56). Wordsworth's apocalyptic moment on Mount Snowdon, like Dillard's "tree with lights," resonates with meaning. Wordsworth writes that when he reached the summit of Snowdon "instantly a light upon the turf / Fell like a flash" (*Prelude* 13.39–40). He continues to emphasize the illuminating aspects of the experience:

> I looked about, and lo,
> The moon stood naked in the heavens at height
> Immense above my head, and on the shore
> I found myself of a huge sea of mist,
> Which meek and silent rested at my feet.
> A hundred hills their dusky backs upheaved
> All over this still ocean, and beyond,
> Far, far beyond, the vapours shot themselves
> In headlands, tongues, and promontory shapes,
> Into the sea, the real sea. (13.40–49)

The mist gathering about his feet and creating shapes in the distance becomes a "deep and gloomy breathing-place" where sounds of roaring "waters, torrents, streams" sound with "one voice" (13.57–59). This literary moment is organic, alive with a sense of panting and breathing, moving with the power of natural phenomena, a transformation the poet's mind has made of the mountain scene. Later he writes that "higher minds" can send forth imagination by "instinct" and "build up greatest things / From least suggestions" (13.90, 96–99). Wordsworth believes that when a sensitive intelligence experiences a natural scene, such as Snowdon's panorama, he will be able to divine a spiritual world behind physical objects; this superior mind will be able to create from even gentle hints. Nature is not a dormant emblem but "thrusts forth upon the senses" its own "strength / Made visible" (13.86–88). The sense of the mind's ability to recreate in its own image, to build up and make new individual experience, to become a "lamp" of illumination rather than a "mirror" of reflection is illustrated in the activity of the Mount Snowdon passage. As M. H. Abrams points out in *The Mirror and the Lamp* (1953), those two objects are analogues for thought as it changed from the eighteenth to the early nineteenth century. The mirror expresses the idea of imitation in the arts, the mind reflecting a larger Platonic universe. The lamp becomes the metaphor for the nineteenth century as the mind was viewed as expressive and creative, reflecting an inner light from the artist. With his "spots of time," Wordsworth falls into the nineteenth-century tradition that suggests a poet has the ability to heighten through language the sensory and spiritual effects of an ordinary scene.

In similar fashion, Coleridge in the "Dejection" ode, pursues the moment when he can feel the "shaping spirit of Imagination" (86) or, as in "The Eolian Harp," feel the "one Life within us and abroad" (26). His "secondary imagination," which molds new entities and creates truly original literature, is an outgrowth of nineteenth-century study in mental processes. For Coleridge the secondary imagination "dissolves, diffuses, dissipates, in order to re-create . . . it struggles to idealize and to unify. It is essentially *vital* . . ." (*Biographia Literaria* 1:304). In "Frost at Midnight" the stilled ice hangs glistening, alive, from the eaves of his cottage, while the "stranger," or the film in the fireplace, flutters like the thoughts of the meditative Coleridge. Both the "film" and "ice" are catalysts for the imagination and important only because the mind works its "shaping spirit" upon them.

This spirit appears in other writers of the romantic period, among them Keats, whose mind works upon the Grecian urn, where the poet perceives spirit music, the "ditties of no tone," not played for the "sensual ear" (*John Keats* 13–14). The urn can "tease us out of thought," an indication of the poet's belief in the mind's ability to imbue the urn with life and to move and shape in infinite patterns, never to end its playing upon the enigma of the "Cold Pastoral" (45). In a letter to Benjamin Bailey, dated November 22, 1817, Keats comments on the activity of the mind as it interacts with outward objects: "the simple imaginative Mind may have its rewards in the repition [repetition] of its own silent Working coming continually on the spirit with a fine suddenness" (*Letters of John Keats* 37).

The contemporary discovery that revealed the human mind as an individual operation, with the ability to shape the object of contemplation, led these romantics to build their poetry about the zenith of an organic "shaping" experience. The romantic concept of understanding the integrated whole of an object through the vehicle of imagination came from the doctrine of "coalescence," which was assumed by Wordsworth and Coleridge and which represents more than a combination of simple into complex ideas, but instead describes the actual creation of an "entirely new and irreducible whole" (Bate 118). The idea comes from a logical process whereby logical steps lead to a conclusion, which after a while loses sight of steps and conclusion and becomes an intuitive whole; for example, coalescence might be applied to language: letter < words < phrases, the latter being something different from a random, albeit large, collection of letters. Another example might be several colors mixed to form a new color. Wordsworth and Coleridge applied the concept to epistemology; they believed that out of each experience, although the mind depended on a natural scene or an object such as an urn for basic perceptions, for understanding it derived "new and characteristic melodies from its own unique framing" (Elder 377).

John Holloway notes that the romantic poem became a vehicle for the poet to explore truth, to experience it, rather than a means merely to "present truth" (58). In a moment of intense apprehension each poet could frame through his own imagination another segment of truth; but the truth, in this sense, is not a preformed system or platonic idea readily mirrored by the poet, but a truth newly discovered in each mind-object experience. The poet's task, Holloway explains, was not "to master mankind's accumulated wisdom...but rather to engage in a pilgrimage through experience, so as to win from it a vital and hitherto uncollected insight.... [This] surely marks a profound transition occurring in our civilization between the Renaissance and the nineteenth century" (64).

When Dillard feels she is "more alive than all the world" in the puppy epiphany (*Pilgrim* 78), she is linking her mind with the object of contemplation, the puppy, just as her romantic forebears linked their minds with urns, or moonlit mountain turfs, or icicles on eaves. In these moments when the "great door opens on the present, [and] illuminates it as with a multitude of flashing torches" (80), she relives the nineteenth-century ideal of mental organicism; the moment creates a new "truth" by combining mind and object.

Also in nineteenth-century fashion, Dillard creates for herself a persona who defies institution. This romantic stance is necessary so that the writer can work from a kind of tabula rasa on which the epiphany can act. The writer's attitude is this: If God, or any spirit, will show itself, then let it do so. This defiant attitude is necessary for the eventual epiphany to be meaningful. A passivity predominates which has included ridding the mind of knowledge acquired by institutions or systems. The romantic writer "values experience over system, whether the system be causal-chronological, logical, theological, or ethical" (Langbaum 345). Thus, Dillard frequently reminds the reader she is not a moralist, not religious; she insists she does not write from Biblical theology but from "natural" theology. She is verifying her own clear psyche, which, the persona claims, has not been tampered with. This echoes the poetic claims of Blake, Wordsworth, and Coleridge (in most of his early poetry).

These writers frequently created their own poetic structures. They desired, echoing the spirit of the French Revolution, a breakdown of institutional values and a construction of values found in Rousseau's natural man and a natural environment. In a 1988 interview Dillard admits to a similar bent when she advocates "skinning off the protective layers that prevent you from feeling and seeing more totally" (Krauth 2). The "protective layers," in most cases for the Dillard persona, are religious systems, although she eventually allows her epiphanic experience to carve out and prove a Christian theology in much of her work. But her initial stance creates her as natural, naive; she is "writer-recorder" seeking only to write about a "few vivid, equivocal moments in the days of some of earth's people in the twentieth century." With this stance she reasserts "the ability of the individual mind to come to terms with murky complexities . . . without the mediation of specialized or institutionalized knowledge" (Hoffman 87).

In a 1978 interview, Dillard also asserted her own natural mind and her avoidance of any knowledge which has been formally institutionalized: "I don't write at all about ethics. I try to do right and rarely do so. The kind of art I write is shockingly uncommitted—appallingly isolated from political, social, and economic affairs" ("A Face Aflame" 960). The denial of preconceived ideas is necessary for this romantic, for then the incursion of the spirit can be validated. It secures the concept of a spirit which arrives by its own means, is not ushered in, perhaps falsely, by mortal knowledge which is always suspect. Epiphany often becomes, as Robert Langbaum observes, the "Romantic substitute for religion" and can, in fact, become "the means of returning to and revalidating dogma as experience" (356), which is what Dillard eventually does, as on many occasions she links her illuminations with Christian doctrine.

One avenue of Christian thought often entertains Dillard's wide range of allusions: fundamentalism. Although she grew up in a Presbyterian church attended by the rich and powerful families of Pittsburgh, she resented the lack of emotion she saw in the service and the bigotry she observed in fur-draped members who tilted their hatted heads and looked at the rural man (Christ) on the golden wall (*American Childhood* 193). The stiff worship and hypocritical alliance of money with only a gesture of caring for the poor, sick, or otherwise troubled peoples of the earth, both of which Dillard the child saw in her church, plant in the writer a need for passion in worship or praise; hence, her fascination with fundamentalism is an outgrowth of this reaction. Wordsworth's fascination with and belief in the "essential passions of the heart" he found in rustics and solitaries is similar to Dillard's approval of the naive joy and unquestioning dedication she finds in Christian fundamentalists. Dillard, purporting her weakness in theology and her dedication to art, praises fundamentalists as bold, dedicated people who have chosen the "narrow way" ("A Face Aflame" 959). She reverses the usual logic by chiding agnostics, for they are illogical and fear-bound, having chosen the "safe" path of no belief rather than the perilous path of belief in God.

In her article "Singing with the Fundamentalists" Dillard narrates an incident in which she joins a group of Christian fundamentalists who have gathered about a university fountain to sing hymns in the early morning. She insists that they are individualists who can pray "privately" in public (320). As craggy, peculiar nonconformists who "pile up money, vote in blocs, and elect right-wing crazies . . . censor books . . . carry handguns . . . fight fluoride in the drinking water and evolution in the schools," they represent, to Dillard, strength and determination; she is "drawn to their very absurdity, their innocent indifference to what people think" (312). They sing out their needs with the phrases, "Broken people! Ruined lives" (317). Dillard's intellectual colleagues join in a "frieze" (her comment on the detached uninvolvement of cold idea) at the windows of nearby buildings (318). These observers, too, fall under the spell of the groupy-individualists who mouth songs in the early morning. This scene reiterates Dillard's concern for dedication and sacrifice for causes. The irate man who chases Dillard the child through a Pittsburgh snow *(American Childhood),* the moth or artist-nun who burns to provide light *(Holy the Firm),* the Chinese writer who would sacrifice literary standards for the workers' state *(Encounters with Chinese Writers),* and the weasel that clings to the throat of the eagle to be borne aloft over fields and trees ("Living like Weasels" in *Teaching a Stone to Talk*)— they are individuals who dedicate themselves single-mindedly and endure alone, as do these fundamentalists. They are Dillard's passionate model for living, a contemporary version of Wordsworth's rustics. David Miller, noting Dillard's proclivity toward dedication, calls her evangelical and finds this a surprising aspect of the "modern literary intellectual" (164). But in this passionate and primitive atmosphere, where, as Wordsworth writes, "the essential passions of the heart" can "find a better soil" to thrive (preface to *Lyrical Ballads* 125), Dillard believes the opportunity for epiphany exists.

The theme of dedication spreads out in many avenues throughout Dillard's work, but essentially it translates into this logic: dedication can make one passionate; passion brings excess; excess is never "pure" for it brings with it "extra baggage" or ideas; but in the "extra" or the excess, one can mill around with idea, intellect, and emotion; all of this excess, because it supplies myriad intricacy, is itself a mystery, a characteristic integral to Dillardian thought. And out of this passionately developed and mysterious excess can rise, if one is fortunate, the pivotal moment, although it can never be understood by intellect, which gives form and meaning to life—the epiphany. This reasoning process begins with the anti-intellectual, the Wordsworthian rustic, or for twentieth-century purposes, the unbiased individual "unfrozen" by intellect, living with emotions open to the vagaries of life, open to pain and beauty. The idea appears in almost allegorical form in *The Living,* Dillard's most sustained attempt at fiction. Although this study is primarily concerned with Dillard's nonfiction, a perusal of the novella can provide some important information about the writer's preoccupation with illumination.

Dillard's style, particularly the motion of the language in *The Living,* is disconcertingly removed from the lyricism of *Pilgrim at Tinker Creek, Holy the Firm,* or even *Living by Fiction;* nonetheless, the subject matter or philosophical approach is vintage Dillard. She begins with a doggedness for repetition and simplicity in language reminiscent of Hemingway and evolves into a stark Hardyesque lyricism as the story progresses.

The Living is essentially an allegory or morality tale which slowly unfolds against the backdrop of Puget Sound at the beginning of the twentieth century. The unusual plot presents a stance initiated in *Living by Fiction* on the subject of purity versus perfection, the two main characters, Beal Obenchain and Clare Fishburn, representing these two qualities, respectively. Obenchain, an intellectual who "liked ideas, purity, and little else" decides *not* to kill a man; "He had killed a man last week and just decided not to kill another" (48). Instead of killing Clare Fishburn, Obenchain will threaten him with death. In doing this, he will control Fishburn without "lifting a finger," for a man, Obenchain reasons, cannot continue to live with the fear of death continually at his heels; if you "tell a man his life is in your hands. . . his life is actually in your hands. You own him insofar as he believes you; you own him as God owns people, to the degree of their faith" (48). But for Obenchain, who believes "Life is mind" (48), the plan is aborted. Fishburn not only does not come to fear Obenchain but is exhilarated by his insight into the possibility of his own death. Consistent with Dillard's final acceptance of her own mortality, her fringed and frayed life in the cruel and mysterious universe of *Pilgrim,* she concludes her morality tale with a suggestion that life, this "living," has its own inexplicable and glorious moments which create for Fishburn, even as he recognizes his diminutive place in eternity and space, a sense of euphoria. Fishburn sees the "broken earth" which buries the men, the horses, and the plows of all ages; yet at the end of the story he turns toward the "light upstream" (64) with an intensified sense of life. Obenchain, recognizing that his plan has misfired in a final attempt to maintain power over Fishburn, announces that he will not kill Fishburn. But Fishburn will not give back his knowledge of death, for this painful awareness of mortality has released him to live:

> Clare felt as wide and spread as the sky. He had a family in his skull; his legs were moving. He knew he was walking as if he were opening something as a boat's bow opens the water. He himself was being opened, as if Obenchain were a table saw. He was a clod of dirt that the light splits, or a peeled fish. Time kept rolling back and bearing him: he was as porous as clouds or bones. (64)

Fishburn, who represents the openness, extravagance, and accumulation of life, who "enjoyed enjoyment," who "never answered letters . . . never deliberately told a lie, but never happened to keep a promise . . . smoked in bed . . . hated schedules, planning, appointments, finances—anything fussy or detailed" (50) is Dillard's representation of "perfection." Perfection allows the stuff of life to invade and engorge. And eventually the very pleasure of life is made more acute by the knowledge of its transitory nature. Clare Fishburn can "burrow in light upstream" as Dillard in *Pilgrim* faces upstream to the unknown future where the "wave that explodes over my head . . . the live water and light" from "undisclosed sources" brings her renewed "world without end" (103). Fishburn has learned a lesson, advanced in *Pilgrim*, that the "terms are clear: if you want to live, you have to die; you cannot have mountains and creeks without space, and space is a beauty married to a blind man. The blind man is Freedom, or Time, and he does not go anywhere without his great dog Death" (*Pilgrim* 181). In the conclusion Fishburn has allowed all knowledge to invade, even the knowledge of death, and finds himself "porous as clouds or bones" with the acceptance of both the beauty and pain of living.

Dillard's allegory is borne out in the characters' names. Obenchain becomes the "chain" of rigidity and bare-bone ideas in language. He is the purity of idea exclusive of the fleshiness of life. Fishburn, on the other hand, is associated with Christ in the symbol of the fish. "Burn" becomes a symbol of God burning like a fireball, or hoop of fire, the holiness of the spirit in the Pentecostal flame. Fishburn is literally "Christ aflame," while "Clare" represents "clear," the full name becoming "clear Christ aflame," suggestive of abundant life and increased knowledge springing out of sacrificial death. Out of the knowledge that life contains death arises perfection and mystery, a burgeoning of antithetical conditions that produce the illuminated moment. As Fishburn's name suggests, one understands the fullness of life, represented by "fish" or Christ, only when one comprehends the limitations of death, signified by "burn" or Christ's sacrifice. Like the finch perched on the thistle erupting the seed to the wind, the moment of "seeing" must necessarily be composed of both beauty and sorrow.

Dillard, without benefit of plot or character, repeats this idea in *Living by Fiction:*

> Material complexity is the truth of the world, even the workable world of idea, and must be the truth of the art object which would imitate, order, and penetrate that world: complexity, and contradiction, and repetition, diversity, energy, and largesse. I am as attracted to purity as the next guy. But it must not happen here. (172)

Dillard maintains that life, and it follows for art, discloses itself through "perfection," the excess, and the chaos of complex and contradictory materials. She defines "perfection" as "fullness," while "purity" is "absence" (171), suggesting that humanity should accept and celebrate both the positive and negative aspects of life; unplanned and chaotic events, which at first seem intrusive, should be welcomed as well as planned and pleasant occurrences. When a person allows these events, and with them many ideas, to invade, Dillard believes the resulting condition is the "soil" in which the spirit hides and grows. Purity, on the other hand, delimits and theorizes, allowing only bloodless concepts, "various irreducible nubs," to stand where once the organic wealth of "material messes" provided an environment in which knowledge could expand (170). While Obenchain selected a purified theory, hoping to gain power through his threat to kill Fishburn, it is the latter man who perceives the full pleasure and pathos of life and, consequently, experiences the illuminated moment. Understanding that he must die, he felt his body change from a mirror's opacity to a window's transparency: "And Clare changed. He walked from the long habit of walking, and he changed as a pane of glass changes when you walk beside it—from reflecting as a mirror to transparent as air" (64). Even this metaphor, the reflected versus the internal light, intimates Dillard's romanticism. While she is "attracted" by the classical idea of balance and order or "purity," she believes in the superiority of the "messy" and contradictory "perfection" that yields God.

Clare Fishburn is a simple man who "feels" life rather than "thinks" it. He sees with a child's eye, another of Dillard's literary preoccupations linking her with nineteenth-century romantics. In romantic literature, children, along with solitary and rustic figures, represent a class of "natural" persons, the unsophisticated who, because they are untainted by institutions, are able, as Wordsworth says, to see clearly "into the life of things" ("Tintern Abbey" 49).[2] Dillard "tries to achieve an innocent eye akin to the child's," according to James Aton, "and figures this in numerous examples of childhood memories" (80). *American Childhood* is predicated on this "innocent eye" and sifts through the fine shavings of consciousness to present an accurate account of Dillard's awakening mind. When the young Dillard tries to identify the luminous "swift spirit" which invades her bedroom where she lies in fear daring neither to blink nor to breathe and trying to "hush" her "whooping blood" (21), she parallels Wordsworth's childhood fear when he, lost on the heath, looks "around for [his] lost guide" and finds instead a "gibbet-mast . . . mouldered down" and a murderer's name etched into the turf (*Prelude* 11.311, 290–93). Dillard eventually "figured it out one night" (21). The oblong light was the reflection from a passing car which "reflected the corner light outside," but Dillard writes that "figuring it out was as memorable as the oblong itself. Figuring it out was a long and forced ascent to the very rim of being, to the membrane of skin that both separates and connects the inner life and the outer world" (21). This is seeing for the first time, seeing shapes of light without the ability to connect these shapes with sources. Here is the innocent eye which can come upon a scene and react with wonder, and with that wonder and freshness see more clearly than the eye of the jaded adult.

Dillard writes in *Pilgrim* about a blind girl whose sight is restored through surgery. When the bandages are removed the girl sees "the tree with the lights in it" (33). The child sees the world as a "dazzle of color-patches," the same way Dillard would see the world, a world "unraveled from reason" (27, 30), for reason, like the purity of Beal Obenchain, takes away our ability to see into the heart of things. Reason, like cataracts, places scales on our eyes, and Dillard would drop these scales of reason in order to see color-patches of beauty. Her search for the "tree with the lights" is the pursuit of seeing like a child in the epiphanic moment. Wordsworth laments the loss of the "celestial light," those "things which I have seen I now can see no more" ("Intimations" 4, 9); Dillard laments with him when she eats the "bittersweet fruit" of recognition identifying the car lights. She "put two and two together and puckered forever" her brain (*Pilgrim* 30). But even with her puckered brain, which symbolizes her increased sophistication and decreased ability to experience beauty, she continues to search for the "vision which comes and goes" (*Pilgrim* 34) when she, with the true vision of a child, can see even momentarily into the life of things.

In line with nineteenth-century romanticism Dillard emphasizes the particular rather than the general. Wordsworth makes a microcosm of a mossy ledge and lichen-covered thornbush where a desolate mother wails for her child in "The Thorn"; in "Resolution and Independence" he finds significance in the peculiarities of an old leechgatherer "bent double" who prides himself in his occupation; and in "Simon Lee" a crippled huntsman who hacks at a decaying stump with little hope of success is the stimulus for an insight into the life of things. Similarly, in *Pilgrim at Tinker Creek* Dillard lists the minutiae of insect and plant life and presents her emotional responses to these details. In the chapter entitled "Spring" she writes of burgeoning life—both vegetables and animal. Millions of rotifers, pond dwellers, tulip trees—all must be admitted into the scheme along with the writer. She cannot hide her eyes from that which cannot be seen readily by the unaided eye. Dillard concludes the chapter: "If I did not know about the rotifers and paramecia, and all the bloom of plankton clogging the dying pond, fine; but since I've seen it I must somehow deal with it, take it into account" (122). The particular or the small world will, she believes, lead her on to the meaning of her life.

This fine detail, however, reveals an intricately beautiful and yet appallingly "fixed" world (67). An illustration of this emphasis on detail is Dillard's childhood memory of a Polyphemus moth which hatches in her schoolroom, an incident that appears in both *Pilgrim* and *American Childhood,* indicating its importance to the writer. The children look on as the huge moth struggles to discard its cocoon. It emerges "at last, a sodden crumple" (*Pilgrim* 61), but expands quickly in the Mason jar. The moth, however, with "multijointed legs, pale and powerful . . . shaggy as a bear's," could not expand to its full width: "He couldn't spread his wings. There was no room. The chemical that coated his wings like varnish, stiffening them permanently, dried, and hardened his wings as they were. He was a monster in a Mason jar" (61). Horrified by the creature's inability to do anything but crawl away, Dillard, in her memory, sees the monstrous image of the moth "crawling down the driveway, crawling down the driveway hunched, crawling down the driveway on six furred feet, forever" (61). Although the details of the moth are painful for

Dillard to recall, she is compelled to search out these details in order to make a faithful account of life's scheme, and all of this detail is necessary for her search. As Margaret Loewen Reimer notes, "her attention is focused always on the most minute detail, the most particular of objects"; thus, desiring to "become lost in the particular instead of the universal" Dillard "experiences the divine" (188–89).

Among Dillard's other romantic characteristics is a certain spirit, specifically an anti-neoclassicism, that shows itself when she laments years of attention given to the polishing of literary surfaces rather than literary content: "That so many critics and poets have for so many years devoted so much attention to poetry's surface accounts for the gradual erosion of any standards but polish" ("Purification of Poetry" 299). Polish and control of material is connected with purity of form, which represents to Dillard a wall against excess, and, consequently, the incursion of the Spirit.

Dillard comments directly on nineteenth-century romanticism specifically in *Pilgrim*. She notes the reliance on smooth, classical forms in eighteenth-century society. But, "after the Romantic Revolution, and after Darwin . . . our conscious notions of beauty changed" (139). Humankind admitted then the beauty of irregularity of form. The mystery of ridges and hide-a-ways keeps the mind awake. In accepting irregularity and unclassical forms humankind also recognized death. "Did those eighteenth-century people think they were immortal?" she asks (140). Answering her own rhetorical question, she concludes that they "blindfolded" their eyes rather than looked at the irregularity of mountains. The romantic revolution dismissed the notion that beauty was always a product of smooth forms.

Finally, in noting these associations with nineteenth-century romanticism, Dillard views herself through much of her work as a poet-priestess, a visionary artist intent on receiving the vision, or epiphany, and then transmitting the moment through her exquisite prose. Wordsworth as a young man is "visited" on the early morning road of his Lake District and "vows were made" for him, although he made no vows for himself. The spirit comes to Wordsworth in order to announce the poet's calling, the vocation of bard:

> I made no vows, but vows
> Were then made for me: bond unknown to me
> Was given, that I should be—else sinning greatly—
> A dedicated spirit. On I walked
> In blessedness, which even yet remains.
> (*Prelude* 4.341–45)

Dillard in similar fashion, because vision is a "deliberate gift," reels under her illumination of the tree with lights and reveals that "it was less like seeing than like being for the first time seen, knocked breathless by a powerful glance" (*Pilgrim* 33). Both artists are passive at the moment of this "vocational" epiphany, open to the greater power which chooses them.

In addition to answering a spiritual calling, Dillard suggests in *Living by Fiction* that the artist, particularly the literary artist, can best interpret the world. Artists, as opposed to theologians and philosophers, deal with the raw material of existence and thereafter interpret it (*Living* 146). She writes that the literary arts in general "are in a better position to interpret the world in all its breadth than are the other arts" (146–47); further, from among these literary arts the best interpreter is lyric poetry. It has been able to "function quite directly as human interpretation of the raw, loose universe" because "it is a mixture . . . of journalism and metaphysics, or of science and religion" (147). Although Dillard's own work is predominantly nonfiction, she tries to maintain the condensation and tenor of lyric poetry. "The idea of non-fiction as an art form interests me," she commented in an interview. "The idea of the non-fictional essay's having the abstract intellectual structures of poetry interests me" ("Drawing the Curtains" 35), verifying the poetic proclivities of her prose.

As an artist called to her work, a holy bard, she believes, like Wordsworth, that not all people are capable of the divine moment of inspiration or illumination. She says she gets "angry at God" when she sees "so many good people who appear to lack an organ by which they can perceive God" ("A Face Aflame" 963). Therefore, since much of the world lacks this visionary organ, she, in the company of Wordsworth and Coleridge, will become a "Prophet of Nature" who will "speak / A lasting inspiration, sanctified / By reason and by truth" to the world (*Prelude* 13.442–44).

While this discussion focuses on the relationship between nineteenth-century British romantics and Dillard, no thorough study of her work can exclude her connections with nineteenth-century American romantics—the Transcendentalists. In the hands of Emerson and Thoreau, the illuminated moment becomes a different experience, or at least a different literary experience, from that expressed by Wordsworth. The change might be summed up by stating that in general these Americans lost immediacy and gained philosophic exposition in the matter of illumination. Emerson's well-known "transparent eyeball" section in "Nature" provides an illustration.

Emerson writes in "Nature" of "Crossing a bare common, in snow puddles, at twilight, under a clouded sky" when, without any expectations, he has "enjoyed a perfect exhilaration" which brings joy laced with fear (10). Following this personal note, Emerson lapses immediately into the third person, assuming the persona of a generic man who "casts off his years, as the snake his slough" when he takes to the woods (10). Expanding on the rejuvenating powers of the woods, he writes:

> Within these plantations of God, a decorum and sanctity rein, a
> perennial festival is dressed, and the guest sees not how he should
> tire of them in a thousand years. In the woods, we return to
> reason and faith. There I feel that nothing can befall me in life—no
> disgrace, no calamity (leaving me my eyes), which nature cannot
> repair. (10)

In attempting to translate the transcendant experience in nature, Emerson is most powerful when he can place himself in a real setting of a bare common with snow puddles; but he begins to lose epiphanic power when he depersonalizes this experience by using a third-person Everyman and changes the setting to an unspecified woods. Further, he scatters the power of illumination by explaining to the reader the meaning of the woods as the "plantations of God." Once again he changes the pronoun, referring to a collective "we," returning again to a personal "I," when he moves into the metaphor of the "transparent eyeball": "Standing on the bare ground,—my head bathed by the blithe air, and uplifted into infinite space,—all mean egotism vanishes. I become a transparent eyeball; I am nothing; I see all. The currents of the Universal Being circulate through me; I am part or particle of God" (10). By shifting out of a personal narrative, a single incident, by changing voices, and by offering meanings to his reader, Emerson is not acting substantially different from his fellow Transcendentalists, but he is changing the mysterious power of the illumination as it appears in Wordsworth's "spots of time."

Thoreau in *Walden* offers several moments which verge on the visionary but also differ from the British epiphanies. One must take into account that Thoreau's magnificent piece is an artifice built around his conflated two-year stay in a cabin near Concord. Knowing, then, that *Walden* is not a strict narrative, the reader can expect to find less detail in the illuminations; and, like Emerson, Thoreau does take pains not to highlight personal responses in these moments. In "Baker Farm" he suggests initially that the experience is a singular real event when he begins with "Once," but he gives no more substantial or immediate detail about the event:

> Once it chanced that I stood in the very abutment of a rainbow's
> arch, which filled the lower stratum of the atmosphere, tinging the
> grass and leaves around, and dazzling me as if I looked through
> colored crystal. It was a lake of rainbow light, in which, for a short
> while, I lived like a dolphin. If it had lasted longer it might have
> tinged my employments and life. (202)

The narrator's singular experience, resonating color and light through
its poetic prose, qualifies as an illumination, but it does not convey the
sense of narrative immediacy, a real place and time, which occurs in
"Frost at Midnight" or the "spot of time" concerning Wordsworth's
childhood fear as he sees in the distance a gibbet mast, a beacon, and a
woman bearing a pitcher on her head. In "Spring" Thoreau composes a
literary moment which becomes more nearly epiphanic in character.
"On the 29th of April," Thoreau writes, identifying a real time, and creating expectancy in the reader, "as I was fishing from the bank of the
river near the Nine-Acre-Corner bridge, standing on the quaking grass
and willow roots, where the muskrats lurk...I observed a very slight
and graceful hawk..." (*Walden* 316). He watches the hawk tumbling
over in the sky, the "under side of its wings" gleaming "like satin ribbon
in the sun, or like the pearly inside of a shell" and considers the origin
of the bird, suggesting it might have been hatched in the "angle of a
cloud, woven of the rainbow's trimmings and the sunset sky, and lined
with some soft midsummer haze caught up from earth" (316–17). This
bright tumbling bird, the wild river valley and woods, suggest to the
writer the renewal of life in spring and he exclaims, "There need no
stronger proof of immortality. All things must live in such a light. O
Death, where was thy sting? O Grave, where was thy victory, then?"
(317). The moment becomes an exemplar of eternal life while the explanation of its meaning lies neatly at the end of the passage. Again, the
gilded poetry of the language is a lovely and fitting extension of Walden's
themes but does not lift it fully into the epiphanic tensions of a
Wordsworth or Dillard illumination.

One quality, often a part of epiphany, which is absent in this Thoreau-
vian moment is fear. When Thoreau does include fear as a part of an illuminary moment, his ascension to the summit of Katahdin, he, like
Emerson, changes voices from the personal "I" to a weaker third-person
"he" or "man":

> I reached the summit of the ridge, which those who have seen in
> clearer weather say is about five miles long, and contains a
> thousand acres of table-land, I was deep within the hostile ranks of
> clouds, and all objects were obscured by them. Now the wind

would blow me out a yard of clear sunlight, wherein I stood; then a gray, dawning light was all it could accomplish, the cloud-line ever rising and falling with the wind's intensity. Sometimes it seemed as if the summit would be cleared in a few moments and smile in sunshine: but what was gained on one side was lost on another. . . . Occasionally, when the windy columns broke in to me, I caught sight of a far, damp crag to the right or left; the mist driving ceaselessly between it and me. It reminded me of the creations of the old epic and dramatic poets, of Atlas, Vulcan, the Cyclops, and Prometheus. Such was Caucasus and the rock where Prometheus was bound. Aeschylus had no doubt visited such scenery as this. It was vast, Titanic, and such as man never inhabits. Some part of the beholder, even some vital part, seems to escape through the loose grating of his ribs as he ascends. He is more lone than you can imagine. (*Maine Woods* 63–64)

Not only does Thoreau change voices, but he breaks into classical allusions about mountaintops, thus mitigating the power of a personal account and thereby weakening epiphany. He further distances himself from the moments by personifying the environment as Mother Nature as she speaks "sternly" to the man who dares climb a mountain. To the personification he enjoins an archaic language with which Mother Nature rebuffs her aggressive man-child, and, finally, Thoreau feels he must explain the meaning of the fear he felt when he reached the summit of Katahdin. Nature, he writes,

does not smile on him as in the plains. She seems to say sternly, why came ye here before your time? This ground is not prepared for you. . . . I cannot pity nor fondle thee here, but forever relentlessly drive thee hence to where I *am* kind. Why seek me where I have not called thee, and then complain because you find me but a stepmother? . . .

The tops of mountains are among the unfinished parts of the globe, whither it is a slight insult to the gods to climb and pry into their secrets, and try their effect on our humanity. . . . Pomola is always angry with those who climb to the summit of Ktaadn. (64–65)

Taken together, these characteristics of American Transcendental illumination—loss of narrative immediacy, masking of the personal experience through voice changes, and metaphoric explanations—set the American "epiphany" apart from earlier British offerings. Emerson and Thoreau create a substantially different literary experience, and, although, Dillard takes much of her love of environment, particularly wilderness, from the cues of these Transcendentalists, the tensions of her epiphanic moments are those tensions of the earlier British romantics. She shares with this form of romanticism the luminous organicism of the mind working upon a natural scene, the defiance of religious-social-political institutions and the advocacy of "natural theology," the analysis of the peculiar detail, the desire for the virgin insights of child or rustic, and the belief that the poet or the literary artisan can be called to her work in order to illuminate the world.

Modern Romanticism

The development of literary romanticism and its attendant epiphanic mode in the early twentieth century and throughout the modern period has been analyzed by so many scholars—including Morris Beja, George Bornstein, and Robert Langbaum—that it does not need an intense perusal here. Several aspects of modern romanticism, however, are significant as they bear upon Dillard's preoccupation with epiphany.

Although the most conspicuous figures of the early twentieth-century "classical" period, including T. E. Hulme, Ezra Pound, and T. S. Eliot, denied that they were involved with romanticism in any way, and although they openly eschewed the use of personal voices and public emotion, literary hindsight and poetic product give evidence of romantic tenets at the center of their work. Beja notes that even a "cursory examination" of Hulme's theories will prove that he is not as "classical" as he wants to believe (64). Hulme believed that images were to be more than "decorative" but should play an "essential role in intuition" (Beja 64). The image, according to Pound, is "that which presents an intellectual and emotional complex in an instant of time" (quoted in Beja 65). These references to "intuition" and "emotional complex" as they occur in "an instant of time" are relevant to the operations of the epiphany.

Eliot, of course, spent a lifetime denying his romanticism, although he admitted that he was its victim during his adolescence, which he connected with "illicit sexuality" and the loss of "rational control" (Bornstein 97). But Eliot, who, according to Bornstein distorted literary history by denying romanticism and carrying with him a plethora of critics who falsely promoted anti-romantic elements in poetry, was himself a romantic (15). Eliot "destroyed romantic tenements only to clear the ground for new pleasure domes" (Bornstein 95). No greater evidence could be admitted for Eliot's romanticism than his final work in the *Four Quartets*, specifically the epiphanic moments in "Burnt Norton" and "Little Gidding."

Bornstein has composed an extensive and helpful list of romantic tenets which are common to both nineteenth- and twentieth-century writers. The main tenet is that literary romanticism involves an "act of the mind" (Wallace Stevens's phrase in "Of Modern Poetry"): "romantic poems are less about their ostensible subjects than about a psyche interacting with them"; the mind itself is not a "narrow denominator of a few mechanistic intellectual operations" but a "psyche or complex of creative, perceptual, and organizational powers" (Bornstein 2, 8). Other common denominators of romanticism are the use of topology or a definite locale; a revitalized language with an emphasis on common style; a desire to play to the "delicatest ear of the mind" or to unify reality and imagination; an emphasis on the "quest" rather than on the "grail"; and the creation of limited imaginative areas in a poem which are "charged with significance" because imagination cannot carry a poetic form for a long period (Bornstein 2–11). This last point speaks to the nature of epiphany for this is the imaginative area "charged with significance" which provides the central "structure" for the romantic piece; this is the "charged" moment in "Tintern Abbey" when the poet enters into "Thoughts of more deep seclusion" to "see into the life of things" (7, 49). Moreover, this is Dillard's sudden recognition of the "tree with lights."

So the moderns, with or without their admission of romantic interests, carried forward the "act of mind." Wallace Stevens recognized during the height of modernism that romanticism "looks like something completely contemptible in the light of literary intellectualism and cynicism. The romantic, however, has a way of renewing itself" (*Opus Posthumous* 215). And, so, romanticism did renew itself in this period but with some alterations which Stevens points out in "Of Modern Poetry":

> The poem of the mind in the act of finding
> What will suffice. It has not always had
> To find: the scene was set; it repeated what
> Was in the script.
>   Then the theatre was changed
> To something else. Its past was a souvenir.
> It has to be living, to learn the speech of the place.
> It has to face the men of the time and to meet
> The women of the time. It has to think about war
> And it has to find what will suffice. It has
> To construct a new stage.
>   (*Collected Poems* 1–10)

These opening lines indicate that the entire backdrop of life had changed for this poet and for his literary companions. Though the poem has a constant, it is "of the mind," now it must find images and forms beyond what was previously poetic material, when there was a "script" from which poets could draw. Images of nightingales or urns or other romantic icons will not suffice when the entire "theatre" has been changed. In learning the "speech of the place," the new language which could make poems create an emotional response in the contemporary reader, the writer, Stevens continues, must "speak words that in the ear, / In the delicatest ear of the mind, / repeat, / Exactly, that which it wants to hear." What the new audience, which is actually the mind, wants to hear is "itself, expressed / In an emotion as of two people, as of two / Emotions coming together" (12–14). Here Stevens indicates that his contemporaries realize even more urgently than did their nineteenth-century counterparts that the poem is of the mind. While Keats sends his mind outward with the nightingale into the dark perfume of the "thicket, and the fruit-tree wild," in a sprawling, frantic search, so that he might forget the "fever" of the world, Stevens, Yeats, and Eliot on most occasions gather the poetic material closer about them, tightening and honing the poem into an obelisk of form and emotion. The poem comes back to the mind, and the mind acting upon itself undergoes epiphanic moments of a different character than those of the nineteenth century. These epiphanies, however, were even more consistently sought by the moderns than by nineteenth-century romantics, including those writers working in fiction and poetry, for their need for spiritual affirmation was greater.

The moderns, turning inward on their material, created literary works more sculptural in character than their romantic forebears. Having turned from the "nine bean-rows" of Yeats's Innisfree to the golden bird set "upon a golden bough" in Byzantium, these modern poets were no longer mesmerized and comforted by natural elements. Keats's dark "muskrose" forest was no longer a balm for these writers. Beja notes that the epiphany became "immensely important and unique" to twentieth-century literature because individuals were "no longer confident. . .of a divine answer" and therefore sought their own answers (18, 21). Nor could reason or rationalism provide answers: "The conviction that enlightenment is no more likely to come from rationalism and logic than it is from God makes the need for instantaneous, intuitive illumination seem all the more critical" (Beja 21). In addition to the "loss" of God and the distrust of reason the moderns showed an increased interest in psychology and the "subjective processes of the mind" (Beja 21). Particularly interesting to them was the human reaction to detail and trivia or the seemingly unimportant details of life. These developments taken together initiated the writer's focus on finding his own spritual enlightenment within the confines of the sculpted art piece.

Illustrating this movement away from the natural, Yeats writes in "Sailing to Byzantium" that "Once out of nature I shall never take / My bodily form from any natural thing" (*Collected Works* 25–26) while Stevens believes that the mind and nature are not suited for one another; "One must have a mind of winter," the mind of a snowman in the poem of the same name (*Collected Works* 1). Langbaum suggests that Stevens is using here a kind of "negative epiphany" which "reverses Wordsworth's idea that mind and nature are admirably suited to each other" (340). The same conviction is voiced in "Man and Bottle" when Stevens writes,

> The mind is the great poem of winter, the man,
> Who, to find what will suffice,
> Destroys romantic tenements
> Of rose and ice . . .
> (*Collected Poems* 1–4)

Although Eliot's hard, intellectual, disjointed images in "The Wasteland" do meekly revert to natural images in "Burnt Norton" as he enters "through the first gate" into the rose garden, the images in the poem present an almost institutionalized nature as the poet walks "in a formal pattern, / Along the empty alley, into the box circle" (20, 31–32). He looks down into a manmade dry concrete pool, and out of this formal, manicured greenery comes the sound of children's laughter which is for the poet the beginning of epiphany (34–41). This garden, which has been prepared and kept by humankind, is not the raging Welsh wilderness where the divine, uncivilized spirit speaks to Wordsworth off the misty promontories of Mt. Snowdon. With these various approaches the moderns eliminated a natural environment which no longer held a voice that could speak to them of spiritual hope; their attention was necessarily given to the art object, the poem, and the novel.

In "The Purification of Poetry Right Out of the Ballpark" Dillard makes some significant comments about the moderns which reiterate the notion of the loss of spiritual identity with nature and the emergence of a new poetic approach. She says that the modernists took fragments of the world, referential things, and united these with "imaginary objects" to construct a "complex, reflexive, internally coherent plan for beauty, the poem" (293). They could no longer write epics or successful narratives because the religious-social structures on which those storylines existed were gone. Their "great theme," according to Dillard, became "the relationship between time and eternity" (293). This theme of time and eternity, then, becomes the springboard for the recurring epiphanic moments in modern literature.

Because these poets had lost their religious undergirdings, and because they needed to maintain some unity, which by its very definition calls for balance, coherence, and meaning, they, according to Dillard, developed eccentricities, indeed, quirky personalities. They brought "embarrassing" and "crackpot" meanings of philosophies to their new forms—Pound's Mussolini, Eliot's Christ, and Yeats's spiritualism (295). Thus, the greatness of these poets, Dillard believes, lies not in their ideas, but in their ideas as they appear on the page. It is the language and the coherence of their forms that make these poets great literary figures (293).

Dillard in this article reveals her own predilections and, one might say, her own eccentricities, for who is to say what content makes up the less "quirky" work? It does appear true that each of these major figures—Pound, Eliot, Stevens, and Yeats—brought an exceedingly individual formula of meaning to his work and carried that formula forward in an aggressive manner. But Wordsworth, Coleridge, and Keats also brought their own meanings: generally that a divine spirit inhabited a natural environment, among other things, and, thus, these nineteenth-century poets could also be construed by many readers to be equally as eccentric. The difference for Dillard is that these earlier views are more homogeneous and, in the long run, more compatible with her own views of universal structures. What Dillard brings to her own writing, specifically the epiphany, with some variations to be discussed later, is a combination of nineteenth-century and modern romanticism, the very traditional epistemology of Wordsworth, Coleridge, Keats, Shelley, and Hopkins united with the highly wrought and unified language of Stevens, Yeats, and Eliot. One other literary tradition provides the variation which creates the unique Dillardian prose-poetry studded with illumination: the Muir-wilderness tradition.

The Muir-Wilderness Tradition

Annie Dillard has been linked with a genre called "naturalist autobiography," or "wilderness literature," a genre that has its roots, according to John Elder, in the writings of John Muir (1838–1914), American naturalist and ecologist. Elder believes that Muir stands at midpoint between nineteenth-century transcendentalists and contemporary nature writers like Dillard. Other writers working in the same genre are Aldo Leopold *(Sand County Almanac)*, Edward Abbey *(Desert Solitaire)*, Rachel Carson *(The Sea Around Us)*, Barry Lopez *(Of Wolves and Men)*, and Peter Matthiessen *(The Snow Leopard)*. During the last several decades this wilderness material has reached a popularity which allows its writers to be deemed, as Elder notes, the equivalent of "updated Victorian Sages" (375).

This literature is characterized by certain common elements, according to Elder: (1) it is marked by "close observation of nature, within an awareness of the modern science of ecology"; (2) it is a "journal of the author's own growth, by means of the intense relation to nature"; (3) it is a "speculation about larger religious and political issues connected with the cause of wilderness-preservation" (375). Its major difference with the transcendental literature which preceded it is that, in the tradition of Muir, it uses accurate, in-the-field description which ultimately tips the balance toward the side of ecological concerns rather than literary or transcendental musings. Muir knew that it is "immediate experience, not its literary reflection, that finally has transforming power" (Elder 377).

A brief examination of Muir's approach to the natural world and his attendant philosophy would be helpful to highlight Dillard's emergence from this literature and then her eventual divergence from it, particularly as that divergence affects her use of illumination. First, John Muir was concerned, as Elder points out, with "immediate experience" rather than "literary reflection." Muir was not, however, unconcerned with philosophical reflection in general which, of course, did make its way into his literature whether the writer desired this vehicle or not. Muir's writings reveal a man consumed with touching the earth directly, botanizing, collecting, studying rocks, plants, and animal life in their natural settings; his beloved Sierra Nevada became the focus of his life. But Muir gave almost equal attention to fitting his field descriptions into a harmonious and quasi-religious plan which he reveals intermittently throughout such pieces as *My First Summer in the Sierra* and *The Mountains of California.*

This harmonious plan, though, should be viewed alongside the work of the preeminent American Transcendentalists, Emerson and Thoreau, to see how Muir's vision fits into its own genre. Direct examination of nature came first for Muir, and for this reason he cannot be found in the same transcendental tradition as Emerson and Thoreau. Muir biographer Stephen Fox observes that "both Emerson and Thoreau seemed insufficiently wild to him. . . . both appreciated nature from a base in abstract metaphysics. To Muir this seemed to reverse a proper, more reverent approach. Always he began with the natural world and judged everything in its terms" (83). Even though Muir believed that "Any philosophical baggage brought to the wilderness merely impeded a true appreciation of nature's handiwork" (Fox 83), he did indeed bring a great deal of philosophical baggage with him, a peculiar type of philosophy which sets him apart in a fundamental way from Emerson, Thoreau, and, in essential epiphanic matters, Dillard. In Muir's mind this baggage, although not necessarily Christian, was marked "Goodness," "Unerring Plan," "Nature's Benevolence," terms characterizing the sentiment of his work. For Muir, this philosophy was concluded at the outset; not the philosophical structure but the plants, animals, and rocks needed to be studied in detail, directly, to observe how they might fulfill the criterion of that philosophy.

There were no accidents or disunity in nature for John Muir, "no dissonance, no absolute separations. Everything, from the man on the mountain down to the smallest speck, was arranged and loved *in equal measure* by the creator" (Fox 13). An exemplar of Muir's thought, a benevolent unity linked with the natural detail he found in his ramblings, lies in the writer's preoccupation with glacial history in the Sierra. Believing that the glacier, as an agent of God, had carved out the Yosemite Valley, Muir maintained that he had found remnants of living, ancient glaciers in the deep crevasses of the valley. His search for glacial work represented his search for harmony and purpose in nature. It was, in fact, as Fox notes, "an act of devotion for him" (21). If the valleys had been formed cataclysmically, the "theory made God prankster," a view of the universe unacceptable to Muir (21). Even though Muir made a break with formal Christianity in 1867, he maintained a belief in the benevolence of a Creator, one who had made the earth for all of its inhabitants (50). What repelled Muir in Christian orthodoxy was that Man was made Lord Man, subjecting all of the "lower orders" to his power. Muir could never accept the dominance of the human species over even the mighty rock formations he encountered on his mountain climbs. Nature was even-handed and unwaveringly benevolent to all forms on the earth; in the Muir philosophy there was a gracious Mind with a grand Plan at work.

Although Dillard takes away from the Muir tradition her close observation of natural phenomena, her reaction to those details is essentially different from Muir's response. Dillard is also seeking a philosophical unity in her literary worlds; however, the placement of that unity in these two observers of the natural world lies in distinct areas of the resultant literature. Muir finds unity in the landscape itself and in its natural processes, that is, in the exterior world. Dillard, on the other hand, must find unity in a kind of philosophical justification within her own mind, an operation which is interior, that is, essentially occurring within the intellect, as the writer observes so often a chaotic world at her feet. Dillard's action of unification must take place in the mind because the natural world is not reasonable, albeit the landscape is excruciatingly beautiful at times. While she recognizes beauty, she must filter it through the painful knowledge of the Fall. Her epiphanic moments, then, are supreme moments of unification, flashing upon her through elements of the landscape but essentially birthed in her mind. Chaos, or at least chaotic antilogic, is dominant until unity—or as Keats would suggest, Beauty and Truth—are clearly and suddenly apprehended in an illumination, a brightening of the mind.

Muir does not have Dillard's need to break through the chaos of fecundity and predation because he does not perceive these processes as irregular. In *My First Summer in the Sierra* he writes that

> the best gains of this trip were the lessons of unity and interrelation of all the features of the landscape revealed in general views. . . . How interesting everything is! Every rock, mountain, stream, plant, lake, lawn, forest, garden, beast, insect seems to call and invite us to come and learn something of its history and relationship. (145)

Here he is revealing a mind already settled on the question of pain; for him, unity and interrelationship are necessarily worked out through the activities of predator and prey. While Dillard writes about the vast waste of reproduction which feeds upon itself, Muir finds harmony in seeds and animals falling away, making a bed for the next generation: "How lavish is Nature building, pulling down, creating, destroying, chasing every material particle from form to form, ever changing, ever beautiful" (*My First Summer* 144). There is little wonder that for Dillard the illuminary moment is crucial and for Muir it is a pleasant and gentle verification of what he already knows or accepts.

The difference becomes even more apparent in a comparison of Muir's reveling in the process of nature with Dillard's utter dismay in the same world. In *My First Summer* Muir writes:

> One is constantly reminded of the infinite lavishness and fertility of Nature—inexhaustible amid what seems enormous waste. And yet when we look into any of her operations that lie within reach of our minds, we learn that no particle of her material is wasted or worn out. It is eternally flowing from use to use, beauty to yet higher beauty; and we soon cease to lament waste and death, and rather rejoice and exult in the imperishable, unspendable wealth of the universe, and faithfully watch and wait the reappearance of everything that melts and fades and dies about us, feeling sure that its next appearance will be better and more beautiful than the last. (146)

But Dillard, questioning, does lament "waste and death" when she cries, "I want out of this still air . . . . It is the fixed that horrifies us, the fixed that assails us with the tremendous force of its mindlessness . . . . The fixed is the world without fire—dead flint, dead tinder, and nowhere a spark. It is a motion without direction" (*Pilgrim* 67–68), and later, "In this repetition of individuals is a mindless stutter, an imbecilic fixedness that must be taken into account" (161). The unity sought by these artists, then, takes place in separate areas. For Muir unity exists in a plan which he accepts as universally good, making the landscape and all of the natural world an active correspondent to the plan. For Dillard the landscape and its processes are often counter to symmetry, illogical and wasted; therefore her unity comes through a trick of mind, a flash of timelessness, a tiny yet sufficient glimpse into an alogical but holy plan which cannot be explained except by the appearance of the next illumination.

Muir interestingly reveals early his speculative assurance in his own brand of illumination when he writes that "we never know where we must go nor what guides we are to get,—men, storms, guardian angels, or sheep" (*My First Summer* 148). It is his "guardian angel" which later saves him from a fall from Mount Ritter in *The Mountains of California*. Muir lapses into epiphanic language in a passage where he feels himself splayed Christlike against the side of Mount Ritter. He can neither climb forward nor backward and has literally become a cross on the rocks "with arms outspread, clinging close to the face of the rocks, unable to move hand or foot either up or down" (*Mountains* 64). But Muir is rescued by his "other self, bygone experiences, Instinct, or Guardian Angel,—call it what you will" and is magically retrieved from disaster (64–65). He writes that had he "been borne aloft upon wings, [his] deliverance could not have been more complete" (65). He had already worked out the theology which would save him; he had already created a beneficent God who might sweep in to catch the writer as he climbs along dangerous rocks. This God is no surprise in the Muir illumination; he is a metaphoric capstone to a theological cathedral already erected. Muir believes that "All the wilderness seems to be full of tricks and plans to drive and draw us up into God's Light" (*My First Summer* 148), while Dillard suggests that if a "trick" does occur it might possibly be malevolent or, at the least, unintended for human ears, as a tree falling in the forest with no one there to hear. Her hope is that she might be present if a trick of beauty does occur.

"Sermons in stone" and mountain cathedrals are the furniture of Muir's landscape where Nature provides her "best masonry"; the writer repeats the comparison often that "the world seems a church and the mountains altars" (*My First Summer* 150) and thus the reader cannot possibly be surprised when the great natural cathedrals house the showing forth of God. But this metaphor with its attendant illumination, its draining of surprise, is exactly what separates Dillard's epiphany from the homogenized moments of Muir. Michael Cohen writes that Muir, in his *Studies in the Sierra*, "immersed himself in the divine truth of the Book of Nature, and read it largely as an early nineteenth-century scientist might, with the assurance that it was a sacred book" (109). Dillard does not assume that her environment is this holy volume.

Dillard, although she often calls on Muir's wilderness tonality for her prose, does not limit herself to the ecologist's landscape as the source of illumination, while Muir's awakenings, on the other hand, most often occur in the mountains. In the tenuous moments when Muir almost falls from Mount Ritter, he receives salvation from an exterior power, perhaps his Guardian Angel. Cohen believes that Muir's letting go of self, the passive quality which ensues in this moment, is the central part of the Mount Ritter illumination and, further, he connects this with the "ecologist's flexibility" which requires "that there was no 'myself' different from the rest of the cosmos" (70–71). Oddly, perhaps paradoxically, Cohen suggests that the moment is cosmic and yet habitual for those who pursue the mountains like Muir. Cohen writes that the "law which let him live was no more an idle chance than the law which might have let him fall":

> Perhaps we could call this mystical mountaineering; those who know something about this experience insist...that it is a normal state of mind, that it happens every day. Bateson believed that he had not accomplished such an "other way to thinking," but still suggested that "we should trust no policy decisions which emanate from persons who do not yet have that habit." Such a state of mind, then, is a *powerful source* for human action, and should be recognized as such. For those who accept it, it represents a commerce between the human mind and the Mind of the Universe. (71)

This passage from Cohen, particularly the phrase "policy decisions," gives the sensation of group epiphany, or at least a prescribed epiphany from the Sierra Club. Cohen directly links ecology and illumination when he cites Bateson's belief that "this fusion of self and other [is] a key step to ecological thinking, where ontology and epistemology could not be separated" (70). This mental state, which is linked directly to mountaineering in the Cohen context, is "necessary to the ecologist's flexibility, to his '*uncommitted potentiality for change*' " (70). Almost suggesting a "good old boy" network of mountain-climbers, Cohen brings together politics and illumination, a connection which no doubt has its place in the physical world of mountain-ecologists but should not be joined to the literary device under discussion. Prescription cannot work in the kind of illumination of which Dillard writes; Muir and Cohen are certainly sincere, but the prescriptive quality, which by its very nature follows metaphor, attenuates literary epiphany.

Not only does Muir find his awakenings most often on mountains, but his moments seem a concomitant of physical acts, as Dillard's do not. He confronts these physical tasks, such as hanging precariously on small ledges behind waterfalls or climbing dangerous mountain passes, in order to feel the rush of power which he interprets as an otherworldly moment. "Danger increasing is met with increasing power," Muir writes, "and when thus successfully met, produces an exalted exhilaration joined with an increase of power over every muscle far beyond the experience possible in flat lowlands, where hidden dangers destroy without calling forth any strength to resist or enjoy" (*John of the Mountains* 296). Here Muir readily admits that his moments are best achieved by arranging danger which in turn activates energy and exhilaration. Further, he suggests that this illumination cannot successfully take place on "flat lowlands." Dillard's "danger," that is, the danger which activates her illumination, is a danger for the spirit, not the body. She questions the entire philosophical setup, the big picture, the gnawing and fighting and death. Hers is the energy encountered by defying it all, a fist at the sky, a heaving of the sacrificed "shoulder of the ram of consecration" (*Pilgrim* 264). She does not have to climb mountains to feel dangerous energy when she cries, "We are people; we are permitted to have dealings with the creator and we must speak up for the creation. God *look* at what you've done to this creature, look at the sorrow, the cruelty, the long damned waste!" (*Pilgrim* 264). Consequently, her epiphany can occur in a gas station on a Virginia highway or in a grove of trees encumbered with doves. John Muir calls for his own illumination and receives it in a kind of orchestrated mountain drama. Annie Dillard desperately desires illumination but recognizes that the moment can only be given and it throws her back; for "although the pearl may be found, it may not be sought. . . . although it comes to those who wait for it, it is always, even to the most practiced and adept, a gift and a total surprise . . . I cannot cause light; the most I can do is try to put myself in the path of its beam" (*Pilgrim* 33).

Muir's anticipation of illumination also does not belong in Dillardian epiphany. Cohen writes that Muir already knew that the Mount Ritter peak experience would be illuminating: "Why did he know this place would be special, before he arrived on its summit?" (72). The answer is that Muir would create the circumstances in which the "special" event could occur. Cohen says, Muir made a "deliberate choice of a route on the North Face" which would lead "him through the darkness and into the light" (73), a path that makes Muir's "rebirth determined by the structure of the mountain" (73). This preparation for rebirth, this determination to climb where he believes he can undergo a "religious conversion" is exactly the matter which separates Muir from Dillard, who cannot allow preparation for the event itself or in the literary narrative that succeeds the event. But most significantly, the literary epiphanist senses that an illumination's effect cannot be the by-product of "selected setting," in Muir's case, the mountain. For a man like Muir, who shared the Victorian predilection for mountain experiences, the encounter with illumination in this active role is almost predictable; for Dillard, however, the epiphanic stance must be one of passivity, openness to spirit but not high-powered physical forays into wilderness which can be noted, even before the event occurs, as significant.

Frederick Turner places Muir within the tradition of the hero myth, insisting that Muir followed the paradigm which includes the figure's "retreat from the ordinary world and his solitary testing in high places; the confrontation with the specter of death and his triumph over it," and finally the hero returning with his knowledge to share with the world ("Foreword," *My First Summer* viii). This pattern, although it allows for what Turner calls a moment of transcendental bliss which produces "a brief moment in the condition of nonattachment to the world" (x), remains a structure too restrictive for the appearance of the Dillardian literary epiphany. Too much emphasis is placed upon a pattern, which suggests anticipation of a known, a tendency which obliterates spontaneity. Also, the literary epiphanist would not necessarily be ordained a hero, or heroine. To be ordained hero requires some communication from a supernatural entity, but the literary epiphanist generally presents himself as a nonassuming everyman (even though the epiphanist later might be known as "bard") who is suddenly struck by the moment, the moment itself as reason for living; that is, the moment can be individual and self-sufficient. There is no need to take this knowledge down from the mountain, as missionary or Moses or Muir, to save the world.

At the same time that Muir insisted on being in the mountains, on examining the smallest variation in glacial rock and boughs of pines, he insisted on casting all his findings into a harmonious plan. This combination does not appear to have brought the writer much intellectual difficulty; but when he was forced to bring these two elements together in the artifice of language, he rebelled. Although his nature descriptions were much sought after by a Victorian audience who desired to "rough it" in the wilderness vicariously, Muir fought the writer in himself, often asserting that language was artificial and could not capture his scenes. Fox points out Muir's desire that his ideas be drawn "from direct experience in nature, not from books, so contrary arguments evolved from books carried no weight with him" (13). Muir himself writes in the journals:

> I have a low opinion of books; they are but piles of stones set up to show coming travelers where other minds have been, or at best signal smokes to call attention. . . . No amount of word-making will ever make a single soul to *know* these mountains. As well seek to warm the naked and frostbitten by lectures on caloric and pictures of flame. One day's exposure to mountains is better than cartloads of books. . . . No earthy chemicals are so sensitive as those of the human soul. All that is required is exposure, and purity of material. (*John* 94–95)

Muir's proclivity is toward mountain experience over literary illumination; as Fox notes, Muir "Always . . . favored direct immersion over the written word" (20).

Emerson played an important part in linking the literary world and the conservationist world by encouraging Thoreau, Whitman, and Muir on various occasions. Primarily, though, Emerson's concerns were literary, like Dillard's, while Muir's were environmental. Emerson found it difficult to touch nature with Muir even when Muir pleaded for Emerson to join him, on their first meeting, in "'a month's worship with Nature in the high temples of the great Sierra Crown beyond our holy Yosemite" (quoted in Fox 5). But the artifice of literature, rather than prolonged immersion in trees and mountains, was the product Emerson desired.

Dillard is an amalgam of the extremes represented by Muir and Emerson in that she joins both ideas—artifice and natural detail—to establish her literature. She works in the American Transcendental tradition while incorporating the spirit of the Muir-wilderness tradition and its propensity for close examination. She is a descendent of both schools, using the methods of Muir but applying, with Emersonian relish, a more probing and questioning philosophical approach to her environment. She is essentially interested in artifice, a point which shall be developed later in this study.

Although many contemporary wilderness writers are quite artful and apparently conscious of literary design, most of Muir's wilderness "descendents" retain a similar balance of art and ecology, the scale tipping toward ecological and environmental concerns. Leopold's *Sand*

County Almanac, for example, develops primarily in strong, poetic prose a year's observation by Leopold on his land in Wisconsin. The chapters are divided by month; "February" describes the sawing of a huge oak tree that has been struck down by lightning, and Leopold, recognizing and appreciating the great antiquity of the tree, comments ring by ring on the historical analogues of its formation:

> We sensed that these two piles of sawdust were something more than wood: that they were the integrated transect of a century; that our saw was biting its way, stroke by stroke, decade by decade, into the chronology of a lifetime, written in concentric annual rings of good oak. (9)

But there is no doubt that Leopold's book was designed for practical purposes when he writes in the foreword, "That land is a community is the basic concept of ecology, but that land is to be loved and respected is an extension of ethics" (viii–ix).

Another wilderness writer who balances art and ecology is Barry Lopez, whose treatise on the preservation of the endangered wolf is a combination of mythology, mysticism, ecology, and religious premise; native Americans and wolves are interlocked as predator and prey, a mystical relationship "based on the penetrating perception" of the wolf's "gestalt" (Of Wolves and Men 101). But finally, even with the advocation of "mystery" as a viable, acceptable energy on the earth, Lopez emphasizes "the separate realities enjoyed by other organisms," a plea to protect the dwindling wolf population of the earth (285).

Although John C. Elder, among other critics, has identified Dillard with this wilderness tradition, she is, in fact, transcribing her own circle, making her own way, in a new literary movement. She has been identified with these wilderness writers because on the surface of the writing her intent appears ecological. Her year's sojourn at Tinker Creek finds her relating in minute detail the habits and life patterns of coots, frogs, and muskrats. She investigates the creek water and the surrounding woods daily, calling up with obvious far-reaching knowledge and skill, scientific data on the ecology of her environment. In Teaching a Stone to Talk she develops her material in similar fashion, encountering weasels, observing deer in Ecuador, and tramping to a hillside in Washington State in order that she might observe firsthand a total eclipse of the sun. Holy the Firm conforms to this search-and-retrieve data technique as does Encounters with Chinese Writers, although these two books appear less "environmental" than her other writings. Even Dillard's short treatise on the art of composition, The Writing Life, is woven with insect analogies, as in her comparison of an inchworm's slow advance from grass blade to grass blade with a writer's thrust of words, "a fiber optic" that seeks out and "illumines the path just before its fragile tip" (7–8). Finally, *An American Childhood* scrutinizes the data of consciousness with microscopic vision. Even here the bold strokes of river information (her father's explanation of the building of dams, the currents of the Mississippi), rock collections, and water habitats (her favorite childhood book was *The Field Book of Ponds and Streams*) seem to link her with environmental causes. But Dillard's cause is not environment, at least not in the ecological sense; it is art. Dillard's nature-trekking and data-gathering are primarily for the purpose of "literary reflection" and it is this reflection which reveals her power. For Dillard, art has primacy over journalism or science or the raw "historical data of a given day" ("Drawing the Curtains" 35). She approaches the world as if it were a work of art and uses "literary critical methods on it" (35). She is an "artist / catalyst," according to McConahay, less interested in giving a "factual account of a wilderness experience than a summons to share a similar experience of self through literary work" (106). Dillard finds harmony and coherence in the "essay itself" (McIlroy 86). She is an excruciatingly conscious artisan whose search for unity of art form and revelation of art source, which she consistently seeks in a divine presence, is the wellspring and purpose of all of her work.

The Muir-wilderness tradition finds its way into her material because she is a self-conscious child of the postmodern period, a writer who has gone to the quotidian of existence and has attempted to wrench it into some logical, unified whole which could affirm the very nature and reason for art. Dillard, carrying with her the coherent, compact language of the modernists, has returned to the natural environs of Wordsworth, but, because she is a contemporary data collector, in the manner of Muir, she has applied a rational overlay to her material. In the end, however, Dillard breaks through all rationality, substantiating her position by referring to physicists as "wild-eyed raving maniacs" because they themselves cannot infer a rational answer and have, indeed, embraced "mystery"; by embracing mystery herself through means of the most irrational of literary devices, she has become a neoromantic.

Neoromanticism

Annie Dillard's brand of neoromanticism, which incorporates nineteenth-century romanticism, the modernist movement, and the Muir-wilderness tradition, is best characterized by her consistent reliance on literary illumination. These illuminations, resulting from merging literary traditions and historical needs, have found fruition in the last half of the twentieth century in a new romanticism with a strong reliance on epiphany, with Dillard as its major practitioner.

As previously discussed, Dillard's illuminations have the tone of nineteenth-century ones; that is, they are epiphanic rather than visionary in structure, moments that reveal a divine source of power in the universe, God rolling along the mountains as a hoop of flame in *Pilgrim*, or, at the least, a sense that the self and the day are holy and connected, as in *Holy the Firm*. The use of illumination which results in a narrator's admission of divinity can make a piece appear archaic, an anachronism, and Dillard has, in fact, been called "a displaced romantic, out of touch with the fashion of the time" (McIlroy 114). But to raise the question of existence and its meaning, indeed, in nineteenth-century fashion, is the hallmark of Dillard's neoromanticism and, according to Eleanor B. Wymard, "in an age of disbelief, it is refreshing that the quarrel can even be rekindled" (496).

Further, the new romanticism adds to Dillard's "nineteenth-century" illumination a modernist's interest in the controlled language of the moment's setting. Although Wordsworth, almost unwittingly, initiated the modern mode of the epiphany through his odd juxtapositions of objects and his elimination of logical verbal transitions (e.g., the "spot" with the woman bearing a pitcher on her head, the pool, and the beacon on the hill), Joyce, Woolf, Stevens, Yeats, and Eliot developed and refined the mechanics of epiphany in both poetic prose and poetry centered on the art object (e.g., Yeats's golden bird in Byzantium). These same writers, while they honed their craft and created the tight, unified moment, generally dispensed with the natural environment which had unleashed a divine spirit for their romantic predecessors.

Like her modern forebears, Dillard believes in a highly structured and unified art piece. She speaks of her use of hundreds of index cards which enabled her to write *Pilgrim at Tinker Creek* consciously and carefully (Major 364); she also notes that she painstakingly balanced the book's structure around the *via negativa* and *via positiva*, honing the work into its form: "Usually I'd write each sentence 7 or 8 times before I went on—or, 3 or 4 times on the spot, & 3 or 4 times as each section of a chapter underwent revision. Each page must have been handwritten, re-written, at least 8 times, and the outlines hundreds of times, for the book, and chapter by chapter, both before & during" (personal correspondence to William Reyer). Wordsworth and Coleridge shared a predilection for fragments of work, unfinished pieces that may have been in one way the psychic mirrors of their century's fascination with architectural ruins. Dillard, on the other hand, is a careful builder who consciously structures her work with a clearly defined beginning, middle, and end. She admits to the grueling work of composition, a kind of denial of the nineteenth-century notion of Imagination or Inspiration, a denial she expresses in *Living by Fiction* when she laments the perception of contemporary nonfiction as "sincere and artless" (83). Her retort to those who expect less art from the essay genre is her own intricately balanced and refined nonfiction which can be described as sincere and *artful*.

Dillard speaks at length about the unity of art in *Living by Fiction*. Her main point is that when systems and structures fall apart, as they did for the modernists, the artist fragments the literary work. She writes that following World War I:

> we lost our context, we lost our meaning. We became, all of us in the West, more impoverished and in one sense more ignorant than pygmies, who, like the hedgehog, know one great thing: in this case, why they are here. We no longer know why we are here. (26)

The modernist who could not conclude "why we are here" created a fragmented space, time, and object to imitate the perceived world. But in fragmenting so much of the internal order of art, the very order which allowed Coleridge and Wordsworth to offer fragments, the modernist was obliged to produce coherence, unity of form, and balance of a new kind in order to encompass the fragmented parts. For as Dillard writes, "Art may imitate anything but disorder. The work of art may, like a magician's act, pretend to any degree of spontaneity, randomality, or whimsy, so long as the effect of the whole is calculated and unified" (*Living* 28).

This statement of aesthetics prevails also for the kind of artist whom Dillard names the "contemporary modernist." She writes that "Modernism is not over. . . . contemporary writers are carrying on, with new emphasis and further developments, the Modernists' techniques" (*Living* 20). Dillard's nonfiction adheres, in part, to her own definition of contemporary modernism, for she creates a glittering collage of material often fragmented and splintered, its surface transitions eradicated; at the same time she applies her own unifying device, the epiphany, to make the narrative cohere.

Finally, Annie Dillard, the neoromantic, with an illumination devised from nineteenth- and twentieth-century models, applies the Muir-wilderness tradition to her work; she brings a barrage of accurate data to the page. In one sense she is acting out the role of the consummate epiphanist, for she is throwing the painful details of existence into the face of any entity, any god that might be watching or listening; she does this in order to elicit illumination. She speaks to this in *Pilgrim* when she writes of the living organisms of the creek:

> I might as well include these creatures in this moment, as best I can. My ignoring them won't strip them of their reality, and admitting them, one by one, into my consciousness might heighten mine, might add their dim awareness to my human consciousness, such as it is, and set up a buzz, a vibration like the beating ripples a submerged muskrat makes on the water, from this particular moment. . . . (94)

One further illustration of this accumulation of detail is an account Dillard attributed to J. Henri Fabre and recounts in *Pilgrim*, of moth caterpillars parading hopelessly and mindlessly about the rim of a vase. Even when the insects are given an escape from their circular route they simply move on destroying themselves; the caterpillars, as Dillard quotes Fabre, "starved, shelterless, chilled with cold at night, cling obstinately to the silk ribbon covered hundreds of times, because they lack the rudimentary glimmers of reason which would advise them to abandon it" (67), a fixed march that moves Dillard to shout from the page, "I want out of this still air" (67). She is afraid that she too is somehow fixed and stepping to "that charmed and glistening thread" (68).

The fixed details, the data Dillard lists in the manner of the field scientist or the wilderness ecologist, give the reader the sense that nothing will be overlooked or dismissed when this writer asks essential questions. In the face of undeniable horror, when the writer has the boldness to confront nothingness, when she has taken an agnostic's stance and has wiped her slate clean of foregone conclusions, the moment of epiphany can show itself:

> I sit on a bridge as on Pisgah or Sinai, and I am both waiting becalmed in a clift of the rock and banging with all my will, calling like a child beating on a door: Come on out! . . . I know you're there.
> And then occasionally the mountains part. The tree with the lights in it appears, the mockingbird falls, and time unfurls across space like an oriflamme. (*Pilgrim* 205)

The sense that a writer dares the spirit to reveal itself at the darkest moment, a moment littered with the carnage of human desolation, gives the epiphany its seemingly unattached, self-engendering, metaphysical organicism. Because the epiphany lives by rising out of its own power it serves as testimony to something beyond human knowledge. The Muir-wilderness tradition, which, as Elder writes, engages the "close observation of nature, within an awareness of the modern science of ecology" (375), becomes the foil for this self-engendered moment.

In addition to data recitation, a kind of literary nonchalance often accompanies Dillard's preparation for the occurrence of illumination. Dillard will set up a narrative situation in which she least suspects an unusual moment, as in her introductory comments for the "tree with lights": "It was for this tree I searched through the peach orchards of summer, in the forests of fall and down winter and spring for years. Then one day I was walking along Tinker Creek *thinking of nothing at all* and I saw the tree with the lights in it" (33; emphasis added). Or in *An American Childhood*, when she highlights the heightened moment by observing that one can "notice *unbidden* that you are afoot on this particular mountain on this particular day in the company of these particular changing fragments of clouds. . ." (248; emphasis added). This is reminiscent of Wordsworth's narrative preparation for the epiphany of his young manhood when "vows were made" for him as he walked home from a night of dance. He writes that he "had passed / The night in dancing" with "unaimed prattle flying up and down" when the "empyrean" sunrise, a part of what formerly had been a "common dawn," created the moment in which he became "a dedicated spirit" (*Prelude* 4.319–44). Dillard and Wordsworth consciously paint the setting for epiphany as placid, unattended, unworthy of notice. This, of course, creates the sensation, once again, of the moment as self-engendering and self-motivating, something visited upon the recipient. In addition, the placid setting creates a verbal foil for the epiphany; that is, the images provided by the writer for the moment itself become startlingly significant against the less sensuous images in the setting.

It is interesting to note that Dillard echoes the objective approach of the field scientist even when she concludes *Living by Fiction*. This book, touted by the author as a work of literary theory, rapidly becomes a philosophical treatise on the meaning of human existence. The final chapter "Does the World Have Meaning?" questions the significance of the human mind to find unity. Dillard's fear is that the brain finds unity in art and world only because it is copying its own internal proclivity. She writes that it "is an appalling possibility" that "our minds are selected for inventing bits of order" and "art's highest function is to shed light on the mind" (180). If this is true, then, "any human artifact is the mind's own simulacrum." Dillard continues with a tone reminiscent of Tennyson's *In Memoriam:*

And if *this* is true, and the natural world which churned out the mind is a wreck and a chaos, like a rock slide, then the mind is a

marvelous monster indeed. And the work of art (in addition to
being the least of our worries) is always a tour de force in which
the mind displays abilities absurdly in excess of, or at least
incidental to, their survival function. For the ability to conceive
and execute murals and epic poems and symphonies and novels is
a grotesque trick of tissue which sprang from the pot of the
possible, like the grossly overdeveloped antlers of the extinct Irish
elk. (180–81)

This "grotesque trick of tissue" is appalling because the premise eradicates a higher order to which art objects aspire. It eradicates a creator.
It assumes that the mind is its own ventriloquist, speaking to itself,
making itself.

Dillard investigates this premise until the last sentence of the book
where she anticipates the reader's question: "What shall it be? Do art's
complex and balanced relationships among all parts, its purpose, significance, and harmony, exist in nature? Is nature whole, like a completed
thought? Is history purposeful? Is the universe of matter significant? I
am sorry; I do not know" (*Living* 185). Dillard's simplistic answer, "I do
not know," after a 185-page analysis, is a correlative to her reference in
Pilgrim to physicists who have become "wild-eyed raving maniacs" after
they have "whisked away" the last "crucial veil" and have found only
the "Cheshire cat's grin" (202). Dillard's "I don't know" is her response
after whisking away all of the epistemological veils she can postulate. In
the final words of *Living* she becomes the persona of the maniacal literary physicist who has no answers. But this abandonment of all knowledge, the careful arrangement of data, and building of theory, is the
perfect and, indeed, necessary groundwork for the epiphanic moment
which denies all twentieth-century rationality. The speculation that
there is no greater power focusing the world—or, more specifically, the
world of art—makes the appearance of some element beyond the reasoning, ordering senses of the mind necessary. This element is Dillard's
epiphany. It is beyond knowledge and learning; it is unreasonable; it
leaves questions unanswered and that is its hope.

A comment about Dillard's position regarding women's perspectives
or feminism in general should be made here. She avoids being defined as
"feminist." Her reasoning here appears to be the same as that which
causes her to present herself as apolitical and uninvolved with institutional guidelines and battle lines. It is the same reasoning which leads
her to list data which in the end will be shattered because it is ineffective
in the face of epiphany. Dillard in a 1981 interview said, "I want to
divorce myself from the notion of the female writer right away and then
not elaborate" ("Drawing the Curtains" 35). If she were to accept the

categorization as "woman writer" she would undermine the very heart of her material: Homo sapiens in touch with the merging of time and eternity, unpolitical, leaping beyond the idea of gender into the idea of the artist in touch with the infinite. She is artist above all, coming to eternity not as a political/cultural victim but as a mind expanded by the moment filled with light, the genderless moment of merging with God.

Annie Dillard takes romanticism to its furthest extreme; she must be extreme because she combats decades of spiritless scientific data; she faces the abyss created by the notion of no external meaning. With the literary epiphany she is able to experience divinity individually, without institutional mediation. She sets her moment against the harsh realities of death and pain; further, she scrutinizes the moment with the verbal surgery of twentieth-century language. She takes it apart, light particle, root hair, and pulse. In addition, she has returned nature to the moment, just as the modern epiphanist eliminated it; Yeats's golden bird has become the warm, living doves in the cedar tree. Dillard is both mystic and romantic, moving between these traditions with ease. Although she has been called a "nature writer," while others edge toward the nature-philosophic essay, employing scientific data to support ecological issues, Dillard is more purely the artist, language-conscious, bound up with the topic of aestheticism and artistic development. She explores and presents the epiphany as the ultimate form of beauty and mystery. Dillard's neoromanticism is a reworking of traditional romanticism; in the face of skepticism and fragmentation she throws science, fact, dismal forecasts to the wind and embraces mystery, a mystery made visible in a moment when "the tree with the lights in it buzzes into flame and cast-rock mountains ring" (*Pilgrim* 271).

3

The Circle is Unbroken

The Shape of Epiphanic Time

Annie Dillard has said that the "relationship between time and eternity" is the "single question" which artistically interests her most ("A Face Aflame" 961). For Dillard each day is filled with the acts of pagan gods and her interest lies in the ways these "small" gods relate to a holy and presumably higher Christian god ("A Face Aflame" 961), a relationship which she examines scrupulously in *Holy the Firm*. The daily gods, reminiscent of Wordsworth's pagan "old Triton," are here symbols of Dillard's conception of diachronic or Newtonian time, while the highest God or Absolute becomes representative of eternity, or what could be more accurately described as timelessness or "untime."

Although Dillard has repeatedly emphasized her preoccupation with time, critics have not given much attention to this aspect of her work: Patricia Ward comments that Dillard deals with the present moment when, seeing eternity or God, she "transcend[s] her time-bound position to experience eternity within the present moment and to capture that moment" (974), but little else has been promulgated on this topic, the majority of critics preferring to highlight aspects of Dillard's interest in the natural environment or her alignment with mysticism. In her foreword to *Wind on the Sand,* a devotional written by an English anchoress, Dillard writes that the single holy life is one which dips into eternity from one point in time: "My favorite aspect of the book, and of the anchoress' life, is the running paradox involved in leading a life that partakes of the eternal, right here in funny old time" (v). In a short prose piece appearing in *Ploughshares* Dillard comments on the importance of her own "spots of time" and how these spots bear upon the entire question of time. She speaks of moments when one travels and is suddenly laid bare to the world; senses open up:

These times are points on which a great many pressures bear
down. The mind returns to them; their meaning is never resolved.
They are doors banging on their hinges, disturbing the
peace. . . . They are one of literature's few subjects. There is, after
all, time, eternity, and nothing else. And time, like light, is both
particle and wave. These times are particles—particles wedged,
perhaps, in the trough of a wave. ("Four Bits" 69)

This statement is particularly significant as it mentions so many key elements in the Dillardian epiphany: times, points, doors, eternity, particle,
and wave are indicators of Dillard's preoccupation with the concept of
entering the precise moment of illumination and the sensations that
evolve from immersion in its center.

The subject of time is admittedly a difficult and amorphous topic; a
quagmire of intersecting approaches and disciplines, philosophic, scientific, and artistic approaches awaits the unwary. But Dillard must be examined foremost as an artist, an artist with a broad knowledge of
scientific matters. Dillard, using the concept of time as the modernists
did, follows the same formula which she notes for Stevens, Yeats, and
Eliot, who took fragments of the world, referential objects, and united
these with imaginary objects of thought to express ideas concerning the
"relationship between time and eternity" ("Purification" 293). Dillard
has united the idea of time with the process of artistic composition on
various occasions, the art piece echoing the idea of time and eternity.
While the artistic vision is eternity, the artistic product is temporality;
the "relationship to the vision which impelled it is the relationship between any energy and work, anything unchanging to anything temporal"
("A Note on Process" 25). This temporality, though, is not a negative aspect of time for Dillard, since it is through time, or the real, that the art-
work comes to fruition. This same logic applies to the evidence of
eternity available in time, that is, the epiphanic moment. Without the reality or mortality produced by time's passage there could be no epiphanic moment. Both the artpiece and the epiphany are clues to eternity
or timelessness; in the literary epiphany these two elements are united.
"We are down here in time," Dillard writes, "where beauty grows"
(*Teaching* 152); time has given beauty an opportunity to flower and
Dillard has consistently sought to examine that flower through her repeated application of literary epiphany.

Several scholars have advanced epiphanic formulas which must be examined to understand the critical groundwork underlying Dillard's concepts of time and epiphany. Martin Bidney has drawn upon Gaston
Bachelard's work on "reverie" to complete several explications of
Wordsworth and Coleridge poems.[3] Basing his study of reverie on

"characteristic patterns of motion, form, and elemental affinity," Bidney explains that Bachelard advances the notion that the literary epiphany, or "reverie," is vital and alive ("Radiant" 114). Bidney, then, studies epiphany in the light of these three patterns: motion, geometric shapes, and elemental substances. His theory of radiant geometry, based on Bachelard's theory of reverie, is offered as an anti-theory because it promotes looking at the structure of the epiphanic moment rather than the commentary the poet might make on the meaning of the epiphany. Bidney goes on to say that Bachelard "has provided a methodology whereby such deeper structures may be allowed to emerge from poetic texts in the clearest way." He rightly suggests that the scene of the spot or reverie is less important than the structure or internal workings of the reverie, since "motion, patterns of form, and the dynamism of elemental substances" create the tension of the epiphany (114). These emphases, however, do not consider the element of time; the relevance of time to Bachelard's patterns of motion and shapes will be a later consideration in this study.

It is true that the motion of the scene and the physical elements included by the epiphanist are vital to the epiphanic structure, but the writer's perception of time's dimension is equally as vital to epiphany. Since time cannot be held or seen with the eye, the epiphanist creates its effects on objects within the moment or by poetic abstractions such as Dillard presents through her metaphysical telescoping into micro- and macrocosms. Generally, time is felt and described as motion, which makes its effects on the landscape or setting of the epiphany.

Morris Beja has offered another set of criteria for the literary epiphany in *Epiphany in the Modern Novel*. These criteria have been expanded by Robert Langbaum; a complete listing of all three scholars appears this way:

Martin Bidney (from Bachelard)
  Epiphany has these patterns:
    1. Motion
    2. Geometric shapes
    3. Elemental substances

Morris Beja
  Epiphany has these criteria:
    1. Incongruity: Epiphany is "not strictly relevant to whatever produces it" (16).
    2. Insignificance: Epiphany is triggered by a trivial object or incident (16).

Robert Langbaum
  Epiphany has these criteria:
    1. Incongruity (from Beja)
    2. Insignificance (from Beja)

3. Psychological Association: The epiphany is "not an incursion of God from outside; it is a psychological phenomenon arising from a real sensuous experience, either present or recollected" (341).

4. Momentaneousness: The epiphany "lasts only a moment, but leaves an enduring effect" (341).

5. Suddenness: "A sudden change in external conditions causes a shift in sensuous perception that sensitizes the observer for epiphany" (341).

6. Fragmentation or the Epiphanic Leap: "The text never quite equals the epiphany; the poetry, as Browning put it, consists in the reader's leap" (341).

These studies of Bidney, Beja, and Langbaum are insightful and provide detailed analyses of epiphanic structures, but these scholars fail to fully include in their criteria what must be an essential element in epiphany—the "shape" which rises out of time's fragmentation. Langbaum recognizes that time is involved in some ways when he lists his criteria of Momentaneousness and of Suddenness; both concepts edge toward aspects of time but deal primarily with time's duration rather than its manifestation in external objects. Beja provides an excellent historical discussion of epiphanic time and the psychological aberrations which occur in the novel's narrator *(Epiphany in the Modern Novel)*, but fails to include a criterion in his list which might clarify time's physical manifestation in the literary epiphany. The criteria which have been composed by these scholars are not enough to explain the pattern which evolves as the epiphanist moves suddenly into another sphere to participate in epiphany. Since Dillard works so intensely with the subject of time, using it repeatedly within the illumination itself and digressing upon its importance in the explanatory sections which surround the epiphanies, it becomes clear that distinct physical operations of time manipulation occur on the borders of diachronic time as it merges with the circle of synchronic time, or timelessness. The emphasis, then, in this and the following chapter will be on Dillard's uses of time within the epiphanic structure, the writer's perceptions best transcribed by recurring motifs. These motifs fall generally into three categories: shape, surfaces, and directions in time.

Epiphanic Temporality: Past, Present, and Future

Every epiphanic moment necessarily alters time, writers instinctively suggesting a realignment of temporality as they cross the "border" into the center of the illumination. What new "time" this crossing may engender, however, is determined by the individual writer's need and preoccupation, although much of time-structure is revealingly similar in all epiphany. Generally, the interior of the moment must be examined by its relationship to past, present, or future time, or, often, by its complete elimination of all time. Beja has suggested that some writers have vacillated between two types of epiphany (past and present) and have used these "according to whichever happened to suit the works . . . at hand" (57). Beja's characterization of the epiphanist as vacillating and arbitrary in selecting a time, past or present, for the epiphany fails to consider either the writer's deep-seated perception of time intrinsic to all of his or her work, the writer's historical milieu, or the striving toward the state of timelessness in all epiphany. Dillard has, indeed, offered two types of epiphanic moments in her work, but has, in addition, provided extended expositions on time's realignment within the moment which will reveal the sophisticated psychological machinery of this illumination.

Dillard deals almost exclusively with time in chapter 6, "The Present," of *Pilgrim at Tinker Creek,* where the puppy epiphany occurs. In this epiphany, time is considered first by the movement of the "sun's wild wheel"; but Dillard in her "blank" preparatory state for epiphany says that her mind had "been a blank slab of black asphalt for hours" (78). In this way Dillard places the tabula rasa of her mind against the "wild" reeling of time; the movement of diachronic time is thus emphasized so that when the cessation of time occurs the effect is even more dramatic. The narrator rubs the puppy's fur, the landscape changes vividly and violently with the sunset, colors change and vibrate, and she feels that "the bare forest folds and pleats itself like living protoplasm before my eyes, like a running chart, a wildly scrawling oscillograph on the present moment" (78). The writer provides a very dense image here; it synthesizes what she so often returns to: in her "bare forest" we see the wild and gorgeous natural environment which becomes Beauty; the ever-present inspection of scientific data, an outgrowth of the Muir tradition, exhibits itself in the "living protoplasm," the "running chart," and the "wildly scrawling oscillograph"; and the element of time appears in her "present moment". The epiphany's purpose is, of course, to achieve this synergy, but for our purposes here time can be identified and extricated from the tendril and snarl of such an image in order to pinpoint Dillard's perception of its operations.

Dillard writes that in this "present moment" she is "more alive than all the world. This is it, I think, this is it, right now, the present, this empty gas station, here, this western wind, this tang of coffee on the tongue, and I am patting the puppy, I am watching the mountain" (78–79). But as soon as she verbalizes the present moment everything fades;

once again she becomes "opaque, so much black asphalt" when she becomes conscious that she is conscious, a state which Dillard calls "self-consciousness" (79). In this state of self-consciousness she knows that she is feeling the moment and this is something less than experiencing the moment.

It becomes clear that Dillard's epiphany can be subdivided in its relationship to time as she writes an exposition on the distinctions of illumination following the puppy epiphany in "The Present." The moment when she saw the cedar tree filled with mourning doves is one type and will be identified in this study as Epiphany 1; the second type is represented by the puppy epiphany and will be called Epiphany 2.

Epiphany 1 occurs when the doors of eternity open onto the present; the moment flames with a sense of holiness and is usually painted as still, or silent. Dillard writes that "On that cedar tree shone, however briefly, the steady, inward flames of eternity..." (*Pilgrim* 80). When the door opens it opens onto linear time, or what at first appears to be linear time, as it must always be constructed of the earthly and human objects which fill linear time. It is, like Christ's incarnation, the "scandal of particularity"; that is, no matter how holy or divine or other-worldly the moment might be it still must take the accoutrements of human life to make it visible to humanity. Just as Christ became flesh so that humanity could be saved, according to Christian theology, so the timeless moment must be evidenced in the "flesh" of the material world so that humanity can experience it.

The second type, Epiphany 2, is "vastly different in quality as well as in import" from the first type (*Pilgrim* 80). The puppy epiphany represents this second type in that it catches the present moment with the writer's complete consciousness, which allows all the senses to experience the here-and-now. Dillard herself emphasizes that these two types of experience differ. When she felt the present with the puppy in the gas station she was acutely aware of time, symbolized by the metaphor of the sunset: "across the mountain by the gas station raced the familiar flames of the falling sun" (80). This kind of moment finds the narrator racing to catch up with time, the time which seems to be associated, for Dillard, with the speed of the earth's rotation. She very often, throughout the spectrum of her work, is jumping to catch hold of the planet or running to attach herself to an enormous fleeting power which seems to be moving at an arbitrary speed, a speed which she attaches to the notion of the present. Yet Dillard often manipulates the speed of the rotating planets herself. She pulls back from the scene of the earth like an omnipresent and omnipotent god and watches the planets revolve metaphysically in fast-forward, reeling out the ages of the earth under her gaze, as a time-tampered film can reveal the opening of a blossom or the penetration of the soil by a mushroom cap. In chapter 8 of *Pilgrim*, "Intricacy," she moves the earth's geological changes like the paint on a canvas, ice ages rolling up "grinding green land under water," ice ages rolling back, allowing forests to "erupt and disappear like fairy rings":

> A blue-green streaks the highest ridges, a yellow-green spreads
> from the south like a wave up a strand. A red dye seems to leak
> from the north down the ridges and into the valleys, seeping south;
> a white follows the red, then yellow-green washes north, then red
> spreads again, then white, over and over, making patterns of color
> too swift and intricate to follow. Slow the film. You see dust
> storms, locusts, floods, in dizzying flash-frames. (143)

She continues this fast-forward with the appearance of animals and humans, and the time-spans of these organisms are even more brief than the great geological ages of the earth; they appear as "spirited tissues that roamed the earth's surface," whose time in the light was a "wavering blur . . . too brief an exposure to yield any image but the hunched, shadowless figures of ghosts." Caribou herds "pour into the valleys like slag, and trickle back, and pour, a brown fluid" (143). All of this metaphysical manipulation with time creates the incredible speed that Dillard must achieve if she is to experience the "present" of Epiphany 2.

In *An American Childhood* Dillard portrays herself as being in the center of a hurricane, creating the illusion of speed and illustrating this secondary type of epiphany. She writes, "Can you catch hold of a treetop, or will you fly off the diving planet as she rolls? Can you ride out the big blow on a coconut palm's trunk until you fall asleep again, and the winds let up?" (150). The planet rolls forward at the exact speed of time's movement, although this is indeterminate speed in Dillard's universe; this is time's movement and is what the epiphanist will experience should she "kick into" the present moment.

Slowing the film, and telescoping once again into diachronic time from her position high above the earth, the epiphanist might actually catch a glimpse of the individual life that is so essential to Dillard: "Slow it down more, come closer still. A dot appears, a flesh-flake. It swells like a balloon; it moves, circles, slows, and vanishes. This is your life" (*Pilgrim* 143).

Thus, it is apparent that for Dillard the door on time opens in several ways. It can illuminate from eternity, from a timeless state where nothing is measurable, but it must use the matter and space of earth to register this moment with humankind. Dillard makes this clear when she writes that "although the door to the tree with the lights in it was opened *from* eternity, as it were, and shone on that tree eternal lights, it nevertheless opened on the real and present cedar. It opened on time . . ." (*Pilgrim* 80). The other kind of opening can best be described not as an opening but as increased speed achieved through the senses which locks the recipient into the "true" speed of diachronic time as she perceives it, however fantastic and metaphysically skewed that time might be. Both kinds of epiphany are generally felt by the epiphanist to be the exact present, although the "present" of Epiphany 1 is, in Dillard's epiphanic world, timelessness, or eternity. In any case, both types of epiphany release Dillard from daily time and fill her with "rising exultation": "Experiencing the present purely is being emptied and hollow; you catch grace as a man fills his cup under a waterfall" (*Pilgrim* 80–81).

The eclipse in "A Total Eclipse" of *Teaching a Stone to Talk* makes an almost perfect paradigm for epiphany because it deals with aspects of physicality which designate and create human time: the sun, the darkened air, and the position of the planets. Dillard provides great detail about the exact date of the eclipse as her narrative purpose is to set up a foil for the spiritual illumination which will occur during the physical illumination. She provides facts which surround her determination to be there during the darkening of the sun and then emphasizes that all was ordinary:

> Early the next morning we checked out. It was February 26, 1979, a Monday morning. We would drive out of town, find a hilltop, watch the eclipse, and then drive back over the mountains and home to the coast. How familiar things are here; how adept we are; how smoothly and professionally we check out. (87)

Dillard emphasizes what the plan is for seeing the eclipse; this, of course, is a backdrop for what will really happen during the illumination. She is characterizing this moment as one lived self-consciously, for she is thinking, anticipating, and planning for the spectacle—all functions which cannot induce the true illumination. When the eclipse finally comes, "It began with no ado." But she notes that this atmosphere, with "no overture" and "no introductory speaker," has been a preliminary to the indefinable moment she has known before: "I should have known right then that I was out of my depth" (89).

Again she begins building upon the idea that this type of experience, that is, the full eclipse, is beyond knowledge, her familiar stance. The partial eclipse, Dillard notes, bears "almost no relation to a total eclipse" (89); thus the latter is almost beyond comprehension, and the partial eclipse becomes symbolic of the secondary epiphany. It also represents the moment for which she has made great conscious plans on the Washington hillside, while the total eclipse is representative of the epiphany that will explode upon her without any preparation for such an insight: "What you see in an eclipse is entirely different from what you know" (90). Once again Dillard points out the relationship between human knowledge and that supra-knowledge acquired by experiencing epiphany. Echoing her phrase from *Pilgrim*, she writes that "What you see is much more convincing than any wild-eyed theory you may know" (*Teaching* 90). Here seeing refers to viewing into the world beyond knowledge, a metaphysical world which lies even beyond the most extreme theory. Seeing is more than physical eyesight and is set against the word "know," indicating that one is the polar opposite of the other. To "know," in Dillard's lexicon, on most occasions, is not to see, but to be blind.

"Total Eclipse," then, presents both types of epiphany within one narrated scene: the desired for and planned moment of watching the eclipse on the hillside in Washington State and the unsought and unexpected illumination of the true epiphany during the eclipse. The present can be caught by planning, as Dillard seems to suggest by her detailed scheme to see the eclipse, but something greater than the present can be experienced only when one is least aware. The secondary moment will "chute" her to time's metaphysical speed, but the primary moment of full epiphany will take her mind "light-years distant, forgetful of almost everything" (*Teaching* 93).

Dillard makes a distinction between two types of awakening in *An American Childhood,* but both types of illumination are lifted out of time by the narrator. One awakening is electric and wild and is usually represented by spinning globes or active, violent waters and speed in general. The planet is spinning in space, a recurring image that Dillard builds through telescoping to macrocosms and then reversing to microcosms. The narrator portrays herself jumping onto the globe and riding it as a child might leap onto a merry-go-round while it is moving. This attachment gives the sensation that she is traveling at great speeds with wind in her hair and loud sounds roaring in her ears. She writes that "Knowing you are alive is feeling the planet buck under you, rear, kick, and try to throw you; you hang on to the ring. It is riding the planet like a log downstream, whooping" (151). The second type of awakening is quiet and still, filled with the sense that time is passing, that this life is like "a weekend in the country," when she understands that she is mortal (151). Both types of illumination, though, are awakenings from a dream land of diachronic time into a real world; both are, for Dillard, turning "on the lights" or stepping "aside from the dreaming fast loud routine" (150–51).

It was noted earlier that the entrance into the epiphanic moment always involves a realignment of time, which may be sought out or may be received, as has been suggested by the narration in "Total Eclipse"; these two methods of tampering with time are frequently advanced by Dillard as "active stalking" and "passive stalking." Stalking muskrats or stalking the spirit can be achieved through either means. Dillard realizes that passivity, or following the *via negativa,* is the superior method because in this way she might achieve the preferred full epiphany. One must be ready to receive it, but one cannot actively catch the moment. Acting to grasp the moment only drives it further out of reach.

Passive stalking requires unself-consciousness, a state in which the narrator is no longer in an interior dialogue with self, but is fully sensitized, a "tissue of senses" (*Pilgrim* 201) exposed to the stimuli of the exterior world; if the writer moves, she might scare the muskrat, which becomes the major metaphor in the "Stalking" chapter in *Pilgrim.* Once again, activity has the potential of destroying the moment. Thus, the realignment of time through epiphany cannot be managed or planned, only hoped for with a receptive spirit.

Dillard's emphasis in "Living Like Weasels" is also on passivity, and this applies to time as well as to all other elements. She wants to be like a weasel because the animal lives purely in the moment, a moment which Dillard witnessed as their eyes locked in the epiphany in the woods. For the weasel, time is "poured," as the weasel is receptive, not anticipatory. When time can be "unremarked" and "ingested directly," as it is for the weasel, each moment becomes epiphanic. The weasel's mind is smooth, a blank slate on which the spirit can write. To live like the weasel is Dillard's ideal for epiphanic time: "A weasel doesn't 'attack' anything; a weasel lives as he's meant to, yielding at every moment to the perfect freedom of single necessity" (16).

Dillard speaks of innocence as "the spirit's unself-conscious state at any moment of pure devotion to any object. It is at once a receptiveness and total concentration" ("Drawing the Curtains" 38), a path by which the borders into the timelessness of the full epiphany may be traversed. When the body begins to leave the senses and live in thought, then something is lost. Therefore, a person should rely on the life of the spirit, for "there is a higher innocence, a new innocence: the redemption of knowledge, the rough merger of the complex products of thought with the simple and received sensations of life in time" (38). This innocence is the opposite of self-consciousness; one must lose all of the thought-laden inhibitions which are associated with knowledge and become totally conscious.

Dillard has illustrated Epiphany 1 with these images: (1) passive stalking; (2) the *via negativa;* (3) the opening of a "door" from eternity on the "real"; (4) full epiphany. "Looking upstream" and the exact present sustained by facing into the future are elements that will be discussed subsequently. Epiphany 2 can be identified by these images: (1) active stalking; (2) the *via positiva;* (3) the achievement of the "true" speed of diachronic time as the narrator latches onto the planet; (4) the "lesser" epiphany. Other metaphors include "looking downstream" and the exact present networking into past memories.

Motion

Motion is the dynamic which underlies epiphany. Its force can be understood to appear in three ways: the flow of diachronic time as its moves toward, around, and beyond the moment of epiphany, the rapid flux within the epiphanic moment itself, and the recurrent psychological motion of the reader's epiphany. Dillard's work gives strong evidence of these three movements.

Dillard has emphasized repeatedly time's flux, which in her view, allows beauty to exist. Using animal metaphors in *Pilgrim*, she illustrates the constant roll of time: "If the sharks cease roving, if they still their twist and rest for a moment, they die. They need new water pushed into their gills; they need dance" (98). The creek, like a shark, pushing forward relentlessly with its "live water . . . from undisclosed sources," is a metaphor for diachronic time, which also flows from "undisclosed sources" that can be assumed to be the Absolute. This motion is the necessary dynamic on which the epiphany will act.

But it is the motion within the moment which is most interesting. After Dillard is released from the moment in "A Field of Silence" she realizes that the stillness she perceived was not actually still; that, in fact, the moment had been in incredibly rapid motion. This motion is represented by the presence of angels: "My impression now of those fields is of thousands of spirits—spirits trapped, perhaps, by my refusal to call them more fully, or by the paralysis of my own spirit at that time— thousands of spirits, angels in fact, almost discernible to the eye, and whirling" (*Teaching* 137). The motion of the angels' wings is so rapid that, like that of a hummingbird or bumblebee, the wings seem to be still. Hence, the intense, hypnotizing power of the moment is created by vibration and "whirling" at such accelerated speed that it is only felt as power, or holiness, but is, in fact, a motion fluctuating faster than humankind can perceive with the physical eye. Thus, when epiphany appears to set up a still tableau, such as the Jo Ann Sheehy ice skating/streetlight illumination in *An American Childhood* or the disturbing silence in the pastures of "A Field of Silence," the moment of timelessness is actually "whirling."

Diachronic time lies outside the circle and is perceived as linear movement, as in the creek, while, traditionally, the epiphany as it crosses the borders into timelessness has been thought to be "stilled" with no movement. Langbaum suggests that the moment is static, believing that the epiphany reorders the parts of poems and novels "backwards and forwards in the direction of lyrical stasis" (346), while Beja calls epiphany a "frozen tableau" (22). But epiphanic moments, not only in Dillard, but also in such other epiphanists as Wordsworth and Eliot, suggest instead that untime or timelessness, as it is perceived and written within the literary piece, is, indeed, movement in extremity. On this point Bidney is correct, as he applies Bachelard's theory of motion to Coleridge's conversation poems:

> Bachelard's real contribution is twofold: he gives one the
> confidence that underlying patterns unify the privileged
> imaginative moments even of the most diversified of poetic
> imaginers (such as Coleridge); and he shows, too, that imagery
> means more than simply pictures, that characteristic
> reverie-structures may involve more abstract components such as
> patterns of motion, geometric shapes, and the dynamism of
> elemental substances. ("Structure of Epiphanic Imagery" 45)

Perhaps this motion can best be compared to the circling of atomic particles about a nucleus. This concept of rapid, "divine" motion in the center of the epiphanic circle makes appropriate the use of buzzing, drowsy flies, an efficient image of slowed motion at the borders of the circle, or moment, in "A Field of Silence." Dillard notes that the moment itself is "eternity's outpost in time" and, further, occurs on a "God-blasted; paralyzed day" (*Teaching* 136), reinforcing the misconception that time is still within the moment, while later in the scene she introduces the idea of rapid movement in the angel wings which whirled "three or four feet from the ground" in clockwise fashion (138). The paralysis of the day set against the interior of the moment with its rapid circular movement suggests the altered state of time within epiphany. Timelessness is not icy stillness, not even in Coleridge's icicle in "Frost at Midnight." For even in the stillness of ice, the true epiphany vibrates, as his "silent icicles" glint in the light of the "quiet Moon" (*Complete Poetical* 73–74); likewise, Dillard's Jo Ann Sheehy turns in the cone of streetlight under "cold stars" which "speckle" the street "without moving" (*American Childhood* 31).

The sense of movement is even further developed in images of sparks and electricity. In *An American Childhood* Dillard combines several epiphanic moments with the images of a downed power line that spits a "thick sheaf of useless yellow sparks that hissed" and a trolley car creating a "radiant fistful of sparks at every crossing of wires" (101, 105). The point here is that these glinting, sparking, speckling images suggest motion, and, although this motion is radiated from physical objects within the epiphany, the sense of rapid interchanges of light and fire must be applied to the dynamic of time within the moment. For it is time which is first altered, and which provides the initial structure of the epiphany. This sensation of movement will be discussed again under the rubric of landscape within the epiphany, but it must be applied first to time as it is managed by the epiphanist.

Langbaum discusses at length what he perceives to be the stasis of the epiphany in Woolf's *To the Lighthouse:*

> Lily Briscoe, the painter, arrives at a theory of epiphany by asking:
> "What is the meaning of life?. . . The great revelation perhaps
> never did come. Instead there were little daily miracles,
> illuminations, matches struck unexpectedly in the dark." Mrs.
> Ramsay unconsciously does in life what Lily necessarily does in
> painting and what Virginia Woolf chooses to do in this novel: they
> give meaning to life by spatializing and silencing it, while
> suggesting its noisy movement. "Beauty," Lily thinks, "stilled
> life—froze it." (346)

Mrs. Ramsey recognizes the vision of the dinner party as "the still space about the heart of things" (Langbaum 346). But this stasis or stilled space, even in Woolf, is like the angel wings, the same rapid movement that appears to be still because it is so rapid, suggested here by Lily's reference about "matches struck unexpectedly in the dark," the flame becoming the rapid intermittent movement of light.

Thus, diachronic time should be seen as passing by the circle of timelessness which is a motion beyond human recognition and is perceived at first to be frozen but is in fact vibrating or fluctuating rapidly within an enclosure. It can be viewed as all time—past, present, and future—within a contained space, or the total elimination of time's rolling movement. This internal epiphanic time feeds on itself, rotating and vibrating off its own synchronization. It is eternal, perpetual.

Finally, motion occurs, not only suggested by the whirling of angel wings, or by the sparks from loose electrical wires, but in the mental motion which occurs between reader and writer during the rereading of the literary epiphany. The movement of the moment within the reader's psyche is violent activity. Keats speaks of the silence of the urn, "still unravish'd bride of quietness," the "foster-child of silence and slow time," ("Grecian Urn" 1–2) but actually the urn, representing an epiphanic moment, is set off from the "slow time" which surrounds it by a complete eruption and recombination of the time, which at first appears as a tableau of maidens and men in a pastoral "mad pursuit" (9). Keats's scene continues to "live" because it "teases" the mind "out of thought / As doth eternity" (44–45). It performs a psychological amalgamation. Like a compound rather than a mixture it forms the resulting new material, the epiphany. And like all good art it happens over and over, each time the observer-reader experiences it. The moment has been set loose by the writer; it waits on the page, and springs to life in the mind of the reader each time it is encountered.

One might argue here that this "springing to life" is exactly what all good literature does, but the epiphany is a device which goes beyond the "good read." Its combination of recurrent patterns and motions, as suggested by Bachelard, and its intensity sets it aside as a literary device that deserves close analysis; it is peculiarly contemporary and invigorating, rising out of language's power to create something more than symbol and metaphor. Coleridge hints at this idea when he writes in a letter that the poet's *"Heart & Intellect* should be *combined, intimately* combined & *unified,* with the great appearances in Nature—& not merely held in solution & loose mixture with them, in the shape of formal Similes" (September 10, 1802, *Collected Letters* 2:864). But what goes beyond Coleridge's recognition of the chemistry of epiphany is that rather than the mingling of mind and object creating a third entity, the combination which cannot be returned to the components of a mixture, a mingling of mind and object *and reader* occurs each time a literary epiphany is read. It is a story never finished. This unfinished story begins with the writer's perception and, then, masterful handling of time's flow within the epiphany. Thus, the epiphany continues to live in each rereading because of whirling motion, first suggested by the writer in the epiphanic contents (angels, fields, a woman with a pitcher, e.g.) but then woven into the symbolic and psychological fabric of the language so that each reader, even many years separated from the composer of the epiphany, relives the moment. This concept will be addressed further in chapter 6.

The Shape of Time

Fringe

The image of fringe provides Dillard with a physical notion she can apply to the various dialectics of her art, for it represents a relationship of irregularity, deep cuts and curves swinging along the edges of matter, and, by extension, the edges of time and eternity. She expands upon this idea of a jagged contour in time elsewhere in her work by the use of similar sets of images that involve tangles, twists, and snarls. These images are applied not only to such abstractions as time and eternity, but also to the physical realm of land and sea, which then become metaphors for time and eternity. Further, she carries the image into her world at Tinker Creek, her symbol for time, which runs near the brutal world of Shadow Creek; here there are gaps which repeat in metaphysical geography the fringe of pain and beauty interlocked in human life. When Dillard writes that "Mystery itself is as fringed and intricate as the shape of the air in time" (*Pilgrim* 144), she is uniting her concept of time as it works on matter, and most importantly, her concept of epiphany, which she calls the "intricate fringe of spirit's free incursions into time" (*Pilgrim* 266). When diachronic time is intersected by what could be called synchronic time (eternity or timelessness), the line contour, as it must be imagined for Dillard's world, is made jagged, cut, or irregular at that intersection. When eternity cuts into human time repeatedly the contour becomes fringed; in turn, the fringe becomes tangled and snarled, and all of this twisting, indeed, messy convolution is the outgrowth of epiphanic moments as they act upon human time: "Beauty itself is the fruit of the creator's exuberance that grew such a tangle, and the grotesques and horrors bloom from that same free growth, that intricate scramble and twine up and down the conditions of time" (*Pilgrim* 146). Free growth must allow horrors, the greatest, of course, being mortality. But as Clare Fishburn learned, the horror of death makes the beauty of life exquisite.

The idea of the tangle appears again in "Life on the Rocks: The Galapagos" in *Teaching a Stone to Talk*. There, time pushes evolution onward, an interaction Dillard describes in this way: "rocks shape life, and then life shapes life," and then "life shapes the rocks" (129). All of this occurs in a free tangle of time and matter and has influence because it is free.

Dillard applies a variation of the fringe image to the beautiful metaphoric passage about the weaver's loom in *Pilgrim*. Here, "Time is the warp and matter the weft of the woven texture of beauty in space" and what creates the intricate and finished textile is the "hurtling shuttle" of death (140). Although Dillard here is joining time and matter rather than time and eternity, the irregular, and in this instance, tweedy texture of two intersecting elements builds the artist's idea. She says that she dreams herself dead and watching from high above; in the "many white stars," she sees a "band of color" which she metaphysically approaches (140). When she is drawn closer to the band of color which now looks like a "woman's tweed scarf," she realizes that what she is seeing is "all the time of the planet" where she had lived, "stretched endlessly in either direction":

> At length I started to look for my time, but, although more and
> more specks of color and deeper and more intricate textures
> appeared in the fabric, I couldn't find my time, or any time at all
> that I recognized as being near my time. I couldn't make out so
> much as a pyramid. Yet as I looked at the band of time, all the
> individual people, I understood with special clarity, were living at
> that very moment with great emotion, in intricate detail, in their
> individual times and places, and they were dying and being
> replaced by ever more people, one by one, like stitches in which
> whole worlds of feeling and energy were wrapped, in a
> never-ending cloth. (140)

This nubby texture of time and matter repeats the idea of the irregular
condition of human life, a texture which becomes for Dillard a cloth of
great beauty. Dillard treats the landscape as a vast fabric which has intricate texture, fringe, and fraying; it is the movement of time which has
allowed this intricate texture to evolve. Time changes the landscapes
Dillard is so fond of painting, ages rolling the green and gray and mists
of the earth's evolving terrain, a metaphysically drawn textile viewed
from the narrator's perch above the planet. But once again in the formula for beauty is death, on this occasion painted as the heavy slap of a
hurtling shuttle that tightens the weave and eventually produces the
cloth. Within rough texture lies the "possibility for beauty" (139) and
with this possibility is always the knowledge of mortality.

The jagged contour of time and eternity appears again in *Holy the
Firm,* this time represented by the narrator's view of land—often ren-
dered as islands—and ocean. All of the landscape points to the sea, an
indication that all human time must necessarily end in eternity, and,
specifically, in *Holy the Firm,* eternity is first encountered through death.
That death is probably preceded by pain is suggested by *Holy's* second
section, "God's Tooth," which entails the burning of the child, Julie
Norwich. Even though the land's color is brilliant and riveting, the narrator's eye is drawn again to the sea: "your eye flies up the black beach
to the point, or slides down the green firs to the point, and the point is
an arrow pointing over and over, with its log-strewn beach, its gray sin-
gleness, and its recurved white edging to foam, to sea. . ." (23). Even as
the land holds the eye with its beauty, that is, earthly time rivets our attention for a time, finally we must face the reality that life ends and the
sea of eternity will take us in; this is the reason the narrator sees the
point of land as an "arrow pointing over and over," out to the reality of
the sea's white foam. Dillard's fringe motif is illustrated by the waves lap-
ping at the rim of the islands, "the fringey edge where elements meet

and realms mingle, where time and eternity spatter each other with foam" (21). Very much like Eliot's metaphor in "Dry Salvages" in *Four Quartets*, human time is represented by land mass and eternity, while God's time is represented by ocean.

Another approach to "fringe" in *Holy the Firm* appears in Dillard's characterization of the small pagan gods of daily life. Each individual day is a god, loosed from the great god whose purpose and interaction with humanity is scrutinized throughout the book. The single day is described as a boy, "pagan and fernfoot" who is all the joy and exultation of human life filled with things, "at home in the hundred senses" (30–31). But this represents the kind god of a pleasant day; an unpleasant god is the focus of part 2. The pagan god of day has a fringed foot, a "fernfoot," and Dillard suggests that each day has been chipped away, presumably from a larger piece of eternity: "Every day is a god, each day is a god, and holiness holds forth in time. I worship each god, I praise each day splintered down, splintered down and wrapped in time like a husk, a husk of many colors spreading, at dawn fast over the mountains split" (11).

This pleasant little god, however, becomes a symbol of wretched pain, the narrator admits, when the greater god allows the pagan single days to bring so much meaningless agony in the burning of Julie Norwich:

> Has he no power? Can the other gods carry time and its loves
> upside down like a doll in their blundering arms? As though we
> the people were playing house—when we are serious and do love—
> and not the gods? No, that day's god has no power. No gods have
> power to save. There are only days. The one great god abandoned
> us to days, to time's tumult of occasions, abandoned us to the gods
> of days each brute and amok in his hugeness and idiocy. (43)

The narrator's conclusion is that "God is a brute and traitor" who has abandoned "us to time" (46).

Dillard suggests that this book will contain nothing, "only a little violence here and there in the language, at the corner where eternity clips time" and she presents the pagan god of her first day (of three days) as a "very small man," his hair on fire, and his wingtips "blackened and seared" (24). The singed wing suggests, again, an irregular contour, as does the image of time "clipped" by eternity. This small singed man with a "hot skull...the size of a hazelnut" is a foreshadowing of the pain and burning of Julie Norwich which will occur in part 2.

The gaps of Tinker Creek, which reveal its pain-ridden counterpart, Shadow Creek, provide another fringed element. These gaps, representative of life's unspeakable horrors, are omnipresent: "Somewhere, everywhere, there is a gap, like the shuddering chasm of Shadow Creek which gapes open at my feet, like a sudden split in the window or hull of a high-altitude jet, into which things slip, or are blown, out of sight, vanished in a rush, blasted, gone, and can no more be found" (264–65). These gaps suck out a human life in time without warning as a depressurized plane pulls a victim into a space from which she cannot emerge; she is lost in the gap, just as the innocent Julie Norwich was burned and blasted in her own gap of undeserved pain. But for Dillard, the gaps are necessary, the "gaps are the thing" (269), meaning that within the mortal, painful gaps of time lie either the mystery or the home of the spirit. These gaps are, for Dillard, a kind of cover for a spirit which will emerge from the tangled, twisted foliage of life to reveal itself in epiphany. She calls this the "spirit's one home" and she demands that we "Go up into the gaps" even though they are "clifts in the rock where you cower to see the back parts of God." And if you have gone into the gaps, you have no certainty that you can meet the spirit, for, like a clever animal, it can hide. Furthermore, the gaps themselves can evaporate, "they shift and vanish too"; so you must search out even the gaps. "Stalk the gaps. Squeak into a gap in the soil, turn, and unlock—more than a maple—a universe," Dillard cries in the final chapter of *Pilgrim* (269). And though the gap, the fringe of the land, will most certainly emit pain, this is the condition of life in time, and the only method by which one apprehends beauty, eternity, and the epiphanic moment.

Dillard's controlling premise is that life is "fringed" because it consists of varying elements acting in irregular ways. Human life involves both matter and time, which act upon each other—time permitting the process of growth, dissemination, and dissolution in matter. Time allows the mangrove tree to float, making its own island; time allows the finch to disrupt the thistledown to produce beauty in its free fall; time allows the manifestation of the spirit having arrived from a state where there is no time. Time has, in fact, created beauty, for beauty is a by-product of human life on this reeling planet. And, although the epiphanist knows she pays with a little violence and blood, with the fall of the thistle or the drifting of the maple key, the beauty of the real as it falls is worth its price—mortality. Dillard realizes that life is made up of "waste and extravagance"; these "go together up and down the banks" of the creek, "all along the intricate fringe of spirit's free incursions into time" (*Pilgrim* 266). The epiphanic moment created by this incursion is the doorway into eternity Dillard seeks in all of her writing.

The Line

The "shape" of time begins for Dillard with a single line that will later be the raw material from which the artist will construct epiphany: Diachronic time is the line of the creek's flow where a beginning and an end, a source and a destination, can be marked. At least, this is how the human mind is first cognizant of time. But Dillard's metaphysics, which allows her to drift far above the landscape of time and matter, eventually enables her to see where the creek runs; her planetary ranging reveals that the passage of the creek demarcates a shape far different from a line. But Dillard begins with a line.

The malevolent nature of time's line is illustrated in *Pilgrim* when Tinker Creek floods, its destructive waters coursing fast, wrenching up life, dead horses, muskrats, and trees. The flooding creek represents the inevitability of aging, lives and objects rising and then falling away into nothingness; their passage appears to be linear, with a beginning and an end. Dillard's purpose in describing Tinker Creek at flood is to portray a human perception of time's ability to destroy; the flood is a fitting image to suggest a condensation of that annihilating force. "The creek is more like itself when it floods," Dillard writes, "than at any other time: mediating, bringing things down" (*Pilgrim* 152). The creek, like time, is "more like itself" during this disastrous event because it is a ravager. Dillard's metaphysics conflate time by presenting the unlikely images of John Paul Jones in his ship together with Amelia Earhart in her plane, the Franklin Arctic expedition in snowshoes, and the three magi on camels riding the flooded creek in twentieth-century Virginia. Dillard's purpose in commingling these jarring images is to create a sense that our time is short and death-ridden—from magi to Virginia residents— and, if seen clearly, moves all in a rage like the swollen Tinker Creek moves in a flood. But this flooding prepares the narrator for the *via negativa*, where death is confronted squarely and where epiphany will have to play a crucial role in any meaningful perspective on life.

Dillard conflates time again in "An Expedition to the Pole" as she did in *Pilgrim* when various explorers, the wise men and their camels, and out-of-place historical figures and objects fall into the flood of time together. In this essay she brings together nineteenth-century explorers and persons from the simple Catholic church she attends, repeating the configuration of a single line where time is all of a piece and rapid, this time carried by an ice floe, bearing all material and humanity forward.

Dillardian metaphysics conflates time again in "A Total Eclipse," where the artist combines her own time (i.e., February 1979), the nineteenth century, and the Middle Ages by uniting the contemporaneous real experience of the hillside eclipse, the physical features of a nineteenth-century tinted photograph, and the other-worldly metallic, spun-silver characteristics of a distant Middle Ages:

> This color has never been seen on earth. The hues were metallic; their finish was matte. The hillside was a nineteenth-century tinted photograph from which the tints had faded. All the people you see in the photograph, distinct and detailed as their faces look, are now dead. The sky was navy blue. My hands were silver. All the distant hills' grasses were finespun metal which the wind laid down. I was watching a faded color print of a movie filmed in the Middle Ages. (*Teaching* 91)

This metaphysical melding of all diachronic time gives the impression that human time is entirely insignificant, like the wink of an eye, or that time as we count it is false, or that we are confused as to its measurability.

Dillard telescopes time rapidly in this scene, propelling her husband Gary to "light-years away, gesturing inside a circle of darkness." She seems to lose him in time as she revolves in her own circle of fear and wonder; she is, in fact, separated from all of the other individuals who have come to the hill in order to witness this event:

> The sight of him, familiar and wrong, was something I was remembering from centuries hence, from the other side of death: yes, *that* is the way he used to look, when we were living. When it was our generation's turn to be alive. I could not hear him; the wind was too loud. Behind him the sun was going. We had all started down a chute of time. (92)

As so often occurs, Dillard's psyche leaps across centuries which recede into the distant past, "down the chute of time," with ancient landscapes folding in and out of her moment as if they were painted swirls on canvas. She finds herself standing in "wild barley" and "wild einkorn wheat" in the valley of the Euphrates, which is called simply "River," an indication of its ancient, primal nature. She cuts grass with "stone sickles" and stands beside her "shelter"; she is first woman at the beginning of human time (92).

At this point in the narration of a somewhat extended "moment," the chuting through time is halted as the sun has been entirely blanked out by the moon. The completion of the drop into timelessness results in total darkness: "The sky snapped over the sun like a lens cover." Suiting the film/photo metaphor, a convenient Dillard device for fast-forwarding time, the lens cover removes the light of human time. The people on the hill scream, nothing appears worldly or definable in the human sense, sound ceases, "eyes dried," "arteries drained, the lungs hushed." The world and its time cease to exist: "There was no world. We were the world's dead people rotating and orbiting around and around, embedded in the planet's crust, while the earth rolled down. Our minds were light-years distant, forgetful of almost everything" (93). Dillard has provided the reader with the sensations of an amusement park ride or Marvell's "winged chariot" ("To His Coy Mistress") by flying herself, as narrator, and the other eclipse watchers on that Washington hillside in 1979 through time to a neolithic or preneolithic past, and then beyond that ancient past to a moment which lies outside of time.

Dillard goes on to explain that this moment is beyond interpretation because it has obliterated significant touchstones of human communal experience; "the meaning of the sight overwhelmed its fascination" (94). The event has taken her to a region which lies deeper in the human psyche than "what our sciences" can "locate or name, the substrate, the ocean or matrix or ether which buoys the rest, which gives goodness its power for good, and evil its power for evil, the unified field" (94). This brings the reader once again to the idea that there are hidden areas of experience which cannot be dissected or learned. They lie beyond the material world where escape comes by passing through a doorway into another dimension, just as the narrator has done by experiencing the eclipse.

Dillard the epiphanist is perpetually involved in trying to achieve this idea of the center of the moment by using contexts and words which are necessarily human constructs. One of the ways she takes us out of time, or space, is by accumulating detail, numerical and conceptual, in great masses. In "Eclipse" she juxtaposes descriptions of the exploding star Crab Nebula, expanding "at the rate of seventy million miles a day," and the tiny lichen whose process is cell division; both star and lichen are constantly growing, dividing, and changing and yet they appear not to have changed (*Teaching* 96). This technique has the effect of reducing great lengths of human-calculated time to insignificance and of heightening the drama of "chuting out of time." Our lifetime, the juxtaposition suggests, is miniscule against the measurability of time by stars or lichens, and yet the time of the star or lichen is miniscule when measured against all planetary time; in turn, planetary time, even with all of its incomprehensible length, is nothing when set against "untime" or God's time, eternity. But for the human eye a line of time is the standard; when the mind is pushed beyond this line, it empties into eternity, where conceptualization fails.

Reminiscent of Emily in *Our Town,* Dillard characterizes herself during the epiphany-eclipse as one who watches an event from the viewpoint of the dead; the dead have little care about time or changes because they have knowledge of life's last great mystery, death itself. What the narrator saw or where she seemed to be standing during the eclipse "was all the wrecked light that the memories of the dead could shed upon the living world" (97). All the spectators on that Washington hillside were also like the dead, "alone in eternity": "We remembered our living days wrong. With great effort we had remembered some sort of circular light in the sky—but only the outline." Once again Dillard telescopes in time:

> Oh, then the orchard trees withered, the ground froze, the glaciers slid down the valleys and overlapped the towns. If there had ever been people on earth, nobody knew it. The dead had forgotten those they had loved. The dead were parted one from the other and could no longer remember the faces and lands they had loved in the light. They seemed to stand on darkened hilltops, looking down. (97)

After the sun emerges, the "shadow cone" of the moon "sped away," the tremendous powerful speed of the eclipse making her feel as though "an enormous, loping god in the sky had reached down and slapped the earth's face" (101). But time's flow and the real world commence when the circular "coned" moment has passed. Dillard adjusts herself to daily life and fits herself back into the motion and sequence of common things. She has rejoined the living, in linear time.

"Life on the Rocks: The Galapagos" in *Teaching a Stone to Talk* also deals with telescoping time as Dillard discusses evolutionary processes of plants and animals on one of the islands: "The ice rolled up, the ice rolled back, and I knelt on a plain of lava boulders in the islands called Galapagos, stroking a giant tortoise's neck" (111). Within this one sentence she has transversed back through eons and up to the present moment again.

She deals at some length with the free flow of time through her major theme in the essay, evolution. Darwin, she writes, "gave us time" (122). Before Darwin, the date for the creation of the world has been set at 4004 B.C. by the seventeenth-century Irish Archbishop James Ussher. After Darwin, the boundary that humankind had comforted itself with, that is, the idea of a beginning, a time from which everything could be dated, fell away:

> The Darwinian revolution knocked out the back wall, revealing eerie lighted landscapes as far back as we can see. Almost at once, Albert Einstein and astronomers with reflector telescopes and radio telescopes knocked out the other walls and the ceiling, leaving us

sunlit, exposed, and drifting—leaving us puckers, albeit evolving
puckers, on the inbound curve of space-time. (123)

Darwin and Einstein, having "knocked out" the walls which terminated
time at its source and destination, have expanded the notion of line.
Once again the question of time is larger than humankind can fully con-
template; we can only watch landscapes reeling away from us, eerily lit
because we can no longer cling to our comfortable definition of time
and our place in it. Dillard brings to center front again her "wild-eyed"
scientists to study the situation and to tell us that there is no end to it,
time or space, that the lifted veils will only reveal more veils, as she first
suggested in *Pilgrim*. Here we drift on the "inbound curve of space-
time," the curve suggesting that space and time are circular rather than
linear, a shape without termination. Time joins space or earth on two
occasions, socketed in "twice," she writes in *Holy the Firm* (71). Time, as
it reveals its completed shape in Dillard's universe, does not run in linear
fashion away from earth, but "sockets" down into matter through human creation and circles back again into eternity.

The Arc

Another motif Dillard frequently employs to express her concepts of
time is the arc, a trajectory of rising and falling; grasshoppers, thistledown,
eels, and jugglers' balls are all rising and falling in transparent arcs. The
globe of the earth becomes a juggler's ball which living creatures must
cling to during the performance—the goldfinch, wasps, and the narrator;
"Everybody grab a handle: we're spinning headlong down" (*Pilgrim* 221).
One descending arc of the juggler's ball has created time; this is the Fall
from grace, from humankind's acquired knowledge catapulted time into
being and, with it, death. But for Dillard there is exhilaration in the Fall:
"I am puffed clay, blown up and set down. That I fall like Adam is not surprising: I plunge, waft, arc, pour, and dive. The surprise is how good the
wind feels on my face as I fall" (*Pilgrim* 221). Dillard's fundamental doctrine about experience is reiterated here: she is willing to shed a "little
blood from the wrists and throat" in order to experience the epiphanic
condensation of beauty; to smell the "scent of deserts, groundfire in [her]
ears," to be in the "clustering thick of things, rapt and enwrapped in the
rising and falling real world," to be a participant in the time of the earth,
she is willing to pay with death (221).

The arc should be seen as a continuation of Dillard's line motif. The
line, representing a human and finite perspective on time, a shape with
beginning and end if seen clearly from Dillard's metaphysical planetary

perch, will evolve into the arc, a more completed shape in the artist's spiritual universe. Dillard's arc translates into a "holy" shape, a point which she illustrates beautifully in *Holy the Firm*. Her use of the arc motif, William Scheick notes, suggests the arches of a cathedral (59), a further indication that this curved and elongated line is associated with holy matters.

Dillard's speculation about the arc as it relates to both time and matter is graphically presented in "Sojourners," an essay in *Teaching a Stone to Talk* which examines the floating odyssey of a mangrove tree. The mangrove tree may arrive in a body of water borne by a hurricane, its germinated embryo dropping "onto a dab of floating muck." It may continue to float, its "aerial roots shooting out in all directions" to trap debris. The tree floats and literally accumulates an island about itself, "more seeds and more muck" intertwining within its increased size (149). Finally, it may be found drifting in an "alien ocean, feeding on death and growing, netting a makeshift soil as it goes, shrimp in its toes and terns in its hair" (150). Dillard's point is that the earth, like the mangrove tree, is a sojourner, creating its own soil and drifting endlessly in an alien ocean of space; the earth is a "wet ball flung across nowhere" (151) that has picked up the "soil" of human culture and is, indeed, creating itself. But the problem for Dillard in this essay is that since the earth is "careening through space toward a point east of Hercules," what will happen when it eventually does reach Hercules: "Isn't space curved? When we get 'there,' how will our course change, and why? Will we slide down the universe's inside arc like mud slung at a wall?" (151).

Rhetorically, Dillard has asked a question which posits the vastness of space as arched. Since Darwin and Einstein have knocked out the walls of space and time, the human mind yearns somehow to contain the incomprehensibility of infinity in a form or shape. With no wall at the end of the line, where does the line go? For Dillard, it arcs, a concept she examines in *Holy the Firm*.

After the tragic burning of Julie Norwich in this work, Dillard sets up various spiritual scenarios which might account for the appalling pain of this senseless occurrence. Is this God a "brute and traitor, abandoning us to time" (46)? Has the "one great god abandoned us to days, to time's tumult of occasions, abandoned us to the gods of days each brute and amok in his hugeness and idiocy?" (43). Dillard at first answers her own questions by suggesting these possibilities: God is "self-limited utterly by his creation"; God's "works are as good as we make them"; God is helpless, the baby [Christ] "self-abandoned on the doorstep of time, wondered at by cattle and oxen" (47). She continues with this supposition: "Faith would be that God moved and moves once and for all and 'down,' so to speak, like a diver, like a man who eternally gathers himself for a dive and eternally is diving, and eternally splitting the spread of the water, and eternally drowned" (47). The "diving" of God marks the path of an arc, but an arc which terminates in God's disappearance in the water where he is destroyed. The splitting of waters, which can be designated as the moment of epiphany, a transitory revelation of God's self, does not make up for the terrible burning of Julie Norwich, for after the arched dive toward earth God is hidden once again, drowned.

The main concern in this book, then, is "whether God touches anything. Is anything firm, or is time on the loose?" Do we as human beings have no link with the heavens; did Christ, Dillard asks, make a dive and undergo a "kind of divine and kenotic suicide," or did he ascend and pull "his cross up after him like a rope" (47)? Dillard seeks a link between something at the core of the earth back upward to the Absolute in heaven. This something which she seeks must be alive in our earthly matter and wrapped around the concept of human time. Another image featuring twining and entanglement as it begins to take the shape of an arc appears in the narrator's question, "is there no link at the base of things, some kernel or air deep in the matrix of matter from which universe furls like a ribbon twined into time?" (48).

In part 2 of *Holy the Firm* the sea, the artist's symbol for eternity, is very real for Dillard; the artist's illusion in part 1, of a fertile and happy scene where the sky "gags" on trees and "hedgerows...rose hips, apples, and thorn" which lie near her on the road (29), has been overshadowed by the burning of Julie Norwich. For the artist, Dillard realizes, is only a "pyrotechnic fool" and death is reality (50). "Everything in the landscape points to sea," toward death, toward eternity, but now the narrator perceives that the sea is also "nothing," an indication that eternity itself holds nothing real or hopeful. She writes that the sea is "snipped from the real as a stuff without form, rising up the sides of islands and falling, mineral to mineral, salt" (49). Eternity, which held such promise of God and meaning, is as unreal and unpromising as the land itself. In this sentence, however, appears a hint of what will become the resurrecting force of part 3: "salt."

Something appears on the horizon of the sea; another island, or perhaps a headland. The narrator says she does not know what it might be, but she will, after a day of horrendous pain, call it "Thule, O Julialand, Time's Bad News: I name it Terror, the Farthest Limb of the Day, God's Tooth" (51). Another reference to "salt" occurs with the sighting of a new land mass which lies "beyond the blue veil a sailor said was Salt Spring Island" (50). Dillard will eventually establish "salt" as the element which lies deep in the earth and bears a relationship to "Holy the Firm," the holy entity arcing back to God.

Dillard uses the phrase the "scandal of particularity" in part 3 (55), signifying the material creation of God and the delimiting forces of time for humanity. God is omnipotent and omniscient, an unseen, pure spirit, who has done us the disservice (or service, on other occasions) of making humanity and matter, in general, into objects which are particular and, what is more, must die: "There is an anomalous specificity to all our experience in space, a scandal of particularity, by which God burgeons up or showers down into the shabbiest of occasions, and leaves his creation's dealings with him in the hands of purblind and clumsy amateurs" (55). Dillard, very much like Eliot here, says that this process of particularity of creation "in time is history; in space, at such shocking random . . . is mystery" (56). Eliot writes that "history is a pattern / Of timeless moments. . . . History is now and England" ("Little Gidding" 234–37). But for Dillard, the moment of Julie's burning raises the question of the moment's significance and its connection with anything holy.

Dillard, using her arc motif, suggests that time, including all of its particular, human, finite moments, is free falling, and God has let it be so, an idea she has suggested in *Pilgrim* with the falling maple key. This is almost an eighteenth-century Deistic view of a spiritual entity, a God who mechanically sets the earth in motion but then backs off to let it operate, except that Dillard's God will appear occasionally in wild, tangled moments of epiphany. She writes that God does not choose "to catch time in its free fall" and that the earth is "enormity at random" (*Holy* 61). We "forget ourselves," however, when we believe that we have assurances or that all is going well, when, in fact, we are asleep to "time's hurdy-gurdy"; eventually we will awake and find God is silent (63). Then we rush to find God, to understand, and to attend our churches; "then it's time to break our necks for home" (62).

Dillard in the final episode of *Holy the Firm* is involved with a church for which she has volunteered to purchase communion wine. The narrator walks bearing the wine on her back, carrying "Christ with a cork . . . Holiness splintered into a vessel" (64). The landscape changes brilliantly in the ensuing illumination: "The world is changing. The landscape begins to respond as a current upwells. It is starting to clack with itself, though nothing moves in space and there's no wind. It is starting to utter its infinite particulars, each overlapping and lone, like a hundred hills of hounds all giving tongue" (64–65). The change in landscape produces the sense of epiphany; the exit from epiphany is announced by these words, presumably God's utterance: "You must rest now. I cannot rest you. For me there is, I am trying to tell you, no time" (68). These words indicate that the spirit, Christ, or some holy entity actually ushers Dillard out of the moment. A further indication that the moment was powerful and agitated for the narrator is suggested by the admonition to rest. Finally, this moment is experienced outside of diachronic time, for the voice announces that it knows no time.

Dillard pulls the two subjects of matter and time together through a theory which she has formed from a combination of three existing theories: one from esoteric Christianity, second, a Western ascetic's metaphysic, and third, a "more accessible and universal view, held by Eckhart" (68–69). The theory from Christianity posits a substance which lies below the minerals and metals of the earth; this substance, called "Holy the Firm," connects itself with the Absolute "at base" (69). Lying somewhere in the bowels of the earth, reaching below metals and minerals, Holy the Firm pushes upward through the earth and arcs into the heavens where it is in touch with the eternal, timeless portion of everything, Dillard's "Absolute" (70). The trajectory is eventually circular as the entity which is God arcs downward, specifically through Christ's sacrifice, where it touches again the substance that is the earthly base of God, or Holy the Firm.

With this arc Dillard has combined two thoughts, the emanance and the immanence of God; that is, the world has emanated from God, furling "away from him like the end of a long banner falling" (69), but is linked back to God through Christ, the spirit semi-pantheistically dwelling in all things. Because the spirit is emanent and immanent, the earth can be counted as an important portion of a total spiritual picture.

Dillard, striving to see the earth as vital in heaven's plans, draws this illustration with the arc ascending and descending through time and space:

> since Holy the Firm is in touch with the Absolute at base, then the circle is unbroken. And it is. Thought advances, and the world creates itself, by the gradual positing of, and belief in, a series of bright ideas. Time and space are in touch with the Absolute at base. Eternity sockets twice into time and space curves, bound and bound by idea. (70–71)

Dillard's concept suggests that an eternal sphere enters and exits human life at two points, two sockets which connect with the timeless world of the spirit. The sockets are the bases of two arcs, one ascending and the other descending. Together these two arcs form the completed circle which is Dillard's most holy shape. She rejoices in her conclusion that "subject may know object," that the universe is real, that we can perceive it (71), and that all is not a fantasy of our renegade organ, the brain. The fall of the maple key and the thistledown represent only one side of a circle of time, the descending arc, and we can be assured, Dillard asserts, that "since Holy the Firm is in touch with the Absolute at base, then the circle is unbroken."

The Circle

As we have already seen, Dillard's concept of time evolves from a line of diachronic time which, if seen panoramically, transpires into an arc, this arc ultimately creating the sweep of a full circle, the "holy" shape of eternity and epiphanic time. The circle begins with the "universe's inside arc" which connects with the Absolute on one distant curve and Holy the Firm at its curved extremity. Dillard's cosmography presents all matter and time as circular because, as "a child of the twentieth century" (*American Childhood* 239), she is well aware of Einstein's physical theory which allows that time does not involve a past, present, or future but contains "all time in every moment of time" (Durrell quoted in Beja 217). This dynamic of centering, with all time always present, is best illustrated by a circle, which has, indeed, been the preferred, probably innate, metaphor for many epiphanists. For not only does the universe, its time and space, appear circular as it curves back on itself, but the epiphanic moment, a single universal and "eternal" episode, generally materializes as a circle of time. It is no coincidence that Wordsworth, Eliot, and Dillard, epiphanists concerned with time, describe their respective illuminations as "spots of time" *(Prelude)*, the "still point in time" *(Four Quartets)*, and "dots of self" *(An American Childhood)*, the spot, the point, and the dot all being variations of the circle.

Martin Bidney, taking his cue from Bachelard, notices that Wordsworth uses a "radiant geometry" in several of his poems; that is, Wordsworth uses an image which allows a "movement between widely separated lights, generally the movement between a radiant center and a higher lighted sphere or myriad-lighted circumference by means of a path or line" ("Radiant Geometry" 115). Bidney suggests the presence of three elements in these epiphanies: the initial light, a movement along a straight line, and a sphere (115). He notes a sphere of light at the base of an object in a Wordsworth passage, and then a radiating line which connects to a second sphere above the first. Unfortunately, Bidney works his epiphanic geometry on lesser, if not debatable, epiphanic areas of Wordsworth's poetry, such as the "apocalyptic vision" (Bidney's characterization) of "The Pilgrim's Dream; or, The Star and the Glow-Worm" and the vision of Margaret's "sleep" in the "calm earth" (line 512) in

"The Ruined Cottage" ("Radiant" 118). Further, Bidney suggests that these spheres are physical entities, although they certainly spring from spiritual concerns, and are not referents of time. Nevertheless, Bidney, via Bachelard, verifies the tendency for circular movement within the epiphany.

Although Bachelard, Bidney, and Langbaum have identified the obvious changes which occur on the landscape and in the psyche of the epiphanic writer, they do not emphasize the significance of time's fluctuations, which fall into identifiable patterns within the epiphany. It must be remembered that Wordsworth calls his moments "spots of *time*," rather than spots of landscape, and Eliot consistently refers to his moments as "still points in *time*." Dillard, employing the circle motif most similar to these other epiphanists, calls her moments "dots of self," not specifically naming time, but she certainly infers "time" when she writes that one wonders "where they have gone, those other dim dots that were you" and that one "must take on faith that those apparently discrete dots of you were contiguous" (*American Childhood* 248–49).

The motion of the epiphany, particularly the different movements of Epiphany 1 and 2, has already been established here; however, this movement also applies in terms of the circle's geometry. Diachronic time, which exists outside the borders of the epiphanic circle, seems to flow along undisturbed by the interruption that lies in its midst. Often in Dillard's epiphanics the participant acts as a mime moving silently in an invisible cylinder on a stage. He slowly places his white hands against the imagined wall, up and down, locating the barriers of his invisible cylinder. The audience, watching his strange, dancelike movements amid walls that are not really there, perceive him to be in another world, with other-worldly motions and other-worldly barriers. Similarly, the persons of Dillard's world often seem to rage silently and slowly behind invisible barriers. In *American Childhood,* for example, when Dillard's family watches Jo Ann Sheehy under the streetlight, two invisible barriers emerge: the first represents the time barrier, and the second, which will be discussed in the next section, the literary framing of the moment. The family breaks through the first barrier, time, by watching Jo Ann Sheehy skating in the "streetlight's yellow cone of light—illumined and silent" (30). Dillard writes that this epiphanic moment was "for many years the center of the maze, this still, frozen evening inside, the family's watching through glass the Irish girl skate outside on the street" (31). Regulating time within the epiphany, Dillard has drawn this moment circularly as a "cone" of timelessness. Its internal motion is different from the family's movement inside the house. Her mother's eye had been caught by the motion of the skating, which preceded the family's rising and moving to the window to see Jo Ann "transfigured" (30). Ordinary life moves around the cone, where the movement itself occurs at a different rate.

The speed of the motion within the epiphanic center, as has been discussed earlier, creates a still tableau, which, like the fluttering of angel wings in "A Field of Silence," appears static but is, in epiphanic physics, rapidly vibrating timelessness. Jo Ann Sheehy's ice skating is at once frozen in Dillard's memory and yet suggestive of the cone's internal vibration. In her skating, Jo Ann moves from one streetlight to another, Dillard intimating the different speed within the illuminated cone; the skater turned, "tilted and spun" under the light, but suddenly winged "into the blackness beyond the streetlight" (30–31). Outside of the circle-light, where Jo Ann disappears, there exists the same lack of motion that holds Dillard's family watching from their "tall chilled windows" (30). When Jo Ann does reappear under another light, her quick, darting movements suggest the vitality of the epiphanic center: "Inside that second cone of light she circled backward and leaning. Then she reversed herself in an abrupt half-turn—as if she had skated backward into herself, absorbed her own motion's impetus, and rebounded from it; she shot forward in the dark street" (31). Here Dillard enhances the sense of increased velocity by describing a movement that "absorbs" itself, a familiar whipping motion that occurs so quickly that it appears not to have transpired. When the skater reappears under the first light, she is "becalmed," a signal that the illuminated moment has ended. Jo Ann Sheehy's skating, like the "stilled" moment in the fields of silence where angel wings fluttered, is an example of varying motions within and without the circle of time, which the epiphanist implies.

The circular image is extended in a description of the farm where this moment occurs in "A Field of Silence." Just as she gave the primal Euphrates the generic name "River" in "Total Eclipse," she notes that the farm seems to be a Platonic form, pure idea,

> eternal in the crude way the earth does—extending, that is, a very long time. . . . a piece of land eaten and replenished a billion summers, a piece of land worked on, lived on, grown over, plowed under, and stitched again and again, with fingers or with leaves, in and out and into human life's thin weave. I lived there once. (*Teaching* 133)

Just as she stretched and retracted time in "Total Eclipse," she makes the farm here become the symbol of diachronic time, and onto this she pins the epiphany of the woman in pink pushing a wheelbarrow. While the farm is given a real date, a viable time frame, "Saturday morning late in the summer, in early September" (134), the moment is set off for the narrator by auditory and visual senses which wrap her in a circle of time from which she loses the power to emerge. The sky has "choked the field," the pastures appear as if they are "holding their breaths," the roosters have stopped their crowing, "all the things of the world—the fields and the fencing, the road, a parked orange truck—were stricken and self-conscious" (135). Time's silence in this essay, an idea expanded later in *An American Childhood*, is like a child's emergence from some unconscious area of the psyche suddenly to understand that she is living: "I could see the shape of the land, how it lay holding silence. Its poise and its stillness were unendurable, like the ring of the silence you hear in your skull when you're little and notice you're living, the ring which resumes later in life when you're sick" (*Teaching* 135–36).

Dillard notices, like the Emily Dickinson persona who hears a fly buzz on the day she dies, that in the unspeakable silence of her moment flies are buzzing over the henhouse, "moving in circles and buzzing, black dreams in chips off the one long dream, the dream of the regular world" (136). The regular world is for Dillard the unconscious world of daily living where one is not attuned to the spirit, the flies representing the sleeping world which lies outside the circle of epiphany. Their association with lazy, disagreeable sluggishness is appropriate, particularly as it provides a comparison with what the narrator finds within the circle of epiphany. Inside the circle of timelessness is the real world, "eternity's outpost in time...God's blasted, paralyzed day" (136). The flies, buzzing just outside the narrator's barrier or invisible wall, are placed near the borders separating time from timelessness to heighten the dramatic effect in two senses: auditory, as the low hum of the buzzing flies is set against utter silence, and kinetic, as the slow motion of the sluggish insects becomes the antithesis of fluttering angel wings. Within the circle of epiphany the narrator rises like a pole of extreme consciousness: "I felt myself tall and vertical, in a blue shirt, self-conscious, and wishing to die. I heard the flies again; I looked at the rooster who was frozen looking at me" (136). Far outside of the circle, set at a distance "at the big yellow Charolais farm," there is motion (136). It is there Dillard is able to see the woman in pink pushing a wheelbarrow and hear her whistling. Agonized by her acquisition of supra-knowledge, "sorrow deriving from knowledge," but suspended in time, frozen in a super-conscious state, along with objects and animals, she can only remain locked to the moment. She is compelled to watch from her vertical position, pinned to the center of the ring of silence. What she is compelled to watch is "holiness": "Holiness is a force, and like the others can be resisted. It was given, but I didn't want to see it, God or no God"

(136–37). She does resist, however, and willfully turns away, at which "the whole show" vanishes; it is then that the "realness of things disassembled" and diachronic time takes hold, making the rooster crow, releasing the fields from their pressure of silence and making the whistling "ordinary" (137).

Dillard's circle image appears consistently throughout her work. In *Pilgrim*, time is portrayed as an entity without a terminus, like a hoop or a "Slinky" toy or a snake skin which appears to have no beginning or end, all metaphoric extensions of the "power we seek...[which] seems to be a continuous loop" (76). In "Total Eclipse" the moment becomes literally a circle as the "shadow cone" of the moon speeds away "down the hill and...over the plain" (*Teaching* 101). In *The Writing Life*, Dave Rahm's plane "cleaved the sky like a prow and tossed out time left and right in his wake" (109). But just as the plane's trajectory suggests at first a line, the epiphanic performance eventually reveals the completed shape of illumination, the line lengthening into an arc and then to a full circle when the pilot "piled loops in heaps and praised height"; Dave Rahm is writing a script of "one infinitely recurring utterance" (109). Dillard's cones of light and shadow are cones of time; they are elongated lines, stretching out into arcs and joining in circles, and through this image her time becomes self-perpetuating, complete, having neither beginning nor end—it is eternity.

Frames

"The world at my feet, the world through the window, is an illuminated manuscript whose leaves the wind takes, one by one, whose painted illuminations and halting words draw me, one by one, and I am dazzled in days and lost," Dillard writes in *Holy the Firm* (24), creating an image which metaphorically suggests the writer's artistic structure. Her "world through the window" is a world filled with holy arcs and circles, the arc of the falling maple key and thistle, the hoop of God rolling along the hills, but these holy scenes are framed by the literary act, the epiphany in words. Thus, the window frame in Dillard's work can be seen as a point of epiphanic and altered time; but as a frame it connotes artificiality as a constituent part of its nature. In this way it can be viewed as the artifice of the writer's language architecturally building the epiphany.

"Aces and Eights" is a superb example of the manipulation of time, particularly as time is "framed," which Dillard can effect within the moment. The essay begins almost as a parody of "Tintern Abbey" as the narrator thinks about how she and her nine-year-old child companion will store the vital memories and nostalgia of a weekend at a country cottage. But for Dillard and the child the pathos of these heightened moments is almost too much to bear; Dillard writes that she went to the cottage against her "good judgment" while the child has already become "morbidly nostalgic and given to wringing meaningful moments out of our least occasions" (*Teaching* 153–54). So rather than storing "food for future thought," a balm for days "in the city pent," as Wordsworth suggests for himself and his young sister-companion Dorothy, Dillard and the child fear the food of their intense moments along the riverbank:

> At home at my desk I doodled on tablets and imagined myself and the child standing side by side on the riverbank behind the cottage in the woods, standing on the riverbank and watching the blossoms float down, or the dead leaves float down, or just the water—whatever it would be—and thinking, each of us: remember this, remember this now, this weekend in the country. And I knew that instead of seeing (let alone remembering) the blossoms, or the leaves, or whatever, the child and I would each see and remember some dim picture of our own selves as figures side by side on the riverbank, as figures in our own future memories, as focal points for some absurd, manufactured nostalgia. (154)

This kind of staged moment, already framed by the knowledge that life is passing, that nothing can be repeated, was a concern for Dillard as a child, she reports in *An American Childhood*. As a thirty-five-year-old woman with this tendency for retrieving and recording moments, she says that her "tolerance for poignancy [had] diminished to the vanishing point. If I wish, and I do not, I can have never-to-be-repeated moments, however dreadful, anywhere and anytime, simply by calling that category to mind" (*Teaching* 154).

Here Dillard has skillfully set the stage for complications and sophistication in epiphany by recognizing that moments in a nineteenth-century mode can be ridiculously maudlin, by admitting the presence of a young mind who is equally aware of "moments," by anticipating and fearing the moment which reminds her and the child of transitory life, and by setting these weekend moments in a perspective that could produce bathos (in nineteenth-century fashion). But the narrator will not allow bathos because she is so aware of the possibility of fraud in this framework. Dillard begins, after this initial comment on fearing the moment, to build a series of narrative-expository vignettes which will, at the end of the essay, become the many facets of a central principal epiphany. This final epiphany is, in fact, like an object in a hall of mirrors reflected over and over from various angles and in various sizes; its subject is time.

Two of the child's activities during the weekend help establish the frame that leads to the final illumination. First, the child, with Dillard's assistance, repairs an old bicycle from under the porch. Finding a route through the woods, the girl ascends and descends a hill on the bicycle several times during the course of the weekend. Secondly, Dillard and the child play poker, during which Dillard tells the young girl "we call aces and eights 'dead man's hand' because Wild Bill Hickok was holding them in a poker game when he was shot in the back" (162). The bicycle ride and card game are united when the child asks for clothespins "to fasten some cards to her bicycle so that when the wheels turn the cards will slap in the spokes" (162). This bicycle ride with flapping cards becomes for Dillard a metaphor for time-perception, as it changes from childhood to adulthood. The slow slap of the cards as the bicycle ascends the hill is the slow passage of time for a child; she "cannot imagine how you will save yourself from death by boredom until dinner, until bed, until the next day arrives to be outwaited, and then, slow slap, the next" (167). But the crest of the hill, or the middle of life, is reached almost imperceptibly, and then the descent begins at a furious rate and out of control. It is in the rapid descent that "days start to blur and then, breaking your heart, the seasons"; the "cards click faster in the spokes," becoming the sound of a "bomb's whine," and then you know that "your course is fatal" (167); you hold the dead man's hand after all.

The river beside the cottage represents for Dillard, as it does in *Pilgrim* and *An American Childhood,* the passage of time, and as such serves to reinforce the disparity between a child's and an adult's concept of temporal movement. She anticipates herself and the child as "figures side by side on the riverbank" at the outset of the essay. Later she and the child launch lighted candles onto the night river and watch them "wobble downstream and gutter out, one by one," causing Dillard to reflect on Thoreau's thought, "You cannot kill time without injuring eternity" (159). As she watches the candles float and extinguish themselves down the river, she wonders about the wisdom or value of their efforts in creating the diminutive water spectacle: "It seemed both to take too long and end too soon" (160). This evaluation of the effort and effect with the candles repeats the notion of the bicycle ride; for the child the ascent up the hill took "too long" and for the adult it all ended "too soon."

After Dillard goes to bed that evening, she is aware of the sound of the water outside her window when she consciously remembers to listen, but later, in a state of elation, thinking about the speed of the revolving earth, she "cannot remember to listen for the river" (160). To be aware of the river is to be aware of time's passage, and when she is exhilarated with certain ideas she can momentarily forget that she is mortal.

In another water scene Dillard and a dog sit watching the reflections of clouds in the river's surface and, in the water, some carp with a "loose-knit network of sunlight" on their backs (165). Water striders skim the surface and appear to be foraging on the bottom of the re- flected cloud "like lizards on a ceiling" (166). The narrator is lulled into euphoria by this river beauty until she is abruptly awakened by the "clacking" of the child riding the bicycle up the hill. Here again is the metaphoric reminder of mortality intruding on the pastoral river scene. Here is what she feared at the outset of the weekend—that she would be acutely conscious of life's brevity. What allows Clare Fishburne to be "porous as clouds" in *The Living* creates exquisite pain in the narrator of "Aces and Eights."

Dillard makes two other symbolic gestures to accompany the river motif. First, the cottage becomes a kind of "first garden," an Eden, very similar to the scene which Dillard paints around the Lucas farm in *Pilgrim*. The cottage represents the opening of human time (or birth) on the river, which itself represents the extended passage of time:

> I would say that coming into a cottage is like being born, except
> we do not come into the world with a box of groceries and a
> duffelbag full of books—unless you want to take these as
> metonymic symbols for culture. Opening up a summer cottage is
> like being born in this way: at the moment you enter, you have all
> the time you are ever going to have. (158–59)

A second image accompanying the river motif is the framed window. Dillard writes that she watches the river from the cottage: "Filling the window's frame, crowding each of its nine square panes, is the river, moving down" (159). She has used a similar framing at the Lucas Farm in *Pilgrim* when she watches through the abandoned house window the finch light on the thistle, which results in the scattering of down. In "Aces and Eights" the passage of time, or the river, is being highlighted, and therefore it is set into a frame, a technique that will become an im- portant feature of the major epiphany in this essay. It appears to be Dillard's comment on the process of art as it captures an illumination. To "frame" the moment is to impose a structure upon a wild and cha- otic flurry of spiritual manifestations; this structure becomes a window frame in the narration but an artistic literary device in the architecture of the epiphany.

With all of the preliminary comment in "Aces and Eights" on seizing the moment, sorrowing for the moment, and anticipating future moments, Dillard adds yet another variation on this theme by transporting herself to her own childhood and recalling a moment which, even as a child, she had intentionally set out to keep forever. When she was very young Dillard became aware that everything changes with the passage of time; she questions, then, what will become of her: If all of her passions would one day "be overturned"—her love of Walter Milligan, her hatred of her sister and piano lessons, her love of bicycle rides, then what would she be? (163). There would be nothing left of what she was, the child concludes, and so she vows that she will remain steady, she will buck the system: "I will until I die ride my bike and walk along these very streets, where I belong. I will until I die love Walter Milligan and hate my sister and read and walk in the woods. And I will never, not I, sit and drink and smoke and do nothing but talk" (164). The child demands of herself that she will remember the vow, inscribing upon her memory that scene or landscape which surrounded her when she made the vow. She awakens to the moment and "walking so fiercely uphill" is "illuminated by a powerful energy" (164). So that she will never forget, she "writes" upon her mind the "stone elementary building, deserted on Saturday" and "a dark row of houses, stone and brick, with their pillared porches"; she "committed to memory the look of that block, that neighborhood: the familiar cracked sidewalk, how pale it was, how sand collected in its cracks; the sycamores; the muffled sky" (164). This deliberate recording of a childhood moment is a peculiar type of illumination very similar to Wordsworth's "spot of time" during the waiting for the horses episode in book 11 of the *Prelude*. As a schoolboy, Wordsworth waited for a coach to carry him from school, and, later, when he remembers the scene, he, like Dillard, recalls the landscape punctuated by a sheep, a whistling hawthorne, and a stone wall which appear in memory's high relief.

This moment of avowal for Dillard, however, is not a fully realized epiphany because it is deliberately constructed by the child, a conscious anticipation which, as we have seen, cannot accompany full epiphany. Because she proposes always to remember, it is more like Dillard's attempt to catch the present moment as she did in *Pilgrim*; the child wants to keep the moment by remaining always as she was at the time of the vowing. The older Dillard has, of course, broken these vows, but she retains the ability to look back on the child's moment, which figures as a kind of preshadowing of the many-faceted epiphany of "Aces and Eights."

All of these elements came together in the moment for which Dillard has been laying the literary groundwork. Noah Very, a local eccentric and recluse, visits Dillard and the child at the cottage; he takes sherry and cake with them while night comes on. Noah, reminiscing, remarks to impress the child that he does not know his own age; he "can't keep track" of it (172). The precocious child is not impressed by this remark, but, nevertheless, Noah continues with an anecdote about his life, a time in his married past which he tried to "catch," much like Dillard the child when she made her vow, and much like the present child, who is already "given to wringing meaningful moments out of our least occasions" (154). The scene Noah remembers is from a time when his children were little, when his family all lived together where he is living now. He looked out of his window and "saw the children playing by the river" and told himself that "This is it, now, when the children are little. This will be a time called 'when the children are little'" (173). "I couldn't hear anything through the window," he reports, "I just saw them. It was morning." Dillard, picking up the narration, writes that she "looked closely at Noah, who was looking at the child," and he speaks:

> I said to myself, "Noah, now you remember this sight, the children being so young together and playing by the river this particular morning. You remember it." And I remember it as if it happened this morning. It must have been summer. There are another twenty years in there I don't remember at all. (173)

Significantly, in this scene Noah remembers his own moment which he had tried to "catch," his faraway moment also framed by a "still" window. Once again a framework has been imposed temporarily on the flow of time.

Continuing his conversation with the child, Noah tells of an apple tree which his grandfather had planted outside of the window near where the child now sits. The child, turning around to look out of Noah's window behind her, can only see her own reflection because it is night. The old man wonders if the child knows " 'how long it takes to grow an apple tree?' " (174). In his explanation of the great age of an apple tree he sings that "You'd have to wait until you were ALL grown up and married...and had FOUR children" (174). Sparked by Noah's "grown up" song, the child moves into her own future plans, seeing herself in the window with a "tall, blank husband" and four children, while Dillard, who is sitting at some distance from the window, also looks into the window and catches the reflected gaze of the child. The child's imagining of her future life vanishes and she sees now, "inside the near, shadowed outline of her own reflection in the window, a smaller, distant reflection under a lamp—just me, a woman in her thirties, drinking sherry and smoking a cigarette":

> The child is holding my eye, which she sees inside the lighted scene inside the breast of her dress. She is laughing because I laughed and she knows why. She looks at me deeply, the way she does, smiling enormously. I put out my cigarette. The child turns herself around on the couch, and together we resume listening to Noah. (175)

Dillard, here, with these window reflections, has constructed a many-sided epiphany relating specifically to time. The child looking through the cottage window becomes a piece of Noah's remembered moment from his own past; she subsequently fades out of his moment and into her own solitary present, watching her own reflection in the window. But then she is suddenly transported into her own future by a snatch of Noah's apple tree song, a future that induces the image of a possible scenario of her own husband and children. Into the frame comes another figure, Dillard the narrator, who catches the eye and the mind of the child, and the child and Dillard suddenly cohere in thought. Dillard has brilliantly brought together and framed a past moment (Noah's memory of his children), a present moment (the child's reflection of herself), a future moment (the child's vision of what she might become), and a unifying flash of moment (the narrator and child suddenly locking in their reflections) within this epiphany. The light in the child's "breast of her dress," an illumination significantly occurring over the traditional seat of human spirituality, the heart, is an indication that she is cognizant of time's passage, that Noah has kept his own moment, that Dillard's reflection is a harbinger of a future life, that this very window reflection is a "caught" moment, a spot gelled in time, and that Dillard herself is aware of all that the child feels.

All of the preceding elements were the groundwork for this epiphany centering on time. Time is a commodity that all of the participants in this essay desire. Each comes to realize that he or she has been dealt a "dead man's hand" and is clacking a bicycle of slow ascent or rapid descent, but each in turn has kept a moment. The individual moments are framed by memory and reflected back to the mind by the will of the rememberer. But most significantly for the artist-narrator, the epiphany of self-realization has been framed by art, the epiphany stylistically preserved and framed by language. Time has been caught in words and just as the window reflects light and time to the characters in this essay, so the epiphanic structure reflects for the reader a vibrating, whirling moment that first sprang to life in the mind of the writer.

An epilogue follows the epiphany in part 3 of "Aces and Eights" and reinforces the idea of the caught moment. The child at the end of the weekend does not want to leave the cottage and announces that she is "not going. . . . I'm staying here" (177). But Dillard protests that they must go. Already they are capturing, however, as Wordsworth would say, "food for future thought," for they are imagining themselves "in the future remembering standing here now, the morning light on the green valley and on the clear river, the child playing with the woman's fingers" (177). A "tiny, final event" occurs, a small postlude-epiphany that reiterates the moment of window reflection and the exposition on time. A breeze ripples across the grasses, into the cottage eaves, and onto the river. It is a reminder of fall, of the old story, time's passage; its intrusion confirms what the narrator has so passionately realized during the weekend: the bicycle is clacking its rapid descent. Dillard laments, "I thought I was younger, and would have more time" (177). But the "gust crosses the river and blackens the water where it passes, like a finger closing slats" (177). The "rogue breeze out of the north" tells her the season is changing, her life is dissolving rapidly, and the moment closes like the slats on a blind (177).

The framing of the moment suggests, in Dillard's work, human or cultural structures. It is not only a device that the writer employs to signal epiphany, but is also a commentary on the role of the artist. Dillard is occupied frequently by the operation of the artist, the dedicated work of creating and sculpting the inspired first vision of art. The frame is the artist's scaffolding on which Dillard applies the flesh of her major theme, epiphany. The artist's initial impetus is a "vision of the work," Dillard writes, "not of the world. It is a glowing thing, a blurred thing of beauty. Its structure is at once luminous and translucent; you can see the world through it" ("A Note on Process" 25). The vision, here, has the same characteristics as a window in that it is a pane through which one can view aspects of reality. Dillard refers to the vision as "structure" several times in this article, referring to its "deep structures" and even intensifying the metaphor by painting the vision in the "rooms of time": "The vision is, *sub specie aeternitatis,* a set of mental relationships, a coherent series of formal possibilities. In the actual rooms of time, however, it is a page or two of legal paper filled with questions; it is a terrible doodle. . ." (25). Dillard's thesis is that the vision must be acted upon by finite, worldly artist's materials and, consequently, can never quite reproduce the initial "blurred thing of beauty"; the actual work is, in fact, a "simulacrum...an artifact alongside the vision" (25). In this article Dillard suggests that the vision becomes the imagined frame for the work of art.

Dillard examines in "Wish I Had Pie" the physical accoutrements of the writer's struggle to produce her art, as she gives an account of her stay in a cabin on Puget Sound. The cabin is a "single small room very near the water":

> Its walls were shrunken planks, not insulated; in January and February and March, it was cold. There were two small metal beds in the room, two cupboards, some shelves over a little counter, a woodstove, and a table under a window where I wrote. The window looked out on a bit of sandflat overgrown with thick, varicolored mosses; there were a few small firs where the sandflat met the cobble beach; and there was the water: Puget Sound, and all the sky over it and all the other islands in the distance under the sky. (75)

This presents an allegory of the artist at work: Dillard sits alone, in a pared-down room with a window (the structured vision) that looks out onto the land (earth's time) and the sea (eternity; the same cobble beach and water of *Holy the Firm*), and proposes to write (the art work). The framed window becomes the vision of eternity, the formal structure of art in time, placed around the spirit itself which appears arched and circular through the luminous frame of vision.

A distinction, then, should be made about Dillard's use of circles, arcs, dots, or generally rounded figures, and her use of frames or rectangular figures. Both types of figures involve her portrayal of time and the epiphany, but appear to signal separate ideas. The frame of a window suggests the moment separated from the rest of time through artistic vision; it appears on the surface to be gelled or frozen, and not a part of the flowing river of diachronic time. In *Pilgrim* the finch and thistle are framed at the Lucas farmhouse. In *Holy the Firm* the narrator watches from her cabin window on Puget Sound to see a new island appear; she writes that "now outside the window, deep on the horizon, a new thing appears....It is a new land blue beyond islands, hitherto hidden by haze and now revealed..." (50). In *American Childhood* the family watches from a window to see Jo Ann Sheehy skate under the streetlight. Also, Dillard, as a child, watches the buckeye trees sway through the "windowed sunporch walls" and realizes, "I am awake now forever ...I have converged with myself in the present" (68–69). In *The Writing Life* the frame is a computer's monitor where a "line of words waited still, hushed, pointed with longing" (21), and a "blank screen" where Dillard finds the nebulous words that mark epiphany (89). A frightening vastness of all possibilities lies in the universe behind the screen which attempts to collect and unify language into the artful moment. In "Aces and Eights" the child cannot see the river through the black window and watches her own reflection. Earlier in the essay Dillard has seen the river "filling the window's frame...moving down" (*Teaching* 159), but now the child, losing sight of the river, or time, creates imaginatively her own future time, this frame also preserving the present moment in which she locks eyes with Dillard. Time is stopped (although the reader must remember that "still time" is intense motion), changed, reversed, or thrust into the future by this framing, a motif which signals the altered time of epiphany and the artistic structure of its literary simulacrum.

The circle, on the other hand, seems to be linked with more purely spiritual matters. The spiritual arc and circle can be seen through the windows of cabins and other structures with windows, or at times with no human artifice interfering at all. The loop of the snake in the woods, God as a fireball or a rolling hoop of fire, all from *Pilgrim*, the circuit of Holy the Firm stretching into eternity, touching the Absolute, and arcing back through time to earth—these are all signifiers of the spirit as it gathers to form in the mind of the writer. This is the form of the spirit as it manifests itself outside of human culture or in the natural environment. In "A Field of Silence," when Dillard is visited by angels in the open fields of the farm, the moment is still, "like the ring of the silence you hear in your skull when you're little" (*Teaching* 135). The ring or circle moves the narrator out of human time, as the framed window does, but suggests that outside of human culture, beyond the frame of the window, the spirit arcs and circles.

4

Upstream and Down

Surfaces and Directions in Epiphanic Time

Surfaces of Time

Annie Dillard frequently brings another spatial dimension to her discussion of time, the concept of "surface" and its corresponding active verb "surfacing." Time's surface is intimately linked with the supraconsciousness Dillard passionately seeks. When a child first begins to join the consciousness of living, a process Dillard often presents as converging with a larger stream, Dillard envisions the child as surfacing into the air of awareness, here illustrated by a passage from "Total Eclipse":

> We teach our children one thing only, as we were taught: to wake up. We teach our children to look alive there, to join by words and activities the life of human culture on the planet's crust. As adults we are almost all adept at waking up. We have so mastered the transition we have forgotten we ever learned it. Yet it is a transition we make a hundred times a day, as, like so many will-less dolphins, we plunge and surface, lapse and emerge. We live half our waking lives and all of our sleeping lives in some private, useless, and insensible water we never mention or recall. Useless, I say. Valueless, I might add—until someone hauls their wealth up to the surface and into the wide-awake city, in a form that people can use. (*Teaching* 97–98)

The transition we routinely make is the movement out of our interior, perhaps, subconscious mind, into the air of acute sensory perception to recognize that we are here on the planet and drifting with time. Like arcing dolphins we surface and then plunge downward again into our "private. . . insensible" minds.

Dillard fills out the analogy with these elements: There is a surface barrier, sometimes land, sometimes water (usually a stream, creek, or river), or sometimes even skin, the flesh barrier to the inner person; the barrier can be transected by an upward thrust of the mind, whereupon the one thrusting breaks through into acute consciousness. Below the barrier, however, lies a treasure that Dillard hints at in her use of the word "wealth." The river of diachronic time, having a surface barrier that meets the air above the water, flows on the surface of the land which itself has its own topsoil barrier. When the mind acts below these surfaces it is creating and collecting its own wealth, intricate veins of precious stones, in "underground corridors where spinel crystals [twin] underfoot," a notion Dillard advances in *An American Childhood* (146). The surface represents to Dillard the daily motion of Newtonian time, measured in increments that have become standardized, but the regions below and above the surface move the mind into altered time. In acute consciousness, above the surface, the mind loses its sense of ordinary time, roaring with the speed of the planet (Epiphany 2) or hovering with the stillness of angel wings (Epiphany 1); below the surface the mind is delving into its own treasures unattended by any notion of time whatsoever. This paradigm of mind, almost Freudian in structure, must include time because the mind first loses time's ordinary sense when it plunges or surfaces.

An American Childhood's major theme, built around this surface metaphor, is a child's consciousness as it links itself with time and matter. The narrator generally uses the river to signify time throughout the book, and the landscape, often a child's geography lesson on landscape, is matter as it fills space. This autobiography is permeated with moments that lie outside of time; these occur when the child suddenly realizes that she is part of time's passage. From the beginning of *An American Childhood* to the end, Dillard rises above herself and the landscape of her life, to view the "dot" of herself from "dizzying precipices" where the "distant, glittering world revealed itself as a brooding and separated scene." She becomes both the "observer and the observable" (12).

One of these moments, which also introduces the skin motif, occurs quite early in Dillard's life when her mother dips her into the hot water of a bathtub:

> The skin on my arms pricked up, and the hair rose on the back of my skull. I saw my own firm foot press the tub, and the pale shadows waver over it, as if I were looking down from the sky and remembering this scene forever. The skin on my face tightened, as it had always done whenever I stepped into the tub, and remembering it all drew a swinging line, loops connecting the dots, all the way back. (12)

These dots, figures which in *An American Childhood* suggest Wordsworth's spots and a child's game of "connect the dots," are, of course, circles of time which represent holy moments of illuminated consciousness for Dillard. They are moments that remain exposed in her memory while other moments, days, and years have been lost to the mind; they are circular moments which lie above the surface of diachronic time.

The river of time metaphor is further expanded and intricately developed throughout *An American Childhood*. When the child is just beyond infancy, she sits "mindless and eternal on the kitchen floor, stony of head and solemn, playing with my fingers" (17). Beside her, "Time streamed in full flood" and "roared raging beside me down its swollen banks; and when I woke I was so startled I fell in" (17). Before the child becomes conscious of time she is "eternal" and "stony," having neither joined time, a prerequisite to surfacing, nor gained sufficient sensual knowledge of earth to mine below the surface; but suddenly gaining the concept of linear time she is swept away by the flow of the stream.

But the child's fall into the river of time cannot be considered, except at the point of juncture, to be epiphanic; that is, the river does not churn up perpetual epiphanic moments. The river provides, instead, the communal consciousness of time's passage. It is possible, however, to live deeply in the flow of time. In the sweep of time a life of concentration can be achieved, a life in which "effort draws you down so very deep that when you surface you twist up exhilarated with a yelp and a gasp" (17). This concentrated life, the life of nun or artist, repeats Dillard's theme of dedication, an effort which eventually allows surfacing into the air, with illumination resulting.

When Dillard is ten, after she has watched through the sunporch window the swaying buckeye tree branches, she undergoes an epiphanic moment: she is conscious that she is conscious. She remembers the details of the moment: the buckeye limbs, her cold hands holding the novel *Kidnapped,* her father snapping his fingers and wandering about the house, "blue shadows of fast clouds" running along the walls and floor—all noted and retained in her acute consciousness (68). She writes that it was then she "felt time in full stream" and "felt consciousness in full stream joining it, like the rivers" (69). Here her own consciousness becomes a converging stream with the larger river of time, and at the confluence of the Allegheny and the Monongahela, Pittsburgh's position on the land's surface, she experiences an illumination that will become one of her connecting dots of time.

As the child grows she notices that she is fully conscious of life only at certain moments. She becomes increasingly anxious over the rapid movement of time and the myriad scenes she has already forgotten. She must self-consciously notice it all or her life will be lost; otherwise there would be the "growing size of that blank and ever-darkening past," which frightened her (130). She believes, since she is forgetting so often, that one day she will forget to remember her life and the "blank cave" will "suck me up entirely" (130).

The child, with her predilection for detail and recording, becomes intensely interested in collections and notation. She spends hours in her attic learning to notice and draw pieces of faces, single features, projecting herself as a Holmes character and working toward a final niche in Scotland Yard (130). But she finds that when she attempts to store the moments, or inspect them, they drift from her, or become dim, sliding "dizzyingly away, like a ship's stern yawing down the dark lee slope of a wave" (131).

This growing anxiety is illuminated in *An American Childhood* by an exquisite chapter that is introduced by the question, "What does it feel like to be alive?" (150). The answer comes metaphorically, again, by the river image. Now, however, the narrator suggests that the child can leave the "sleeping shore" of the river and deliberately plunge into the water. Once in the river the child steps into a waterfall where she can feel the dash and power of time:

> The hard water pelts your skull, bangs in bits on your shoulders and arms. The strong water dashes down beside you and you feel it along your calves and thighs rising roughly back up, up to the roiling surface, full of bubbles that slide up your skin or break on you at full speed. Can you breathe here? Here where the force is greatest and only the strength of your neck holds the river out of your face? Yes, you can breathe even here. You can learn to live like this. (150)

This moment under the waterfall is epiphanic (probably of the lesser type because Dillard is *trying* to catch the moment), but, in this instance, it provides an illustration of the way these moments might occur, or the emotion a recipient might feel when experiencing illumination; it is an expository and generic illumination. Dillard narrates, however, an autobiographical epiphany in the pages following the waterfall illumination.

In this passage Dillard writes of her friend Judy Schoyer, whose parents own a farm near Paw Paw, West Virginia. Dillard is invited to spend a weekend there with the family when she becomes suddenly cognizant that life is too brief and that somehow she must catch the moment. For she has arrived at an age when life seems to be "a weekend, a weekend you cannot extend, a weekend in the country" (151). Just as she and the child in "Aces and Eights" begin to regret painfully nostalgic moments, even before the weekend begins, so the young and precocious Dillard envisions herself remembering this Paw Paw weekend: "I imagined myself in the distant future remembering myself now, twelve years old with Judy" (152). She knows she has only these few hours to remember and the minute she sets "foot on that land across the river" she starts "ticking like a timer, fizzing like a fuse" (153). Dillard has become a "noticer"; she realizes that she must keep her own record, she must set it down. She writes that during that weekend she began the "lifelong task of tuning my own gauges. I was there to brace myself for leaving" (155). With a sensation that she is "haunting" her own childhood, Dillard cannot prevent the thought that this is only a weekend in the country or that this life is only a prelude to death.

Furthermore, this noticing, Dillard realizes, could present a severe impediment; it could, she writes, drive her "around the bend," as it prefigures the writer's dilemma of both living life and recording it. For as Thoreau notes in "My Life Has Been the Poem I Would Have Writ," one cannot "both live and utter" life (*Collected Poems* 1–2). Dillard understands that "Too much noticing and I was too self-conscious to live; I trapped and paralyzed myself" (155).

But this self-conscious child does continue to notice, to surface in the river, to realize her dots of self on the landscape. In the concluding pages of *An American Childhood*, in a peculiar expository epiphany, Dillard connects her dots of time by rising again over her own landscape, over mountain ridges and valleys and rivers. She can see herself, her various selves, each self an indicator of momentary consciousness in many positions on the topography of her life. She rises in supra-consciousness again, noticing herself somewhere standing on a mountain, or ridge, and realizes, with the geography of her life laid out before her, that she herself is the dot who is walking there:

> if you notice unbidden that you are afoot on this particular
> mountain on this particular day in the company of these particular
> changing fragments of clouds,—if you pause in your daze to
> connect your own skull-locked and interior mumble with the skin
> of your senses and sense, and notice you are living,—then will you
> not conjure up in imagination a map or a globe and locate this
> low mountain ridge on it, and find on one western slope the dot
> which represents you walking here astonished? (248)

Still, she wonders in this conscious moment where the "other dim dots" which were her have gone (248).

Dillard began this book by saying that she could connect the dots of herself "all the way back," an indication that she is able as the adult writer of this autobiography to understand that she is all of these diverse dots together; and even though she awakes to find herself at great distances from the last awakening, even though the last dot appears to be somewhere on a distant terrain, far from where she stands in the present consciousness, these dots are she. They are Dillard suddenly alert to the spinning globe which she can catch and ride; they are Dillard alive with the "dizzying overreal sensation of noticing" that she is there on this landscape on a particular day at a particular moment; they are Dillard emerging from the river of time, surfacing into the air of epiphany, with a "yelp and a cry" (249). The earth's crust and the body's skin are temporary barriers to the "crystalline intelligence inside" and to the moment under the waterfall where the "strong water dashes down beside you and you feel it along your calves and thighs rising roughly back up, up to the roiling surface, full of bubbles that slide up your skin or break on you at full speed" (139, 150).

Directions in Time

Dillard's imagining of time involves not only geometric shapes, motion, and the concept of surface barriers, but also a sense of direction. Time can be seen in Dillard's world as moving horizontally or vertically, the vertical movement generally a signal of extreme holiness or advancing epiphany. *Pilgrim at Tinker Creek* suggests two analogies which work well for Dillard's conception of direction in time: the horizontal flow of the creek and the vertical growth of a tree. Both physical entities, however, have some combination of directions within their metaphoric structures.

The tree becomes the avenue of Dillard's search for the reality of the moment at hand in "The Present" because, she writes, "Trees have a curious relationship to the subject of the present moment" (*Pilgrim* 86). Because trees are large, reach upward into space and downward into the earth, and are held with intricate root systems, they represent standing firm and planted in the present moment. Dillard elaborates in both scientific data and poetic abstractions about the presence of the tree. She ruminates over Xerxes in Persia having been utterly dumbfounded by his sudden sighting of a tree, halting his army for days to look upon the "beauty of a single sycamore" (87). Xerxes attempts to capture the steadfastness of the sycamore by commanding his goldsmith to pound in gold the emblem of the tree (89). Thus even in ancient times, we are to conclude, the tree represented a link to eternity.

Dillard elaborates upon the intricate root systems which ply their ways under the base of a tree by visualizing aphids and cicadas, webs of filament and minute life which live in planes of soil just below her and in even deeper levels:

> Under my spine, the sycamore roots suck watery salts. Root tips thrust and squirm between particles of soil, probing minutely; from their roving, burgeoning tissues spring infinitesimal root hairs, transparent and hollow, which affix themselves to specks of grit and sip. These runnels run silent and deep; the whole earth trembles, rent and fissured, hurled and drained. (95)

The tree draws her thoughts not only to the region under the surface of the soil but also into the upper atmosphere, as its limbs reach out to find God. Like the world that lies below the surface of the creek and the life illuminated above the water, the tree becomes a paradigm for the paradox of the human mind. The tree has depths and heights, both seen and unlimited; and like the mind, the tree has the power to fabricate something tangible—wooded trunk and leafy growth—from the realm of the invisible: the air itself.

But as the tree branches uncontrolled below and above the surface of the earth, so the mind branches into many thoughts whose paths cannot be checked. Dillard thinks of all that is occurring in that present moment as she, like the tree, stands on the land, and that vision is heavily colored by her sense of time and mortality. Her old tomcat is dead; a steer "stumbles into the creek to drink. . . . The giant water bug I saw is dead. . . . The mockingbird that dropped furled from a roof. . . but this is no time to count my dead. That is nightwork" (98). Dillard's thoughts, branching out like intricate root systems, also cannot avoid their apprehension of the past: "Big trees stir memories," she realizes (99). Like Alice in Wonderland, the narrator is imaginatively reduced in size so that she can bore through the "thickest part of the trunk as though it were a long, dim tunnel" (99). This tree tunnel reminds her of a highway landmark of her childhood, Squirrel Hill Tunnel, and suddenly she has "achieved the past" (99). Having burrowed her way into her own past, she finds herself in "a shady side of town, in a stripped dining room, dancing, years ago. There is a din of trumpets, upbeat and indistinct. . . I stir" (100). She has connected with some dim memory from her past through the wandering roots of her thoughts but, shaking off this memory, she returns "to the present, to the tree, the sycamore" and sets off to seek the "live water," an indication of what she will find at the creek (100).

Dillard, with her characteristic metaphysics, rises above the rotating sphere of earth to investigate what is happening on the surface of this single present moment, just as she previously investigated what lay below the surface in the tree's soil base. The "galaxy is careening in a slow, muffled widening. If a million solar systems are born every hour, then surely hundreds burst into being as I shift my weight to the other elbow" (97). Suns are exploding, meteorites are "arcing to earth," all within this one moment of the present (97). She reels the scene in, bringing it closer to the reader, and imagines a trapper "maddened, crazed" in the far north, thinking of the chinook wind; she thinks of the pampero, the tramontane, the Boro, sirocco, levanter, and mistral—all winds raging about the spinning earth in this one chink of present. These winds allow her to "lick a finger" and "feel the now," to note with her senses, as best she can, the very present moment (97).

In this chapter of *Pilgrim*, Dillard examines the present moment "vertically," with the tree as her symbol. She rises above the moment to note what planets could be achieving in the present; she telescopes closer to the earth to note what other regions might be producing at this one moment; she burrows beneath the earth to consider the substrata life of insect, fungi, and plant. Her burrowing downward, however, led her away from the very present moment to a mind tunnel, a horizontal root that eventually linked her with her Pittsburgh past.

Thus in slicing time vertically into the present, Dillard has inadvertently moved horizontally into time past. This horizontal tendency into the past has grown out of her determination to be "present"; that is, she willed this grappling of the moment; she sought to find present and in the search, which was tainted with desire, she wandered into past. This analysis of the tree as mind can only bring her back to the present and, thus, must be considered as the lesser epiphany. Although the tree is a magnificent image of myriad possibilities in the present moment, it does not yet represent the moment which opens from eternity onto time; it is not the moment of the cedar tree with lights. It is not "live water," the creek that breaks into particles over your head when you face upstream.

Although trees give consciousness to the present moment and "stir memories," it is "live waters" which can heal these memories (103). Dillard shouts from the page:

> Look upstream. Just simply turn around; have you no will? The future is a spirit, or a distillation of *the* spirit, heading my way. It is north. The future is the light on the water; it comes mediated, only on the skin of the real and present creek. My eyes can stand no brighter light than this; nor can they see without it, if only the undersides of leaves. (101)

Looking upstream is predicated on the notion of the creek's horizontal flow. Time is the river; if one can stand in the river of time one can feel the present, the swiftness of the water rolling down. Standing in the river must be preceded by arising from the surface of the water with a "gasp and yelp" to see it rolling by. So the epiphany occurs when an individual can surface above the water. After the surfacing, the narrator can position herself in the water two different ways: she can face down the river or she can turn and face up the river. When she faces down the river she experiences the second type of epiphany; that is, she catches the present, as it is imaged in other portions of Dillard's work. But when she faces up the river she sees the brilliance of water or time flowing and striking her, a vertical thrust upward into the air. The future comes translucent in waves, the past is in fragments: "Here it comes. The particles are broken; the waves are translucent, laving, roiling with beauty like sharks" (103). Overhead she can see the particles of water breaking, shattering, announcing to her nothing but the "now." In the preferred epiphany there is no past, for the epiphanist chooses not to turn and gaze down the river. When she does turn down the river, Dillard the narrator is able to see the particles breaking overhead, an apprehension of present, as in the present of the tree, but she is often distracted by the past, as when her "root thoughts" lead her away into Squirrel Hill Tunnel and her Pittsburgh beginnings. It should be concluded, then, that to look upstream, like Clare Fishburn, is to achieve the spirit of full epiphany.

Looking downstream ignites the "lesser" mood of Epiphany 2, while facing upstream will allow the explosion of Epiphany 1. In Epiphany 2 the epiphanist enters the exact present and casts her eyes toward the past. In Epiphany 1, the epiphanist feels the exact present, but can also examine eternity. Dillard says that by facing the future, upstream, all moments of epiphany can be hers, while she cannot capture the past with "baited hooks and nets" for the past is always flowing away from her vision down the creek (102). To experience this moment is to live fully in the senses for a brief period and to be transported to fragments of the past. It is present plus past. It is, Dillard writes, her "present consciousness . . . a mystery which is . . . always just rounding a bend like a floating branch born by a flood. Where am I? But I'm not" (93). Turning up the river allows moments like the cedar tree filled with mourning doves; turning down the river allows moments like the puppy in the gas station:

> I look up the creek and here it comes, the future, being borne
> aloft as on a winding succession of laden trays. You may wake and
> look from the window and breathe the real air, and say, with

satisfaction or with longing, "This is it." But if you look up the creek, if you look up the creek in any weather, your spirit fills, and you are saying, with an exulting rise of the lungs, "Here it comes!" (100)

Here the narrator suggests that she can stand at the window and look at the creek; she can have longing and satisfaction as she attempts to feel the exact present which results once again in present plus past. But if she turns around and faces upstream she will be filled with the spirit.

Dillard's metaphors are often mixed and dense as she illustrates these distinctions. She writes that the "present is a freely given canvas. That it is constantly being ripped apart and washed downstream goes without saying; it is a canvas, nevertheless" (83). As the canvas of the present breaks into particles or is "being ripped apart," it, too, is washed down the river of time. In this narrative scenario the canvas exists without an "artist"; however, should the artist appear, he could enhance the epiphanic moment by rising in the stream, canvas in hand; by turning to face the stream as it pours over him; and by tossing the canvas over his head in the water so that he can watch the canvas rip into brilliantly colored particles. He should not turn to watch the fragments as they are carried downstream.

The present can be explored in two ways: by apprehending the exact present with all of its branches of organic life, above and below the land's surface and its attachment to the past, or by facing the future and seeing then only the present, with no attachment to the past, only the particles breaking overhead as time rushes toward you. Dillard concludes "The Present" with the exultant comment: "The present is the wave that explodes over my head, flinging the air with particles at the height of its breathless unroll; it is the live water and light that bears from undisclosed sources the freshest news, renewed and renewing, world without end" (103).

Both of these illuminations, the present plus past, or the present plus eternity, with their vertical and horizontal ranging, occur because humankind is set down in a life that is dissolving. Life passes and decays; it is studded with pain and the knowledge of death. Dillard describes its rolling and progression by comparing it to the motion of sharks and muskrats, whose movement is the essence and heart of their lives: "If the sharks cease roving, if they still their twist and rest for a moment, they die. They need new water pushed into their gills; they need dance" (98). This is the paradoxical nature of time, decay and delight, which Dylan Thomas calls the "force that through the green fuse drives the flower" and the poet's "green age"; it is the blind man married to space who takes with him his dog of death (*Pilgrim* 181); it is the thistle that is torn by the finch and scattered to the wind. Time is flux; but with Dillard it will always be redeemed by an epiphany achieved by acknowledging the exact present or by simply being alert when the great door on eternity swings open and light illuminates the landscape of earth.

Epiphany and Vision

One question arises concerning the relationship of full epiphany to the lesser phenomenon of vision, and the manner in which these two illuminations treat time: since Dillard's full epiphany (Epiphany 1) seems concerned with purely spiritual matters, how closely does this epiphany border on the vision? Since, as Dillard says, the door opens from eternity on time, what holy entities (a god-head figure, Christ, small pagan gods) are revealed and, when they are revealed, do these entities mitigate the essence of epiphany, which always involves a rupture in time? The problem here centers on the open-endedness of epiphany versus the fill-in-the-blank allegoric nature of vision.

The rupture in time is in itself a major portion of the mystery or "holiness" of an epiphany. Thus, if a spirit can be defined, even partially by figures or objects, as Dillard does with her god of the day in *Holy the Firm,* these figures necessarily become allegorical or metaphoric; this, of course, leads back to the metaphor of vision rather than to the dynamic of epiphany. It appears, then, that vision has less to do with time than the epiphany; while epiphany breaks or ruptures diachronic time, vision, with its allegoric proclivity, works more with matter than intangible time. So when Dillard moves more toward the full epiphany, a very fine line keeps her from ranging into vision.

As has been noted from the beginning of this study, Dillard is conversant with many types of illuminations, but essentially her moments tend toward these three types, all sculpted primarily by their reliance on time: Epiphany 1 (present and future, the cedar tree with lights), Epiphany 2 (present and past, the puppy in the gas station), and vision (more matter and less time, the finch on the thistle). Finally, the epiphanic moments in general are more powerful because they *do* rupture time; they pull back the curtain on the moment and leave objects open, with little explanation, to the reader's view. Her visions, on the other hand, become explicators of illumination, or didactic. This approach diminishes the power of the moment to involve the reader.

With Wordsworth and Eliot: A Comparison of Epiphanic Times

Wordsworth, Eliot, and Dillard have written seminal works revolving around epiphanies initially achieved by their reorganization of "time." Robert Langbaum says that the epiphany of "Little Gidding" takes its structure from the epiphany of the romantics: "Eliot is a great poet because he embraces the whole of the poetic tradition up to his time and takes it a step forward. Wordsworth is the great seminal Romantic poet who revolutionized the tradition of his time, giving rise to much that is most innovative in Romantic and modern literature" (357). George Bornstein also verifies the similarity between the romantic and the neo-classicist when he writes that in "projecting mental developments as overt subject of a long, first-person poem, *Four Quartets* inevitably recalls *The Prelude*" (154). This similarity is directly linked to these poets' interest in time. Dillard has gone even further in her discussion and development of time, as she does with other elements of epiphany, in that she overtly includes it in most of her work. A comparison between these three epiphanists' use of time reveals their similar innate conception of this difficult element, and, also, their individual insights and preoccupations concerning the subject.

Wordsworth, who was writing at the beginning of what we would later term a literary tradition, had taken his cue, according to Herbert Lindenberger, from Rousseau; both writers were concerned with the "significance of time and memory in their autobiographical works" (139). Memory and the theory of association allowed the writer to return to his past and in some way revive and restore himself with these memories. Wordsworth's spots of time allow a "mysterious and complex transfer of power," according to Lindenberger (154), which exceeds the energy of the usual recaptured memory; this power might only point out that life is different from the way it used to be. Wordsworth's epiphanic door in time, which initiates the "transfer of power," can be considered in three ways in order to highlight Dillard's similarities and differences: the framing devices, the time framed, and the perspective of the writer.

Wordsworth's major framing device for his spots of time can be seen as the memory itself. With a new contemporaneous interest in the association of memory, it would have been a pioneer adventure simply to apply repeatedly, as Wordsworth did, a return to memories which "with distinct preeminence retain / A renovating virtue" (*Prelude* 11.258–59). Among his most memorable spots, and those which he identifies specifically following his epiphanic definition in book 11 of *The Prelude*, are the incident involving the girl with the pitcher, the beacon, and the pool and the incident which finds him waiting for the horses to take him from school. Other spots from book 1 in *The Prelude* include Wordsworth's ice skating on a lake, stealing eggs from a raven's nest, taking woodcocks from another's trap, and drifting in a shepherd's boat when the poet feels the malevolent power of a cliff rising above him. There are yet others which reveal various degrees of spiritual force within the epiphany, but the most overtly spiritual of *The Prelude's* spots, carrying apocalyptic overtones, is the moment of Wordsworth's ascent of Mount Snowdon (book 13). All of these epiphanies are framed initially by the "revolutionary" act of remembering and drifting with that memory.

Perhaps the best illustration of memory as frame is the multidimensional spot involving the girl with the pitcher. Lindenberger quite rightly points out the various levels of time called up here; he also applies an apt metaphor for these variations of time—the refraction of light through a prism (153). The first level of time must be the moment of composition itself, the present time from which the poet writes; this can be called the diachronic time in which the epiphany can act or be released from the ordinary mechanics of Newtonian time. Wordsworth introduces the lines of the spot with "Life with me, / As far as memory can look back, is full / Of this beneficent influence" (11.276–78), thus inserting the first hint that memory is to release him from his current time. He recalls "a time / When scarcely (I was then not six years old) / My hand could hold a bridle, with proud hopes / I mounted, and we rode toward the hills" (11.278–81). The young Wordsworth, with his companion, "honest James," rides into the hills where the boy becomes lost and then disoriented. The lost boy eventually spies a frightening spectacle, a gibbet-mast which has "mouldered down" and, nearby, the turf which had been "lettered" with the name of a murderer. The mouldered mast and lettered turf now provide a further removal to a more distant past when the murderer was hanged.

Wordsworth rides frantically into the hills above the Gothic scene and is there entranced by visually grouping together several objects—the gibbet mast, a beacon on a hill (a stone?), a desolate pool, and "more near / A girl who bore a pitcher on her head" who is making her way against the strong wind that tosses her garments (11.301–08). Thus far, three levels of time have been cited—the present (of the poet's composition), the past (of the hanging), and the nearer past (of the five-year-old Wordsworth). The poet adds yet another facet to the prism by calling up a time of "early love" when he and two beloved companions (his sister Dorothy and future wife Mary Hutchinson) would walk near the gibbet scene:

> When, in the blessed time of early love,
> Long afterwards I roamed about

> In daily presence of this very scene,
> Upon the naked pool and dreary crags,
> And on the melancholy beacon, fell
> The spirit of pleasure and youth's golden gleam...(11.317–22)

In this manner, a fourth time period, a framed memory, is added, which gives the spot a peculiar prismatic character, further enhanced by the fact that Wordsworth does not elucidate what is the specific renovating power of these various times. He only suggests that these "remembrances" have a "radiance more divine" and have left him with a "power" (11:323–24). What gives these various levels of time their power is what is left out, an explanation or exposition on the significance or, as has been offered before, the symbolism or metaphoric quality of the objects as they appear through the four facets of time's prism.

It is as if Wordsworth needs no other device than memory itself to highlight the epiphany when he writes that "The days gone by / Come back upon me from the dawn almost / Of life; the hiding-places of my power / Seem open, I approach, and then they close" (11.333–36). The mind with its powers of association is powerful enough to frame the moment and when the mind or memory is clouded by intervening, perhaps mechanical time, the frame is clouded. Intellectual mist envelopes the memory when the poet attempts to approach too consciously or deliberately his own mind.

It has been noted that Dillard's frame for epiphanic time is often literally a frame in the objective realm as she looks at her own spots of time through windows. Or, the frame becomes another kind of highlighting with the increased speed of the epiphanist, who clings metaphysically to the planet. Dillard does attempt a kind of webbing effect, similar to Wordsworth's refracting prism, when she wanders to her own past through the metaphor of the tree, its branches above and its roots below the surface of understanding. But this kind of webbing becomes less epiphanic because, first, it is associated on its one level by metaphor, and, secondly, because Dillard is always less epiphanic when she deals with the past rather than the future.

In general, a narrator's perspective of the landscape is connected with the type of time found within the epiphany. Wordsworth's distant perspectives within his poetry have often been identified. His eye, with the reader's, is drawn farther and farther over the landscape with the sense of a Turner or a Constable painting, where folds of color envelope one another. "Tintern Abbey" illustrates this painterly technique superbly with its "hedge rows, hardly hedge-rows, little lines / Of sportive wood run wild" (16–17) and smoke that rises from a solitary's hut in the woods (21–23). The same perspective of distance lies in *The Prelude's* spots of time. The girl with the pitcher on her head and the wind-whipped garments appears to be at a nearer distance than the naked pool and the beacon on the hill. When Wordsworth waits for the horses at Christmastime he has "repaired / Up to the highest summit" of a "crag, / An eminence, which from the meeting-point / Of two highways ascending overlooked / At least a long half-mile of those two roads, / By each of which the expected steeds might come" (11.349–55). He ascends Mount Snowdon to watch the mist roll out in promontories and the hills raise their "dusky backs" (13.45). Even in the "lesser" spots such as the theft of the raven's eggs, the poet writes he is a "plunderer . . . In the high places, on the lonesome peaks" and hangs "Above the raven's nest, by knots of grass. . . Shouldering the naked crag" (1.336–46). When he steals the shepherd's boat he has "fixed a steady view / Upon the top of that same craggy ridge, / The bound of the horizon" (1.397–99). When Wordsworth the epiphanist seems to be bound at the center of the epiphany, as in the ice skating spot of book 1, he continues to note the horizon beyond his whirling circle or spot: "With the din, / Meanwhile, the precipices rang aloud; / The leafless trees and every ice crag / Tinkled like iron; while the distant hills / Into the tumult sent an alien sound / Of melancholy" (1.466–71).

The obvious links between these distant perspectives and the poet's engagement with time is that Wordsworth looks to his own distant horizons of past life. In the folds of land stretching beyond the eye he seeks the restorative power of his wild and thoughtless childhood. Although Wordsworth emphasizes that these remembrances will give him aid, that "feeling comes in aid / Of feeling" (11.325–26), thereby anticipating a future time, he is a poet bound up with past. The mists, he realizes, will one day close on his landscapes, and he will only be able to "see by glimpses" and eventually "May scarcely see at all" (11.337–38). When the past is entirely blocked from view he has little hope of his future, although he does resurrect a last hope for sight with the "philosophic mind" of the "Intimations Ode."

Wordsworth's general proclivity within the epiphany is horizontal, time reaching out over his shoulder on the landscape, while Dillard's movement is vertical. She delves underground with the tree roots, she rises out of the creek, she surfaces to take in the full sensuality of the moment. Her perspectives are shorter; she looks from a window to see Jo Ann Sheehy under the streetlight; she watches the diminutive movements of a finch on a thistle; she stands in the middle of a farm field to see angel wings fluttering. Although the "Field of Silence" epiphany contains brief mention of a woman in pink at a distance, the sense of distance is much shorter than Wordsworth's long, sweeping views from a hilltop. The point of this shortened distance is Dillard's sense of time. She wishes to verify the present moment and to do so she stands in the middle of her symbol for time, the creek; out of the "creek" of diachronic time she rises, and at that rising she can apprehend two different times: the past, by looking down the creek, or the future (causing the present moment to be sustained), by looking up the creek. To rise in the middle of the creek puts the writer at the center of her time, at the center of the cone, the cylinder, or the circle.

Dillard reveals her connections with her own historical framework when she writes that she prefers revelation of the present: "There must be something wrong with a creekside person who, all things being equal, chooses to face downstream. It's like fouling your own nest. . . . Look upstream. Just simply turn around; have you no will?" (*Pilgrim* 101). Morris Beja notes Einstein's influence on contemporary writers, as the physicists's time did not involve a past, present, or future but was a "time which contained all time in every moment of time" (217). Thus, Dillard, echoing the spirit of her age, surfaces to the present point of time and does not concern herself with distant perspectives.

T. S. Eliot's contribution to the use of epiphany is interesting to note because he stands between Wordsworth and Dillard. His work is also instructive because it is an emblem of one who tried to deny romanticism, and therefore epiphany, but who apparently clasped it to himself, as evidenced by its obvious importance in the late and very substantial work of *Four Quartets*. Each section of the *Quartets*—"Burnt Norton," "East Coker," "Dry Salvages," and "Little Gidding"—is constructed in five parts about the framework of an epiphanic moment and its relationship to time and eternity, so that a central subject of the *Quartets* is, indeed, time. "Burnt Norton" opens by announcing the subject:

> Time present and time past
> Are both perhaps present in time future,
> And time future contained in time past.
> If all time is eternally present
> All time is unredeemable.
> What might have been is an abstraction
> Remaining a perpetual possibility
> Only in a world of speculation.
> What might have been and what has been
> Point to one end, which is always present.
> Footfalls echo in the memory
> Down the passage which we did not take
> Towards the door we never opened
> Into the rose-garden. (1–14)

Eliot begins here his search for what he calls the "still point," which is the intersection of time with the timeless. It is Einsteinian time where each moment contains all of the past and the future, the eternal present. Finding his way into the rose garden of Burnt Norton, a deserted seventeenth-century estate, Eliot experiences his "still point," or epiphany. He enters through the "first gate," redolent of Eden, following the "deception of the thrush," perhaps like Keats, in his famous ode, followed a nightingale who could not "cheat so well / As she is fam'd to do" (73–74). Eliot's narrator walks an alley of boxwood until he reaches two dry, cement pools ("Burnt" 20–34). The atmosphere is strangely quiet, the roses bearing the look of "flowers that are looked at," and there is "unheard music hidden in the shrubbery" (27–29). In the dry pools the poet apprehends water created "out of sunlight" lifting a "lotos rose" when the surface of the water in the pool glitters "out of heart of light" (35–37). Suddenly a cloud passes, the bird calls, and excited children hidden in the shrubbery laugh (39–42). Eliot concludes section 1 with lines that once again highlight the nature of time:

> Go, go, go, said the bird: human kind
> Cannot bear very much reality.
> Time past and time future
> What might have been and what has been
> Point to one end, which is always present. (42–46)

It is difficult to separate Eliot's landscape from his conception of time within the rose garden epiphany. All epiphanic moments intrinsically rely on the intertwining of these two elements. But if, as Helen Gardner writes of the *Quartets,* "the sense of time is the soul of Eliot's later poetry the sense of place is its body" (320). The "soul" of the moment in the rose garden of Burnt Norton must be gently extricated from the "body" to discover its character.

Eliot, like Wordsworth, looks to his own past within the confines of the rose garden epiphany (Moynihan 82), the poet asking the question, "What might have been?" The laughter of the children in the shrubbery, among other allusions, has been identified with Eliot's early St. Louis life when he would listen through a wall which separated his yard from a schoolyard (Gardner 324). But Eliot is moving ultimately in a different direction from Wordsworth. Eliot looks quickly and quietly at his past, listening to "echoes" which "inhabit the garden," but even this brief moment is almost too overwhelming for the poet, for "human kind / Cannot bear very much reality" (17–18, 42–43). Eliot desires instead to move to the "still point of the turning world," a movement which carries the poet through "Burnt Norton" and the remaining three segments of the *Quartets*. This still point can be identified as a nontemporal moment or an absolute present. Like Dillard, Eliot seeks to stand directly in the present moment which contains, also, all of "time past" and "time future" (1–2). He seeks what Dillard desires as she "faces upstream," where she can watch the translucent wave break into particles over her head. And similarly, Eliot's epiphany, his brief encounter with the lotos rose rising out of sunlight in a dry pool, is only a "hint" of "Incarnation" ("Dry Salvages" 215), for Christian theology is what Eliot is pointing to all the way through the *Quartets*. The moment in the rose garden has opened his eyes just briefly to eternity, but this single fleeting moment for Eliot will eventually open on to all eternity, or a time with no time, when the "fire and the rose are one" ("Little Gidding" 259).

The door into Eliot's timeless moment must be considered through the tone and the setting, to some degree, just as Wordsworth's spots of time must be considered for their position on distant landscapes. Eliot's entry into the rose garden gives evidence of human cultivation. The garden is cultivated even though it is on an unoccupied, seventeenth-century English estate (Hargrove 133–34). Shrubbery, flowers laid out in "a formal pattern," a "dry concrete, brown edged pool," and an "empty alley" of trees—all indicators of human cultivation and established tradition despite the estate's deserted condition at the time of the poet's visit—fill the garden. Eliot stands surrounded by these icons of human order and experiences a quiet, almost timid, illumination. The moment is manicured, an appropriate literary gesture for a poet who disdained emotion and wore an intellectual mask. And although Eliot moved away from dreamscapes and cityscapes as he aged, allowing himself the romanticism of rural life through the setting of Burnt Norton, a movement, according to Gardner, symbolizing some respite from despair (323), his epiphanic vocabulary indicates that he remained an advocate for tradition—literary, religious, and political.[4]

The powerful natural elements in Wordsworth's spots stand in great contrast to the quiet, cultivated still point in "Burnt Norton." The blasts, crags, and eminences, the vast panoramas of Wordsworth's spots, are a necessary facet for a poet who desires to see something in the distance, while the poet who is seeking simply to be brought to a stilled point is comforted by the quietness of a rose garden.

The concept of three separate times is apparent in Wordsworth, Eliot, and Dillard. Wordsworth is most involved with the retrieval of his past, but is also, according to Herbert Lindenberger, aware of a historical time, as illustrated by the Druidic scene on the Salisbury Plain in book 12 of *The Prelude*. This historical time is "unconcerned about the order of public events and unaware of distinctions between public history and private history of self" (Lindenberger 173). This could be called a "spirit of history," as opposed to the factual details of history. Finally, there is a sense of eternity which is always implied by any illumination. Wordsworth, however, does not emphasize eternity, since he does not appear to have worked out the details of eternity's power; he finds his renovating power in the past.

August Nigro claims that Eliot also suggests he understands three levels of time in the *Quartets,* particularly in "Dry Salvages": diachronic time (symbolized by the river), synchronic time (by the surface of the ocean), and nontemporal time or eternity (by the ground swell). In "Dry Salvages" Eliot speaks of the "river...within us, the sea...all about us" (15). Eliot's river is time as it is commonly perceived by humanity, while the sea becomes something just short of epiphany. The sea contains all of the water which has flowed from the rivers; it contains the accumulated debris of nations, empires, and civilizations, which has flowed into it and in turn been thrown onto the beaches. We living have evidence of time before us. Although it appears linear because we see ourselves as products and descendents of these past civilizations, it also appears vast and incomprehensible, vast stretches of eternity before our time. Eliot writes that the "sea is the land's edge also, the granite / Into which it reaches, the beaches where it tosses / Its hints of earlier and other creation" (16–18). Out of the vast, rolling sea has come "our losses, the torn seine, / The shattered lobsterpot, the broken oar / And the gear of foreign dead men" (22–24), all of which indicates that the sea contains human time and its accoutrements. But in the deepest parts of the sea lies the movement of the "ground swell" which is "a time / Older than the time of chronometers," older, even

> Than time counted by anxious worried women
> Lying awake, calculating the future,
> Trying to unweave, unwind, unravel
> And piece together the past and the future,
> Between midnight and dawn, when the past is all deception,
> The future futureless, before the morning watch
> When time stops and time is never ending;
> And the ground swell, that is and was from the beginning,
> Clangs
> The bell. (39–48)

The women waiting for their men on the sea still wait with human longing and sorrow. The sea has taken these sailors and made them a part of the human dilemma; they will become the debris which the sea casts up as signifiers of human passage through time. But swelling and rising in the depths of the sea is the timeless moment, the ground swell, which becomes a larger and more powerful movement than even the ordinary, cyclical rocking of the oceans. This ground swell is the action which lies outside of time, which for Eliot "clangs the bell" to alert humankind to God's timelessness. This clanging of the bell is "perpetual angelus," the moment which can intersect with human time to warn of the rocks that can crush a sailor, the Dry Salvages that can bring death.

As suggested earlier, rapid fluctuation is a central feature of the epiphanic moment, and this principle can be applied to all three epiphanists. Wordsworth's moments obtain, according to Lindenberger, the "rhetoric of interaction"; that is, a sense of gliding in and out of present time underlies the spots (169) creating an illusion of a mind intensely engaged with a process of contemplation.[5] Dillard's epiphanic movement has been identified most significantly in "A Field of Silence," where she has seen the fluttering of angels' wings. Eliot, by his use of the phrase "still point," at first appears to assign epiphany to a "frozen tableau," a recurrent image in many writers. But Eliot dismisses the notion of motionlessness when he writes that the still point is where "the dance is":

> And do not call it fixity,
> Where past and future are gathered. Neither movement from nor
> towards,
> Neither ascent not decline. Except for the point, the still point,
> There would be no dance, and there is only the dance.
> I can only say, *there* we have been: but I cannot say where.
> And I cannot say, how long, for that is to place it in time.
> . . . .
> surrounded
> By a grace of sense, a white light still and moving,
> *Erhebung* [rising] without motion, concentration
> Without elimination, both a new world
> And the old made explicit, understood
> In the completion of its partial ecstasy,
> The resolution of its partial horror.
> ("Burnt Norton" 64–78)

The "white light" of the still point is paradoxically "still and moving"; it is at any point of the "dance" where timelessness invades. But like the dance, its location and duration cannot be measured, for as Eliot writes, "that is to place it in time," and the still point is a circle or cone (or a dot or spot) removed from diachronic time.

But just as Dillard cannot see the completed beauty of the finch until it has torn the thistle seed from its case, just as Clare Fishburn is invigorated and made whole by the knowledge of his own mortality, so Eliot cannot perceive the still point, the nontemporal moment, unless it is set against the foil of temporality and all of the fleshiness and pain which accompanies it:

> But only in time can the moment in the rose-garden,
> The moment in the arbour where the rain beat,
> The moment in the draughty church at smokefall
> Be remembered; involved with past and future.
> Only through time time is conquered.
> ("Burnt Norton" 85–89)

Each of the illuminations Eliot mentions here—the rose garden, the arbor, and the church—all moments of sudden insight, must be encountered through mortal life until this life can merge with the sea of God's timelessness. For Eliot, this is the intertwining, a concept strikingly similar to Dillard's twine of time and matter, or her weft and woof of life's fabric, only in Eliot that intervening is of the "tongues of flame" (God's pentecostal fire, timelessness) with the rose of the garden (human time), so that at last in a "condition of complete simplicity" all sense of time is eradicated:

> And all shall be well and
> All manner of things shall be well
> When the tongues of flame are in-folded
> Into the crowned knot of fire
> And the fire and the rose are one
> ("Little Gidding" 255–59)

The epiphany in "Little Gidding" is centered on the poet's journey to a small Anglican chapel located in a field in Huntingdonshire. This chapel, built by the devout Nicholas Ferrar, was the center of an Anglican community established prior to the English civil war (Hargrove 184); and it was to Little Gidding that Charles I, "a broken king," found his way to pray before his imprisonment by Cromwell ("Little Gidding" 26). The poet-narrator walks along the "rough road" turning "behind the pig-sty to the dull facade / And the tombstone" with little or no purpose in mind (28–30). But this lack of purpose for Eliot is a passivity on which the moment acts, for another eternal "purpose is beyond the end you figured / And is altered in fulfilment" (34–35). Another quiet epiphany ensues on the road to the chapel:

> Midwinter spring is its own season
> Sempiternal though sodden towards sundown,
> Suspended in time, between pole and tropic.
> When the short day is brightest, with frost and fire,

The brief sun flames the ice, on pond and ditches,
In windless cold that is the heart's mirror
Reflecting in a watery mirror
A glare that is blindness in the early afternoon.
And glow more intense than blaze of branch, or brazier,
Stirs the dumb spirit: no wind, but pentecostal fire
In the dark time of the year. Between melting and freezing
The soul's sap quivers. There is no earth smell
Or smell of living thing. This is the spring time
But not in time's covenant. Now the hedgerow
Is blanched for an hour with transitory blossom
Of snow, a bloom more sudden
Than that of summer, neither budding nor fading,
Not in the scheme of generation. (1–18)

Eliot makes it clear that this moment is removed from diachronic time. The sudden appearance of spring within winter characterizes the moment as out of "time's covenant," while it is also "sempiternal," "suspended in time," and "Not in the scheme of generation." This moment, which once more fulfills the pattern of the frozen tableau with its flaming ice and cessation of earth's smell, appears to be stilled from motion in its "windless cold." But the more dominant pattern of fluctuation in timelessness reveals itself with the stirring of the spirit and the quivering of the "soul's sap." However, the quietness of Eliot's epiphany prevails and he completes this section of "Little Gidding" by reaffirming that this was, indeed, his encircled moment, the still point of epiphany: "Here, the intersection of the timeless moment / Is England and nowhere. Never and always" (52–53).

It would do well for the reader to rise imaginatively, or perhaps metaphysically as Dillard does, above the "landscapes of time" as these three writers paint them. Wordsworth watches from craggy eminences and ascends mountains to see his "spot of time"; he looks over vast panoramas seeking that revelation which will provide him with poetic power and insight, which will in turn lead him on to the next spot. Wordsworth's horizontal vision, a vision of a man looking over his shoulder for glimpses of something escaping him, allows him a moment out of time which sometimes hints at eternity, as on Mount Snowdon, but which generally apprehends his early life. He fears a time when he can no longer catch glimpses of the "days gone by" where lie the "hiding-places of my power," for age is clouding the vistas of the poet's mind. Without the circle of past time at his mental disposal there is little hope for an inspired present or future.

Eliot's landscape of time, on the other hand, is drawn in, pulled closer about the narrator. There are enclosed, boundaried rose gardens and narrow English roads. Eliot's hedgerows blossoming with snow are viewed at close enough range to see the transitory nature of the melting blossom, unlike the "sportive lines of hedgerow run wild" which Wordsworth points out in "Tintern Abbey." Eliot's garden has been cultivated, laid out in rows, and he stands in the middle of it. His garden will not provide vast panoramas because it is not the panoramic past he seeks. He stands in the middle because it is there, between past and future, that he will perhaps experience the still point where "time is eternally present." Eliot's hints about time's variation are secret, hidden, and timid within the illumination, the "unheard music hidden in the shrubbery." His is a time which hints at rash disjointedness, strange enjambments; he is vertical within the garden and the "time objects" encircling him are experienced with a sense of misalignment. The dry concrete pool, the empty alley, the box circle, the formal pattern are all slightly ajar with "unheard music" and the "unseen eyebeams" of roses. This smacks of cubism, while Wordsworth's painted scene is Turneresque romanticism.

Eliot's time landscape does, however, maintain a certain realism in its selection of elements; the roses belong in the garden, the hedge is appropriately placed along the road. These real elements, though, are trimmed, close, and traditional, while Wordsworth's epiphanic elements are wild growth, distant, and revolutionary in the late eighteenth century. Eliot, interested in achieving perpetual present through artistic and religious tradition combines the subjects of time, art, and faith in his epiphanic still point.

Eliot can be characterized as a vertical narrator, while Wordsworth remains a horizontal narrator. But Dillard, following Eliot, takes his landscape of time and stretches it vertically to its furthest extreme. She does not keep to the surface of the land (or garden) but delves to subterranean depths and rises to planetary orbits. She searches the webbing of soil under the roots of a tree in *Pilgrim at Tinker Creek;* in *An American Childhood* she pries open the landscape to find "crystal-crusted cavities lined with fire opals and red plume agates" (146); her childhood rock collecting, she writes, "was like diving through my own interior blank blackness to remember the startling pieces of a dream" (139). In *Pilgrim* she rises above the planet to see the earth's ages roll like paint in her fast-forward film. In *Holy the Firm* she speaks of the holy substance that is "lower than salts and earths" and connects with the Absolute, rising through an arc to eternity. Dillard surfaces; she walks on the landscape, but she longs both to penetrate the consciousness that lies below and engage the power that rises above. She is in the creek of time but never ceases her quest for the moment of surfacing to no time, to a present moment which lies outside of time, to the intuitive knowledge that this dot of self is her walking on a "particular mountain on this particular day" (American Childhood 248).

Dillard's landscape of time is filled with people and objects gathered from all time: camels and magi, polar explorers and Keystone Cops, penguins and Christ, a "cello, a basket of breadfruit, a casket of antique coins" (Pilgrim 152)—all are borne by time's flow. Dillard will walk in the woods or the gardens, but eventually she will delve into the depths of the earth or fly into the heavens, for her time must be the very exact present and the exact present can only be found by ranging vertically, metaphysically. She has learned this from Einstein and the "wild-eyed physicists"; the timeless moment, a piece of eternity, remains a difficult prize, but Annie Dillard has skewed language in a new and marvelous way in order to achieve this transitory state.

5

When Everything Else Has Gone
Epiphanic Landscapes

Annie Dillard introduces *An American Childhood* with these words:

> When everything else has gone from my brain—the President's name, the state capitals, the neighborhoods where I lived, and then at length the faces of my friends, and finally the faces of my family—when all this has dissolved, what will be left, I believe, is topology: the dreaming memory of land as it lay this way and that. (3)

Dillard asserts that the topology or landscape of her life will remain the central, sustaining feature in her memory. With individual memories or the "discrete dots of you," Dillard concludes in *An American Childhood*, she can connect herself to herself; she can know that these dots are contiguous even though she must "take on faith that those severed places cohered, too—the dozens of desks, bedrooms, kitchens, yards, landscapes. . . . take it on faith that the multiform and variously lighted latitudes and longitudes were part of one world. . ." (249). Here Dillard confirms the importance of landscape as it relates to her epiphanic moments in that epiphany occurs on the surface of the land, blending the objects of physical scenery into the machinery of illumination. But the epiphany, as Dillard and most other literary epiphanists apprehend and compose it, must be considered in several ways; first, as the illumination occurs to the individual in a real or natural setting (assuming the writer is sincere in asserting that this spiritual moment actually occurred), and, secondly, as it is structured within a work, acting as a literary device within the limitations of language. Thus, if epiphany's landscape is to be considered at all, it must be considered through its interaction with a physical setting and its use of words in a language setting.

With a consideration of epiphanic landscapes, both physical and language-bound, Dillard must be seen as a direct literary descendent of

Gerard Manley Hopkins. Although certain aspects of Dillard's work are clearly linked to the British romantic tradition, Dillard's epiphanic style can be associated with Hopkins's work more than with any other writer. This association between a nineteenth-century British poet-priest and a contemporary American woman prose-poet is, in fact, uncanny in its appropriateness. While Dillard's sense of time within the illumination is best examined in relationship to Wordsworth's and Eliot's epiphanic time, her overall development of epiphany echoes Hopkins, a development that rises out of a combination of literary ingredients that appear in the same ratio in the works of both writers. The tensions between ecstasy, observation, and language are almost identical in Hopkins and Dillard although they are writing one hundred years apart.[6]

These tensions of epiphanic composition grow out of like interests in a spiritual search through nature and language. Hopkins and Dillard have both come to the world of "raw data" and turned this data into the ecstatic language of praise and doubt. Calling for the critic who will use raw data rather than the predigested material of the artifact, Dillard writes:

> We are missing a whole class of investigators: those who interpret the raw universe in terms of meaning. If science will not seek human meaning, and if interpreters (critics, anthropologists, etc.) study human events and human artifacts only, then who will tell us the meaning of the raw universe? By the raw universe I mean here all that we experience, all things cultural and natural, all of the universe that is known, given, made, and changing: the world, and they that dwell therein. (*Living by Fiction* 145)

Dillard and Hopkins are part of the class of investigators Dillard calls for here; that is, both writers have committed themselves to the clear, objective observation of the natural landscape, and based on that objectivity have taken the further step of examining the inner landscape in a quest for meaning. The dynamic is the same: observe meticulously what lies about you and allow the spirit to invade via the avenue of those perceptions.

Along with their meticulous observation of the landscape, Dillard and Hopkins share a Christian theology. Dillard's tendency to move to a visionary, hence metaphoric, illumination in some of her work has already been made clear here; essentially, however, she is a true epiphanist, allowing the materials of the epiphanic moment to remain unremarked or free from analogous meaning. Hopkins, who has been called a "man outside his times" (Beja 43), resigned to the spare existence and dedicated theology of a Jesuit priest, also composed the Wordsworthian type of unresolved epiphany in his work. In many of his poems, however, Hopkins followed the glittering moment of epiphany with an application of his metaphoric Christian equivalencies. This ordering of literary material, the epiphany first and its meaning suggested later, does not diminish Hopkins's legitimate and original use of this literary device. He is, in fact, a master of unresolved thought presented in brilliant language; Morris Beja calls Hopkins the "chief Victorian figure of whom it can be said both that he stands in direct contrast to the increasingly secular outlook and that his work is pervaded with moments of sudden insight" (43). Ashton Nichols, in his excellent study *The Poetics of Epiphany: Nineteenth-Century Origins of the Modern Literary Moment,* assigns the tradition of "theophany" to Hopkins, a tradition in which he also places T. S. Eliot: "In this tendency to emphasize the revelatory quality of the details of ordinary experience, Eliot not only continues the theophany tradition of Hopkins but also advances the development of the secular epiphany in the twentieth century. The theophanic tradition demands that a holy entity be "contained in the experience it records" (Nichols 29), which suggests that an illumination can be experienced at first as an open-ended, unqualified moment but must eventually be counted as evidence for a religious dogma. But Hopkins, as we shall see, manages to keep an illumination free from closed meanings even when he appears to assign a Christian theology to its content.

Dillard and Hopkins can also be compared in their very similar uses of landscape, a key element within the literary epiphany as Bachelard, Beja, and Langbaum suggest (see chapter 3, pp. 64–65). Bachelard's "elemental substances" (earth, wind, water, and fire) are obvious attachments to landscape, while Beja's "Criterion of Insignificance" (epiphany is "triggered by a trivial object or incident") and Langbaum's "Criterion of Suddenness" ("A sudden change in external conditions causes a shift in sensuous perception that sensitizes the observer for epiphany") are usually shifts of conditions which occur on the landscape. M. H. Abrams has suggested similar changes in the epiphanic landscape when he writes that the "Greater Romantic Lyric" usually includes a "particularized, and usually a localized, outdoor setting" which is described by a speaker and which, through the course of the poem, will change, evoking "a varied but integral process of memory, thought, anticipation, and feeling which remains closely intervolved with the outer scene" ("Structure and Style in the Greater Romantic Lyric" 527). Physical and psychological changes occur also in the epiphanist, as Dillard proposes when she writes about attaining the present moment: "I stand. All the blood in my body crashes to my feet and instantly heaves to my head, so I blind and blush, as a tree blasts into leaf spouting water hurled up from roots"

(*Pilgrim* 99). These changes in the speaker's physical and psychological perceptions, although intimately linked with what may or may not be a real, external change on the landscape will be addressed in the final chapter of this book.

Landscape is the key shaping factor for Dillard, for she sees in locus the seed of all life that follows, a seed which allows life to bud and then in a synergistic relationship react to the life it has spawned: "Geography is the key, the crucial accident of birth. A piece of protein could be a snail, a sea lion, or a systems analyst, but it had to start somewhere. This is not science; it is merely metaphor. And the landscape in which the protein 'starts' shapes its end as surely as bowls shape water" (*Teaching* 127). Dillard's "geography" becomes a full-blown motif in *An American Childhood*, with epiphany engaging what lies below and above the surface of the land. But Dillard suggests with the word "metaphor" another kind of landscape that links her with Hopkins—the landscape of language. In these two writers language becomes more than just a system of symbols to represent exterior ideas; language becomes idea, or "the thing" itself. Language takes on texture and form and meaning; it evolves just like the physical landscape, for, Dillard writes, "like languages, ideas evolve. And they evolve . . . not from hardened final forms, but from the softest plasmic germs in a cell's heart, in the nub of a word's root, in the supple flux of an open mind" (*Teaching* 122). Both Dillard and Hopkins react to language as if it is a "hardened" soil, an arena of activity by itself; in this language-rich soil the epiphany of words springs to life.

One further comment should be offered about Hopkins's work and how his literary product compares to Dillard's. Chapter 1 of this book suggested that Dillard's prose could be read as poetry. The same could be said of Hopkins, as his devotional writings, journals, and diaries appear almost interchangeable with his poetry. Patricia Ball writes that

> the Journals join the theory to show that Hopkins's verbal sense is first, highly charged, that he is ready to explore words through their whole aural range and spectrum of implication; and further, that he conceives their interplay to be as potent as their individual force, so that verbal structure takes on a special prestige. (131)

Altogether Hopkins's work comprises one volume of poetry and five volumes of prose, including three books of letters, one of sermons and devotional writings and one notebook.[7] Through all of his "highly charged" poetry and prose Hopkins passes on a theory of poetics which is "invariably assertive, indisputable, and charmingly cocksure" (Ellsberg 5). Hopkins calls some of his rhymes "grubs in amber," something which is past change, a hint at the strange and beautiful solidifying power of language-landscape. But just as Eudora Welty asked of Dillard's work, "What's going on here?" so Hopkins's work has been variously applauded and criticized for its compression and irregular grammatical leaps. When Hopkins's poems finally did appear in 1918, long after his death, they were considered revolutionary. In the 1920s I. A. Richards and William Empson "liked them very much," Yvor Winters disliked them, Yeats called Hopkins a Mannerist, Eliot said he was "minor," and A. E. Houseman criticized the poet as one who did not make his sprung rhythm "audible" (Ellsberg 14). Irving Massey calls Hopkins's compressed style the "touch of just-too-muchedness" in words that make "one wonder what he is really trying to say" (93). These critical reactions reveal that evaluations of Hopkins and Dillard and their compressed language-landscapes are very much a question of taste. But for readers who can catch the inscape of Hopkins and the "snarl" of fringe and matter intertwined in Dillard, the epiphanic moment that engages the mind can be theirs.

Close parallels in the thought processes and language product of Dillard and Hopkins could certainly be the focus of additional study. The scope of this book limits our examination to the obvious similarities of Hopkins and Dillard in their glittering, jeweled, and fiery landscapes and the parallels in notions of language as a second landscape, both reviewed with epiphany as the focus. These similarities both provide insight into Dillard's preoccupation with illumination and reveal subtle differences that have transpired in epiphanic language as it has made its way from the nineteenth to the twentieth century via two strikingly similar writers.

The Physical Landscape of Epiphany

The physical landscapes that appear in the writings of Gerard Manley Hopkins and Annie Dillard are characterized essentially by the same earthy referents. These terrains reflect a similar light which increases in brilliance until it flares into fire. Because they grow out of similar landscapes, the resulting epiphanies in Hopkins and Dillard appear to have the same character.

These landscapes are alive with weeds and water, the "fringe" of the intimate corners of earth which bring forth secret life. Weeds and waters suggest to both epiphanists a sense of contradiction or paradox, spontaneity, and spareness, all of which they value as they search for revelation. Often, these moist lands will carry the reflection and color of gems, silver and gold, or simply the quality of light as it is refracted from sky, trees, or water. But the most significant landscapes, those which explode into epiphany, will eventually release fire. Bachelard's theory of "elemental substances" and "geometric shapes" within "reverie" is certainly supported here, water and fire (and light) becoming the chief elements and irregular, "pointed" contours becoming the shape of the illuminations.

Not only do the landscapes of Hopkins and Dillard bear the same elements and shapes, but they are also described with similar intensity. Dillard's preoccupation with detail will be seen to be Hopkin's preoccupation. To observe all the particulars of a natural scene is the first task of each writer, while the formation of these particulars into the spiritually lighted materials of an illumination is the second. These writers' tendency toward close observation grows out of similar historical circumstances in the nineteenth and twentieth centuries. While Dillard follows the lead of Muir's ecological literature, Hopkins follows the influences of both Charles Darwin and John Ruskin. Just as Dillard takes Muir's observation into the realm of aesthetics with her ornamented prose, so Hopkins carries the detailed observations of Ruskin into some of the most original poetic structures of the nineteenth century. When Dillard called on someone to interpret the "raw material" of the world, she was actually naming her own literary function. She, like Hopkins, goes straight to the "raw" data of the undigested world; that is, they observe closely and then they sculpt their literary pieces directly from their observations. They have done away with the intercession of interpretation, shunning systems that include religious and social dogma, and have instead interpreted for themselves. Although this appears at first to contradict their religious commitments, it is not so, for Hopkins and Dillard insist on seeing for themselves, confronting the actual world; only later do they apply their theology. Dillard has quite clearly stated her belief in this power of observation when she writes about "lyric poetry" as "actual" rather than "fabricated"; it "has been able to function quite directly as human interpretation of the raw, loose universe" (*Living* 147).

Weeds and Water, Fire and Light

The contemporary poet A. R. Ammons writes:

> for the inexcusable (the worthless abundant) the
> merely tiresome, the obviously unimprovable,
> to these and for these and for their undiminishment
> the poets will yelp and hoot forever

probably,
rank as weeds themselves and just as abandoned:
nothing useful is of lasting value:
dry wind only is still talking among the oldest stones.
                ("Conserving the Magnitude of Uselessness" 21–28)

Ammons is suggesting that useless and unlovely things that have no function and cannot be improved are the materials of earth that will outlast the so-called "useful" items. A similar praise of useless life is raised by Hopkins in "Inversnaid" when he writes, "What would the world be, once bereft / Of wet and of wildness? Let them be left, / O let them be left, wildness and wet; / Long live the weeds and the wilderness yet" (*Poetical Works* 13–16). The same message prevails: uselessness, or what appears to the critical world as useless, is in fact of paramount importance. In both poets the image of weeds represents this paradoxical but significant uselessness.

Hopkins relies heavily on this image of weeds in his poetry and prose. In "Binsey Poplars" he laments the felling of aspen trees that have grown along the "wind-wandering weed-winding bank" near the village of Binsey (8). In "Winter with the Gulf Stream" the poet writes of the "brambles" which show "With bills of rime" and "clammy coats / Of foliage fallen in the copse" (4, 11–12). His praise of Duns Scotus, a medieval scholar of Oxford whom he admired, is punctuated by the sentiment that this distant scholar "haunted," like Hopkins, the "weeds and waters" that surround the university city "branchy between towers" ("Duns Scotus's Oxford" 10–11, 1). In "Ribblesdale" he speaks of the "sweet landscape" where "leaves throng" and "louched low grass" make up the scene (1–2). These weeds, usually set against wetness, represent the heart of uselessness, a uselessness which is also echoed by an interest in the "forgotten" or unnoticed, unsymmetrical, or common objects and functions of earth. Hopkins praises all that is "dappled.... counter, original, spare, strange . . . fickle, freckled" in "Pied Beauty" (1, 7–8), an attempt to acknowledge all that might be commonly thought of as unimportant. For Hopkins believed that it was in the center of this speckled and irregular life that holiness hid, writing that "There lives the dearest freshness deep down things" ("God's Grandeur" 10).

Hopkins's proclivity toward this weedy landscape and all other "counter" things calls to mind Dillard's interest in the wild, tangled places which can give rise to epiphany. Peter Milward writes that Hopkins "sees wildness as essential to the world's being.... And through the wildness of nature he looks to something wild and untamed in the human heart . . ." (80). It is as if the irregular contour of the weed represents, as it does for Dillard, gaps in which the spirit can hide. Dillard writes of her desire to live like the weasel in the "mud" and with the "wild rose," living with the mind of a weasel "leaning on mouse fur, sniffing bird bones, blinking, licking, breathing musk, my hair tangled in the roots of grasses" because "Down is a good place to go, where the mind is single" (*Teaching* 15). Down is moving into entanglement, single-mindedness, and spirit for Dillard. In the snarl or tangle of nature there is always the chance that God is present. All of this weediness or interest in the forgotten or the odd, reminiscent of Wordsworth's rustics, and Dillard's insects, shows diversity, an asymmetrical look at life. This diversity is necessary for the unsettling epiphany requires, since the static or balanced form cannot achieve epiphany. Hopkins has "little use for classical simplicity or geometrical balance," Milward comments. "Rather, he delights in the variety and profusion of riches in the natural world, which observe a form of balance but with stresses of a far more complex kind than are to be found in the geometry of Euclid" (41).

The notion that epiphany occurs in unsuspected or lowly places is not original with Hopkins and Dillard. In fact, Beja's "Criterion of Insignificance" marks the lowliness of landscape or object as a hallmark of epiphany. "When one comes across some glorious, earth-shaking moment of revelation, one is not really tempted to speak of epiphany," Beja writes (17). The specific choices of low objects, however, are strangely parallel in Hopkins and Dillard, the fringed weed and the water playing prominent "holy" parts in illumination.

The presence of watery or at least moist landscapes is another common characteristic in the works of these two epiphanists. Using her micro- and macrocosms in an essay entitled "Lenses," Dillard takes the reader to the wet pond landscape of circling, migrating swans and the tiny wet world of a drop of pond water that carries the swim of algae and rotifers. The large and small worlds are drawn together metaphysically, revealing Dillard's intense desire to be "in" the translucent, holy world of water: "How I loved that deep, wet world where the colored algae waved in the water and the rotifers swam" (*Teaching* 106). She waits crouched in the reeds so that she can catch a glimpse of the whistling swans (*Teaching* 107). Now, with the wet world expanded and deflated simultaneously, she creates an epiphany out of the swans' return to the pond:

> I was lost. The reeds in front of me, swaying and out of focus in the binoculars' circular field, were translucent. The reeds were strands of color passing light like cells in water. They were those yellow and green and brown strands of pond algae I had watched

so long in a light-soaked field. My eyes burned; I was watching algae wave in a shrinking drop; they crossed each other and parted wetly. And suddenly into the field swam two whistling swans, two tiny whistling swans. They swam as fast as rotifers; two whistling swans, infinitesimal, beating their tiny wet wings, perfectly formed. (*Teaching* 108–09)

Her "lenses," the microscope and binoculars, have allowed her to undergo an epiphany surrounded by the element of water. It is not surprising that, as Dillard tells us in *An American Childhood*, her favorite book as a child was *The Field Book of Ponds and Streams* (87).

Pilgrim at Tinker Creek deals on many levels with an environment transected by water. The creek is the center of Dillard's world, with a "steep forested bank" on one side and on the other a pasture; the low water between the field and an island is "shallow and sluggish," filled with "flags and bulrushes." Dillard, "drawn to this spot," calls the creek her "oracle" (4–5). The water is "held pellucid as a pane, a gloss on runes of stone, shale and snail-inscribed clay silt . . . flecks of shadow and tatters of sky . . . the waters of beauty and mystery" (266). Mary Davidson McConahay sees the water of Tinker Creek as symbolic of "the inscrutable natural universe that exists as an intermediary between the elements of land and air" (109). Dillard calls the creek her "mediator, benevolent, impartial, subsuming my shabbiest evils and dissolving them, transforming them into live moles, and shiners, and sycamore leaves. It is a place even my faithlessness hasn't offended; it still flashes for me, now and tomorrow" (*Pilgrim* 101–02). This watery world transports Dillard to "higher planes of cosmic awareness," McConahay continues, and finally comes to reflect the "transcendent nature of man" and "ultimately the perfect nature of God" (110).

Hopkins's landscapes, like Dillard's, are often transected by water that becomes, if not the central feature, at least a tonal aspect of the scene. While Hopkins's poems speak of weedy waters, his Binsey poplars dangling their "sandalled / Shadows" in the river (6–7), Dun Scotus haunting the "weeds and waters" near Oxford (10), and the ferny path of Inversnaid Falls rushing onward through "wildness and wet" (15), it is his journals that reveal most his fascination with this element. He repeatedly observes water in its various forms, from the moisture webbed into peat soil to the whorls and lines cut into a bank of snow. "On the Common the snow was channelled all in parallels by the sharp driving wind and upon the tufts of grass (where by the dark colour shewing through it looked greyish) it came to turret-like clusters or like broken shafts of basalt," he wrote in 1870 of a winter landscape (*Journals* 195). Later, he describes the snow in another pattern as it moves along the road: "Nearer at hand . . . it was gliding over the ground in white wisps that between trailing and flying shifted and wimpled like so many silvery worms to and from one another" (196). His entry for September 17, 1872, reveals his close observation of dew, which lingers under a wall's shadow; it appears "chilled and blasted with such well-marked plotting off and bounding line" (226). Hopkins revels in the patterns that radiate from water's various forms, the apparently casual gestures of nature turned into configurations signaling beauty, such as the "chilled and blasted dew" melting in the sun into a meaningful demarcation. He writes of a brook that drains "the bogs on the breadth of the ridge" and in the same entry even notes the "inscape" of dry grass that gives the appearance of water, "flowing and well marked almost as the frosting on glass and slabs" (226). For Hopkins, the free-flowing characteristic of water, allowing it to bend with the wind or to solidify into crystalline patterns, seems to be its appeal; this element's very mutability fascinates the poet because it signifies a life within, a constant display of nature's organic power. Hopkins records minute details about water's fluctuations, its secret and almost hidden changes, such as his notice of the "random clods and broken heaps of snow made by the cast of a broom" and, later, the "path trenched by footsteps in ankledeep snow across the fields leading to Hodder wood through which we went to see the river." At the river, his journal indicates, he observes the bank covered with "broken brambles" and all the boughs "cloyed with white, the brook down the clough pulling its way by drops and by bubbles in turn under a shell of ice" (230). Hopkins's watery landscapes respond to other formations or forces; brambles, weeds, wind, and sun all mingle with streams and snow to create patterns—irregular and natural patterns, jagged edges rising out of moist and possibly holy waters. When he wonders what the world would be if it lost its ability to shape itself, if it was "bereft" of water and weeds, he is suggesting with Dillard that some mysteries must remain, some areas must allow an otherness that is not human.

Besides water itself, other elements in the weedy, wet landscape are significant for Hopkins and Dillard. First, trees can be seen as an extension of the irregular contour of line which allows epiphany. Further, the tree has a kind of elegant stability in the earth, a majesty which, as Dillard has reminded us, reaches into the heavens and roots under the surface of earth. Hopkins, in his "passion for fixing the dissolving moment," is particularly intrigued by the organic life of the tree: "he is drawn . . . to nature's displays of organic form, the rooted life of plants and, especially, the tree, where the harmony of energy and structure is epitomized" (Ball 125). Many intricate, detailed descriptions of trees appear in his journals, but this one from July 11, 1866, is representative of Hopkins:

> Oaks: the organisation of this tree is difficult. Speaking generally no doubt the determining planes are concentric, a system of brief contiguous and continuous tangents, whereas those of the cedar would roughly be called horizontals and those of the beech radiating but modified by droop and by a screw-set towards jutting points. But beyond this since the normal growth of the boughs is radiating and the leaves grow some way in there is of course a system of spoke-wise clubs of green—sleeve-pieces. And since the end shoots curl and carry young and scanty leaf-stars these clubs are tapered, and I have seen also the pieces in profile with chiselled outlines. . . . (*Journals and Papers* 144)

A poetic fragment anthologized as "Ashboughs" reveals again the keen interest in the fringed contour of the tree with Hopkins's intense observation bearing down on it:

> Not of all my eyes see, wandering on the world,
> Is anything a milk to the mind so, so sighs deep
> Poetry to it, as a tree whose boughs break in the sky.
> Say it is ashboughs: whether on a December day and furled
> Fast or they in clammyish lashtender combs creep
> Apart wide and new-nestle at heaven most high.
> They touch heaven, tabour on it; how their talons sweep
> The smouldering enormous winter welkin! May
> Mells blue and showwhite through them, a fringe and fray
> Of greenery: it is old earth's groping towards the steep
>   Heaven whom she childs us by.

Hopkins notes the fringed contour reaching into the heavens and the tree becomes the comforting mental elixir; nature reaches into the heavens which have given it birth. Milward notes that Hopkins has a "kind of fellow-feeling that amounts to love" about trees when he speaks of his "aspens dear" which have been felled along the river (63). This recalls the passionate discussion of trees as the present movement in Dillard when she writes,

> I want to think about trees. . . . There are many created things in the universe that outlive us, that outlive the sun, even, but I can't think about them. I live with trees. . . . trees live quite convincingly in the same filament of air we inhabit, and, in addition, they

extend impressively in both directions, up and down, shearing rock
and fanning air, doing their real business just out of reach.
(*Pilgrim* 86–87)

The tree seen against winter skies suggests another tendency which
accompanies weedy waters and irregular contours; this is a preoccupation with spareness. The spare Dillardian landscape is central to her concept of sloughing off all that impedes the single-mindedness of the
weasel. This is her way on the *via negativa*, when in a "twiggy haze" she
can see all that "summer conceals" and "winter reveals" (*Pilgrim* 38).
Hopkins writes often of the same spare landscape, where the moisture
of summer is now frozen into "frill upon frill of snow" and the "ground
[is] sheeted with taut tattered streaks of crisp gritty snow" (*Journals*
228). Dillard often mentions the cold North or the life of Eskimos because they represent spareness: "I use them and the spare landscape in
which they live as an emblem for the barren landscape of the soul: the
soul's deliberate preparation for the incursions of the Divine" ("Drawing
the Curtains" 32).

For these writers, this wet and irregular landscape sets up contradictions of meaning, the plain object elevated to beauty, the notion of scum
and visually beautiful water life drawn together; these are the gaps,
fringe, twists, snarls, and recesses where God can grow. Both writers insist on the nubby texture, filigree, and complexity of weedy landscapes,
which will eventually "gash gold-vermilion" from "blue-bleak embers."
Hopkins's beautiful sensory image from "The Windhover," which allows
common, dull-surfaced clods of earth to break into "sillion" (a "long,
narrow sub-division of an open field"; see MacKenzie 84) with the passing of the farmer's ploughshare, and faded embers into the renewed,
golden light, is a superb representation of common things giving off the
illumination of light and fire. Referring to the buckling swing of a kes-
trel, the poet speaks first of the sun's fire reflecting on the wing of the
bird as it drops from its high hover; the poet continues with reference to
other materials which similarly appear suddenly to ignite:

> Brute beauty and valour and act, oh, air, pride, plume, here
> Buckle! AND the fire that breaks from thee then, a billion
> Times told lovelier, more dangerous, O my chevalier!

> No wonder of it: sheer plod makes plough down sillion
> Shine, and blue-bleak embers, ah my dear,
> Fall, gall themselves, and gash gold-vermilion.
> ("Windhover" 9–14)

Examples of this gem-and-fire technique are numerous in Hopkins's work. Gemmed surfaces reflecting light can be seen as the use of the same element—fire. "Flash," "beacon," "shivelights," "firedint," "spark," and "wildfire" are all a part of Hopkins's epiphanic language of illumination. In "Il Mystico" the air is filled with an

> air-blended diadem,
> All a sevenfold-single gem,
> Each hue so rarely wrought that where
> It melts, new lights arise as fair,
> Sapphire, jacinth, chrysolite,
> The rim with ruby fringes dight (115–20)

In "God's Grandeur" God "flame[s] out, like shining from shook foil" and the light of morning "springs" off the "bright wings" of the Holy Ghost (2, 12–13). "Kingfishers catch fire, dragonflies draw flame" ("As kingfishers catch fire" 1); the air itself is dazzlingly bright with stars or "fire-folk" that sparkle like jewels and precious metals:

> Look at the stars! look, look up at the skies!
> O look at all the fire-folk sitting in the air!
> The bright boroughs, the circle-citadels there!
> Down in dim woods the diamond delves! the elves'-eyes!
> The grey lawns cold where gold, where quickgold lies!
> Wind-beat whitebeam! airy abeles set on a flare!
> ("The Starlight Night" 1–6)

The images here virtually glitter with sound and sight, the gems of heaven flaring into a fire which becomes the "prize" of salvation in the second section of the poem. "That Nature is a Heraclitean Fire and of the comfort of the Resurrection" becomes the penultimate statement on light and fire in Hopkins. Here the theory of fire from Heraclitus of Ephesus (c. 500 B.C.) is the working dynamic of the poem. Fire appears to be the element itself and also the process of mutability which characterizes all things. Like Eliot's fire in "Little Gidding," this one consumes to recreate itself. Norman MacKenzie suggests that to "Heraclitus fire was the substrate or underlying matter of the universe...intelligence, the substance of the pure soul" (195–96). Like Shelley's west wind, it is destroyer and preserver. The poem is given in its entirety here:

> Cloud-puffball, torn tufts, tossed pillows flaunt forth, then chevy on an air-
> Built thoroughfare: heaven-roysterers, in gay-gangs they throng; they glitter in marches.

Down roughcast, down dazzling whitewash, wherever an
　elm arches,
Shivelights and shadowtackle in long lashes lace, lance, and pair.
Delightfully that bright wind boisterous ropes, wrestles, beats
　earth bare
Of yestertempest's creases; in pool and rutpeel parches
Squandering ooze to squeezed dough, crust, dust; stanches,
　starches
Squadroned masks and manmarks treadmire toil there
Footfretted in it. Million-fueled, nature's bonfire burns on.
But quench her bonniest, dearest to her, her clearest-selved spark
Man, how fast his firedint, his mark on mind, is gone!
Both are in an unfathomable, all is in an enormous dark
Drowned. O pity and indignation! Manshape, that shone
Sheer off, disseveral, a star, death blots black out: nor mark
　　Is any of him at all so stark
But vastness blurs and time beats level. Enough! the Resurrection,
A heart's-clarion! Away grief's gasping, joyless days, dejection.
　　Across my foundering deck shone
A beacon, an eternal beam. Flesh fade, and mortal trash
Fall to the residuary worm; world's wildfire, leave but ash:
　　In a flash, a trumpet crash,
I am all at once what Christ is, since he was what I am, and
This Jack, joke, poor potsherd, patch, matchwood, immortal
　diamond,
　　Is immortal diamond.

This poem engages the activities of the four elements, the mood swing-ing from Hopkins's estatic joy in cloud formations to a lament for hu-manity's brief passage over earth's crust and finally to an exultant cry for the permanence that the Resurrection "fire" brings to the poor "pot-sherd" man. The poet rejoices in cloud puffs that gather and rise from the earth; they are like reveling gangs of youth, "heaven-roysterers" that reflect light in their airy paths. That same light filters back down to earth causing trees to cast "shivelights," or splinters of sunlight, into lacy pat-terns over the landscape. Even the wind is "bright" as it whips down from the clouds above to the earth's surface below; but now the first signs of nature's "Million-fueled...bonfire" appear as the ground's pools of water change from "dough" to "crust" and finally dry com-pletely into "dust." In light and fire nature dissolves and then recreates itself. But now the poet laments that man's individual self does not re-turn in what might be deemed an otherwise beneficent cycle. Even his poor "firedint," the spark that flicked from his mind, is blocked out in the vastness of death. The individual person who during life appeared to be a glorious spectacle, like a "star," the very essence of fire, is lost; even the memory of that star is blurred and eventually beat "level." In the final lines, however, an eternal light appears on the horizon, the beacon which is Christ's resurrection; and the weak, spindly, "matchwood" life of man flames and burns with God's fire, thus having been transmuted into the permanence of a brilliant gem, an "immortal diamond."

Dillard makes her way through similar motifs of gems, brilliance, and fire. The "rock" chapter in *An American Childhood*, for example, is full of gem references. The epiphanic moments in *Pilgrim* are virtually all described in light. The puppy epiphany begins with "brilliant blown lights" and clouds dashed to the "northwest in gold rush" (78). As the moment intensifies, the lights rising off gemlike surfaces fill the air, and

> purple vaults and slides, it tricks out the unleafed forest and rumpled rock in gilt, in shape-shifting patches of glow. These gold lights veer and retract, shatter and glide in a series of dazzling splashes, shrinking, leaking, exploding. The ridge's bosses and hummocks sprout bulging from its side; the whole mountain looms miles closer; the light warms and reddens. . . . (78)

Passages like her description of shiners, little fish, darting about in Tinker Creek are reminiscent of Hopkins's "Windhover," in which a limited perspective, a tiny piece of observation, breaks into light and resolves itself in a majestic comment on eternal matters:

> Again and again, one fish, then another, turned for a split second across the current and flash! the sun shot out from its silver side. . . . flash, like a sudden dazzle of the thinnest blade, a sparking over a dun and olive ground at chance intervals from every direction. Then I noticed white specks, some sort of pale petals, small, floating from under my feet on the creek's surface. . . . I saw the pale white circles roll up, roll up, like the linear flashes, gleaming silver, like stars being born at random down a rolling scroll of time. (33)

The strange and startling imagined epiphany of "silver eels," which Dillard gleaned from the writings of Edwin Way Teale, also uses glimmering light and precious, shiny metal. The eels are seen making their way across a meadow on their way to the sea: "All you see is a silver slither, like twisted ropes of water falling roughly, a one-way milling and mingling over the meadow and slide to the creek. Silver eels in the night: a barely-made-out seething as far as you can squint, a squirming, jostling torrent of silver eels in the grass" (220). Of course, the cedar tree with doves is transfigured with light, every cell of the birds and tree "buzzing with flame" so that the tree becomes for Dillard "the tree with the lights in it." But, as with Hopkins, the light becomes something more than light; it flames into fire: "I stood on the grass with the lights in it, grass that was wholly fire, utterly focused and utterly dreamed. . . . The flood of fire abated, but I'm still spending the power. Gradually the light went out in the cedar, the colors died, the cells unflamed and disappeared" (33–34).

Dillard describes the spirit as a "fireball, shooting off a spray of sparks at random. . . the hoop of flame that shoots the rapids in the creek or spins across the dizzy meadows. . . the arsonist of the sunny woods" (*Pilgrim* 76). In *Holy the Firm* the image of the burned moth and the burned child guides the poetic narrative. The artist's commitment to art burns up life like the moth's burning creates a higher flame. The burning is holiness itself, or the sign of holiness in the artist: "What can any artist set on fire but his world?. . . What can he light but the short string of his gut. . . . His face is flame like a seraph's, lighting the kingdom of God for the people to see; his life goes up in the works. . ." (72). Dillard, like Hopkins, sees holiness, spirit, or God as a flame which appears glancingly on occasions as light. One critic suggests that in Dillard's "mystical perception all of nature burns. . . everything in nature ceaselessly emanates from the dawn of creation at the margin of time" (Scheick 57). When the world is not burning it is for Dillard a landscape which cannot give a showing of God, "dead flint, dead tinder, and nowhere a spark" (*Pilgrim* 67–68).

Particulars and Science

Dillard's preoccupation with accurate observation and in-the-field ecological data has been addressed earlier in this study. This same attention to the details of natural landscape are paramount to Hopkins's building of epiphany. Some further examples of Dillard's notion of seeing will reveal her close connections with Hopkins in this respect. This determination to be accurate in observation is only one underlying aspect of the similarity in both writers, however; their observation is motivated by similar needs and reported in similar language and eventually burgeons into kindred epiphanies.

When Dillard writes of the "ringstreaked, speckled, and spotted" flocks of Jacob, who carried with him into Egypt the cattle that would become Israel's heritage (*Pilgrim* 145), she uses a voice that could be Hopkins's. With her biblical allusion and her love of variegated textures she is repeating Hopkins's praise of "dappled things" in "Pied Beauty." Hopkins praises texture in "rose-moles all in stipple upon trout" and "Landscape plotted and pieced," among other highly irregular surfaces in color and form, and insists that these multifarious and "fickle" forms lie closest to the heart of the creator ("Pied Beauty" 3, 5, 8). Dillard calls this texture "intricacy" and claims it as the birthright of human-kind, the "hardiness of complexity that ensures against the failure of all life. This is our heritage, the piebald landscape of time. We walk around; we see a shred of the infinite possible combinations of an infinite variety of forms" (*Pilgrim* 145). Because there is such a prolific assortment of forms, a variety that can keep two poet-observers occupied for a life-time, Dillard and Hopkins set out to see and record it all. Dillard calls it "seeing," Hopkins, "inscape."

This way of seeing, however, is more than just watching the surface of the land without attention to the way one sees. "Unless I call my atten-tion to what passes before my eyes, I simply won't see it," Dillard writes, and suggests that to see correctly she has to verbalize, put her observa-tions in language; "I have to say the words, describe what I'm seeing" (*Pilgrim* 30). Like Hopkins, Dillard records her forays into nature in lengthy passages. And for both writers, if the description is so correct that it cuts to the heart of the observed subject, then the heart will re-veal itself, a spirit emanating from the interior of its being. But Dillard reminds us of the ultimate seeing, which can never be pursued and caught, when she writes that "the secret of seeing. . .the pearl of great price. . . . although it comes to those who wait for it, it is always, even to the most practiced and adept, a gift and a total surprise" (*Pilgrim* 33). Dillard has been called a "connoisseur of spirit, who knows that seeing, if intense enough, becomes vision" (Hoffman 88). Therefore, Dillard will be patient, meticulously observing and recording all that the land-scape provides, waiting for the moment of epiphanic seeing.

Dillard, with a Hopkinsesque tone, writes later in *Pilgrim* that she wants "to have things as multiply and intricately as possible present and visible in my mind" (137).[8] As she has done throughout all of her work, she brings science to bear on observation, writing that "if I try to keep my eye on quantum physics, if I try to keep up with astronomy and cos-mology, and really believe it all, I might ultimately be able to make out the landscape of the universe" (138). She believes that if she can actively engage every tool of knowledge then the seeing will be an event that has not been romanticized, because it will have grown out of keeping one's eyes open rather than wearing limiting blinders.

Dillard's propensity to see and record began early, a tendency which revealed itself in the farmhouse at Paw Paw, West Virginia, with Judy Schoyer, when Dillard felt as if she were haunting her own childhood with intense seeing (see chapter 3). With the realization that the world had a vast network of further worlds below the surface, areas of knowl-edge about "drawing, painting, rocks, criminology, birds, moths, beetles, stamps, ponds and streams, medicine," Dillard, a thirteen-year-old child, began to takes notes (*American Childhood* 158). And when she finds herself, riding along a rainy Pittsburgh highway, absolutely bored with no book material at hand, only watching the "infuriatingly dull sight" of rainy rivulets poring over the marks builders had left in the stone, she becomes suddenly transported by the thought that even the dull rocks could be fascinating:

> But now I knew that even rock was interesting—at least in theory. . . . Even I could tap some shale just right, rain or shine, and open the rock to bones of fossil fish. There might be trilobites on the hilltops, star sapphires. Right along these wretched rainy roads. . . .
> If even rock was interesting, if even this ugliness was worth whole shelves at the library, required sophisticated tools to study, and inspired grown men to crack mountains and saw crystals—then what wasn't? (158–59)

In this way, and at this early age, the entire world opens to Dillard for the possibility of scrutiny, and, thereafter, epiphany.

Hopkins also watches the world intensely, hoping to find the "inscape" of a tree, a flower, a bird, or anything that exists on the landscape, and, as we will see later, in language. Hopkins's best-known contribution to poetics, his theory of inscape and instress, confirms the concept of language as landscape. The first appearance of these two terms occurs in notes on Parmenedes "which he made early in 1868" (Kitchen 127). By "inscape" Hopkins means "the inherent and distinctive design of an object (be it a group of trees, a frozen clod of earth, or a *poem*) which gives it its 'oneness' and which has to be discovered through concentrated observation" (Kitchen 127; emphasis added). Instress should be seen as the energy which flows from inscape and "determines its inscape, and flows into the senses of the perceiver" (Kitchen 127). What is important to note about these concepts is that the oneness that makes up inscape and releases instress is present for Hopkins in both the physical and the language landscapes of his poetry. Margaret Ellsberg offers a clearly stated definition of "inscape" and "instress," writing that Hopkins invented the terms at least partly to justify the way he saw things—simply, inscape is the form of a thing, especially as it reveals some strain of universal form or harmony; instress is the recognition or feeling of the force of an inscape" (11). For the purposes of this study, then, inscape should be considered the knowledge Hopkins finds in the deep scrutiny of any object/subject, while instress becomes the epiphanic force which is released from the scrutinized object. Inscape is the ability to see the individualized nature of a thing, the ability to see the intricate details and complexity of a shape and yet to see its unity which connects each object with all others. For Hopkins each object is "almost a separate species and the world becomes an endless catalogue of sharply individuated selves" (Pick xvi–xvii). Hopkins, speaking of his need to focus and record his findings, writes in a letter, dated July 10, 1863, to his friend Mowbray Baillie:

> I have particular periods of admiration for particular things in Nature; for a certain time I am astonished at the beauty of a tree, shape, effect etc, then when the passion, so to speak, has subsided, it is consigned to my treasury of explored beauty, and acknowledged with admiration and interest ever after, while something new takes its place in my enthusiasm. The present fury is the ash, and perhaps barley and two shapes of growth in leaves and one in tree boughs and also a conformation of fine-weather cloud. (*Further Letters* 202)

The passion with which Hopkins seeks out the exact shape of a leaf or tree suggests that what he finds is of exquisite beauty and entirely valuable; it becomes part of his cache of "explored beauty." But like Dillard, who becomes overwhelmed with her need to record so many landscapes and objects within those landscapes, Hopkins is almost distressed with his own need to record so much detail. "His microscopic powers of observation were obvious in the landscape sketches published with the journals," Ellsberg notes; "His desire to grasp, in his life and his poetry, reality in its every detail without recourse to fantasy, allusion, or abstraction, his obsession with 'stress,' as well as the special perceptions he sought, all caused him frustration" (89, 90).

These two writers are driven by some internal force which says that "if you are deep enough, accurate enough, thorough beyond even the most dull scientific fact, deliberate in seeing, then a landscape which lies further than knowledge will be opened to you." They have been called to witness the multifarious forms of the earth, and, unlike Wordsworth, they propose to come with no romantic overlays on their vision, no pre-established notions about where the spirit might rise. They intend to be objective. And let the spirit rise where it will. Dillard traveled to the Galapagos Islands to witness the "evolved weird forms" that had grown up in isolation (*Teaching* 73). There she becomes entranced by the palo santo trees crowding the hillsides, doing nothing but standing in witness of the other strange animal life of the islands. She decides, then, that if she can return to life after death, she will return as one of these "leafless, paralyzed, and mute" palo santos, for its only function is to witness, to stand mute and watch (75). This mute observation has become the ultimate goal for Dillard:

> We are here to witness. There is nothing else to do with those mute materials we do not need. . . . all we can do with the whole inhuman array is watch it. We can stage our own act on the planet—build our cities on its plains, dam its rivers, plant its topsoils—but our meaningful activity scarcely covers the terrain. We do not use the songbirds, for instance. We do not eat many of them; we cannot befriend them; we cannot persuade them to eat more mosquitoes or plant fewer weed seeds. We can only witness them—whoever they are. (72–73)

Dillard emphasizes here not only her act of observing, but also the idea that what is witnessed has no practical use to humankind, and, further, these impractical subjects, specifically, songbirds here, are mute, at least to human understanding. Thus, impractical and mute things can and should be observed in the landscape for reasons beyond science, although these things must be approached with a scientific eye; for Dillard and Hopkins, this reason is to find the instress of epiphany.

Hopkins, in an early poem, "Nondum" (1866), which echoes Tennyson's disillusioned tone of *In Memoriam*, writes of a God who does not answer back: "And still th'unbroken silence broods / While ages and while aeons run" (19–20). The poet pleads with this silent God to answer, "Speak! whisper to my watching heart / One word," but apparently only silence is returned to the young Hopkins (49–50). The later Hopkins in his priestly vocation does not look for large, cosmic answers in broad sweeps of language, such as "We see the glories of the earth" ("Nondum" 7), but has instead gone to tiny worlds where the horizons can be as diminutive as "Thrush's eggs [which] look little low heavens" ("Spring" 3). The later Hopkins can observe the landscape closely in prose and poetry, a skill which allows him to burrow into the meaning of nature and emerge with the spirit of his subject.

In these observations Hopkins goes beyond nineteenth-century romanticism, just as Dillard becomes a different kind of romantic in the face of increased scientific discovery. Nichols notes that "Even more than Wordsworth, Hopkins seeks the natural appearance unnoticed by others, the dappled, fickle, freckled thing, the ordinary intensified. Hopkins is perhaps as great a master of naturalistic details as any of his Romantic predecessors" (179). But Hopkins is, of course, the greater detailist, because he, like Dillard, is facing a world which includes a barrage of scientific data. They are calling the entire speckled world to the front so that they can inspect it and read its signs. They are making a juncture of "colloquial-science" and spirit, while Wordsworth is making a juncture of an abstract, almost painterly, natural world and spirit. For this reason, Dillard can be seen as an echo of Hopkins, much more than of Wordsworth.

Hopkins is not satisfied just to give pictorial descriptions of nature's subjects, but knows the names of many types, to which he then adds his own more poetic epithet, as Peter Milward notes in Hopkins's observations of trees:

> The variety of trees mentioned in his poems is indeed impressive. It is not just that he mentions them specifically by name; but whenever he mentions their name, he feels impelled to attach an appropriate epithet. . . . he characterizes the abele (or white poplar) as "airy"; the apple in bloom as "drop-of-blood-and-roam-dapple": the ash as "scrolled," and the mountain ash (or rowan) as "beadbonny." (63)

But still this close observation should be seen as joined with a romantic sensibility. Patricia Ball, in her excellent study *The Science of Aspects: The Changing Role of Fact in the Work of Coleridge, Ruskin and Hopkins*, makes these connections in Hopkins as he moves between high romanticism and later Victorian scrutiny:

> Hopkins draws on the highly developed Romantic awareness of identity, with its emotional force and sense of relationship, and infuses this into his Ruskinian scrutiny of the object. Moved equally by the "taste of self" and the conviction that "things are" he brings the two together in his vision of inscape. (108–09)

Ball suggests that Hopkins took Coleridge's powers of observation and modified the idea that only the self made the difference in the status of the observed object. Without the mind, Coleridge would believe, the object is dead or static. "Coleridge could say," Ball writes, "in the course of working out his theory of imagination, that 'all objects (*as* objects) are essentially fixed and dead'. . . " (1). But Ball sees Ruskin's influence in close observation of object as equally central to Hopkins's development, in that to Ruskin "the object itself was the prize to be grasped as completely as possible by a concentrated study of its qualities. . . " (2). This nineteenth-century combination of inner reflection and intense observation of external objects is paralleled in twentieth-century literature through Dillard's poetic, ecstatic prose and her reliance on ecological and scientific detail.

Hopkins's ability to give a sense of immediacy in a singular event and yet to connect this small event with universal concerns ties him to Dillard. A description of waves breaking is recorded in his journal:

> The wave breaks in this order—the crest of the barrel "doubling" (that, a boatman said, is the word in use) is broken into a bush of foam, which, if you search it, is a lace and tangle of jumping sprays; then breaking down these grow to a sort of shaggy quilt tumbling up the beach; thirdly this unfolds into a sheet of clear foam and running forward in leaves and laps the wave reaches its greatest height upon the shore and at the same time its greatest clearness and simplicity; after that, raking on the shingle and so on, it is forked and torn and, as it commonly has a pitch or lurch to one side besides its backdraught, these rents widen; they spread and mix and the water clears and escapes to the sea transparent and keeping in the end nothing of its white except in long dribble bubble-strings which trace its set and flow. (*Journals* 251)

Ball writes that this passage has a "spontaneity undestroyed" because while Hopkins is a "master of the patterns of its movement...the immediacy of the sensuous encounter with it remains. His power...lies in his ability to keep us in the presence of the thing itself while he demonstrates its properties and exposes the laws of its being" (123). This composition of immediacy verging on ecstasy combined with visual and/or pertinent scientific data also characterizes Dillard's work. Ball calls this tendency a "fine balance between the experience of phenomena in the moment and the perception of enduring laws" (123).

But a great distinction should be made between the observation of Ruskin and Hopkins. Hopkins's journals

> show that Hopkins's verbal sense is first, highly charged, that he is ready to explore words through their whole aural range and spectrum of implication; and further, that he conceives their interplay to be as potent as their individual force, so that verbal structures take on a special prestige. Poetic organization is a goal for him as it is not for Ruskin, a mode of expression capable of bringing unique power to aid the art of description in its revelation of identity. (Ball 131)

Hopkins's notes from his early diaries prefiguring "The Starlight Night" reveal that even in journal form he was more engaged with language than Ruskin:

> The sky minted into golden sequins.
> Stars like gold tufts.
> _____ _____ golden bees.

‗‗‗‗‗‗ ‗‗‗‗‗‗ golden rowels.
Sky peak'd with tiny flames.
Stars like tiny-spoked wheels of fire.
Lantern of night, pierced in eyelets (*or*
eye-lets which avoids ambiguity).
(*Journals* 46–47)

Ruskin, in his reaction against romantic subjectivity, insisted on accurate, painterly description of an object. Onto this accurate, detailed description Ruskin would often "paste" a spiritual meaning. But, as Ball
asserts, this pasted meaning or revelation was not altogether successful,
since "his efforts in *Modern Painters* to show this faith, either as an argument or an experience, tend to be unconvincing, being intellectually
confused and emotionally crude" (144). Further, Ball points to a gap in
Ruskin "between the finely realized object and the much weaker conventional formulae in which he seeks to convey its religious import"
(144).[9] Hopkins found the method to convey the total import of the object, combining as he did his very unconventional poetic language and
his true sense of accuracy in the field.

Hopkins was not afraid to insert his emotional and subjective self into
the rich fabric of his intense factual data. While other Victorians, especially Ruskin, were attempting to keep the romantic self free from the
Coleridgean fusion of subject and object, Hopkins was able to take both
formulae, Ruskinian objectivity and romantic fusion, to create his poetry
and prose. "Hopkins is not troubled by the fear that to admit the subjective response is to muddy the water of pure fact" (Ball 142). This admission of subjectivity allows a narrator's self to emerge, albeit, the voice is
usually not transmitted as "I." Nevertheless, a strong self is present in
Hopkins's work. Ball contends that "the faithful report of what is seen
justifies his emotional comment on it" (143). Just as Dillard piles up
data, providing an ecological format at the outset of the work in order
that it might explode into moments such as the doves in the cedar tree,
Hopkins orders his material, resisting the earlier romantic balance of
"some data with more reaction." Ball insightfully comments that in
Hopkins the balance is "changed from the Romantic apportioning of
fact and reaction, where the latter was paramount" (142). This new balance, in which fact at first seems to take precedence over reaction, finally emerges in the work of Hopkins and Dillard as ecstatic epiphany,
epiphany arriving so profoundly because of these writers' initial desire
to keep the "waters pure." Both writers observe closely so that the thing
itself will show itself. But this close observation also is not released into
formal parallels or meanings; both writers steer away from sewing up a
meaning or finding visionary analogies. Ball observes that "Hopkins

gives himself the opportunity for movement inward, and is ready enough to accept it, but the progression to symbol is not inevitable, the thing seen is allowed to remain itself, and the experience of the poem is that of feeling roused by impassioned observation" (143). Ball here focused upon the central working dynamic of the epiphany—the resistance to metaphor and analogy. Although Dillard and Hopkins certainly have their metaphoric and visionary moments, or the suggestion is strong that a Christian analogy lies somewhere in the offing for both writers, the observed objects of a landscape are frequently allowed to stand separate and reverberating in their own space, the language keeping the division and yet promoting the psychological leap, all of which produces the literary epiphany.

The Language Landscape of Epiphany

The landscapes of Dillard and Hopkins become more than a description of physical matter. They are language landscapes where language does more than describe parallels with the external world, but creates it own tensions, its own hardening of metaphoric soil, from which may spring outgrowths unlike anything that the language has yet produced. In its originality of form and message this language landscape is like the mangrove tree in Dillard's essay "Sojourner," a tree that makes it own floating muck into an island which thereafter carries it forward into random seas. The accumulated debris or "makeshift soil" caught in its "toes" and "hair" (*Teaching* 150) will probably be like no other mangrove island; it has built itself from chance occasions and is not rooted in a larger landscape. And, as Dillard writes, "A mangrove island turns drift to dance" (152), suggesting that entities virtually arising out of chance situations and random accumulations can eventually transform themselves into beautiful shapes. This is the dynamic underlying language in the writings of Dillard and Hopkins.

Language in Dillard and Hopkins creates itself just as the mangrove tree does. Sometimes the meaning comes out of tensions of words and phrases that only become sensible in their own peculiar settings. Dillard "strives toward discoveries of something higher than our ladders of ordinary language seem designed to reach," R. J. Smith comments. "I always get the feeling that she is still seeing 'as' she writes, providing that indispensable element of discovery without which a naturalist or a poet is merely 'an expert' " (95). Dillard does in fact use language in new capabilities, as does Hopkins; both achieve a new landscape, but their verbal territories are strikingly similar because they plant them with similar foliage, they generally use the same proportions of like plants, and they arrange these verbal plants in similar patterns.

The tension between language components in Dillard and Hopkins is achieved through use of many techniques, including colloquialisms, shouts of ecstasy and praise, and ellipsis. Hopkins tends to use grammatical ellipsis, while Dillard, in a more contemporary mode, more frequently uses logical ellipsis. In the works of both writers, sharp-edged, clean, and precise language leads eventually to a tightened or "object-like" moment. This could be said to be a moment when the vehicle and the content of the language make a juncture where both parts arrive in equal proportions, the juncture marking literary epiphany.

Nun and Priest

Dillard has asserted through much of her work that the artist's life, in its purest sense, is much like a nun's: the nun leads a life of focus, dedication, and praise, all of which the artist hopes to achieve. Although Dillard belongs to no official religious order, she would see herself as confined within the structure of her art, her time and effort all given over to the act of creation, just as a nun's days are dedicated to a higher cause. Margaret Loewen Reimer calls Dillard a "religious mystic" who "ordains the ritual and receives the sacrament," acting as "both priest and supplicant" (187). *Pilgrim at Tinker Creek* reveals Dillard's early fascination with the religious life, a circumscribed existence based on observation, its very limitation intensifying experience:

> I live by a creek, Tinker Creek, in a valley in Virginia's Blue Ridge. An anchorite's hermitage is called an anchor-hold; some anchor-holds were simple sheds clamped to the side of a church like a barnacle to a rock. I think of this house clamped to the side of Tinker Creek as an anchor-hold. It holds me at anchor to the rock bottom of the creek itself and it keeps me steadied in the current, as a sea anchor does, facing the stream of light pouring down. (2)

Dillard finds in this constraint of living an anchor-hold to keep her steady and focused, a constraint which she has asserted in most of her work allows the intense moment of seeing. Just as she holds a vertical position in time, she can also be viewed as "vertical" in her apprehension of intense study; that is, she believes that it is better for the artist to range deeply rather than widely. Intensity is of paramount importance to Dillard and this can only be achieved by being focused. If she allows herself to range too far from her "anchor-hold" she might be tempted to see too much, to miss the spirit hiding in small, tangled places. When one insists on knowing each object in such detail, becoming intimately familiar with every contour of a leaf or an insect and every habit these life-forms exhibit, one must limit the broad range of study, as Dillard and Hopkins do, or the sheer volume of work would be too overwhelming.

Dillard's preoccupation with a nun's life is a central motif of *Holy the Firm*. Robert Paul Dunn notes that Dillard uses the three stages of the mystic way—illumination, purgation, and union—to plot the way of artist and nun (18). "A nun lives in the fires of the spirit, a thinker lives in the bright wick of the mind, an artist lives jammed in the pool of materials," Dillard writes, carrying forward the image of the burned moth (*Holy* 22). Julie Norwich represents a nun, her name perhaps an allusion to Juliana of Norwich, a fourteenth-century mystic; even Julie's cat has been dressed in a kind of habit by the child: "And all day she was dressing and undressing the yellow cat, sticking it into a black dress, a black dress long and full as a nun's" (*Holy* 40). Dillard hints at her own identification with Julie, and therefore with a nun, by reminding the reader that Julie and she "looked a bit alike" (41), preparing the way for the final section of the book, in which Dillard says rhetorically to the child, "You might as well be a nun" (74). For the nun's life will bring the child the ecstasy of commitment to something larger than the scattered, unfocused days of life; life will not be squandered on unimportant or nonspiritual matters. Referring to the focus of artist and nun she writes,

> There are two kinds of nun, out of the cloister or in. You can serve or you can sing, and wreck your heart in prayer, working the world's hard work. Forget whistling: you have no lips for that, or for kissing the face of a man or a child. Learn Latin, an it please my Lord, learn the foolish downward look called Custody of the Eyes. (74)

This "cloistered" life will cause the ecstatic moment of epiphany which she describes as

> Mornings, when light spreads over the pastures like wings, and fans a secret color into everything, and beats the trees senseless with beauty, so that you can't tell whether the beauty is *in* the trees—dazzling in cells like yellow sparks or green flashing water—or *on* them—a transfiguring silver air charged with the wings' invisible motion; mornings, you won't be able to walk for the power of it: earth's too round. (75)

This passage describes the sensations she felt when she saw the tree with lights in *Pilgrim,* combining her epiphanic characteristics of light, sparks, metallic surfaces ("silver air"), motion ("wings' invisible motion"), and the circle ("earth's too round"). This moment is the reward for sacrificial living and, although Dillard is not bound to a convent, she has set her own boundaries of focus through her art. She makes this quite clear in her final words to Julie Norwich: "So live. I'll be the nun for you. I am now" (76).

Hopkins was, of course, officially part of a religious community having "Resolved to be a religious" in May of 1868 (Kitchen 105). Hopkins had been under the influence of the Anglican High Church as part of the Oxford Movement when he was a student at Oxford from April 1863 until June 1867, and in this same period, encountered the great Catholic, John Henry Newman (MacKenzie 14). Hopkins joined the Jesuits in September 1868, having burned some copies of his poems as a symbolic gesture of his dedication to his new life; he did not write poetry again until, on the suggestion of a superior, he composed "The Wreck of the Deutschland" in December 1875 (MacKenzie 28). But the structure which he placed about himself, although many critics lament what they consider the loss of time for a great and original talent, did not restrict him in a negative way. A limited life appears to have unleashed an intense poetic power in Hopkins. Sir James Stephen hints at why this power might be increased by limitation when he writes in "Founders of Jesuitism": "Obedience—prompt, absolute, blind and unhesitating. . . such submission, however arduous in appearance, is, in reality, the least irksome of all self-sacrifices. The mysterious gift of free-will is the heaviest burthen of the vast multitude of mankind" (Kitchen 113). Hopkins limited himself by obeying without hesitation a set of rules which would allow him to think deeply rather than broadly. Like Dillard, he needed to see to the least vein of a leaf, a throstle nesting above a "Cluster of bugle blue eggs" ("The May Magnificat" 21), or the "rose-moles all in stipple upon trout" ("Pied Beauty" 3). Rather than crippling his art, the Jesuit structure seemed to be the catalyst to an originality in Hopkins which far outstripped his contemporaries. Hopkins's intellect was not hobbled by his commitment to the Jesuits, and there is evidence he believed in free will. Margaret Ellsberg notes that when the poet used the term "pitch" (both as verb and noun) he was discussing "highly selved and inscaped things":

> A human is "pitched" or intentionally thrown at a certain "pitch" or level of determination. Humans, however, have personality, which is distinct from human nature (which exists prior to the individual human's existence). Personality requires a human nature in order to display itself. . . . And although one's personality is predetermined by one's creator, one has free will. (86)

This is reminiscent of Dillard when she writes, "If I am a maple key falling, at least I can twirl" (*Pilgrim* 268). Just as Hopkins identifies the predetermined elements of human life as "pitched" or thrown at a peculiar angle so that one must respond in a prescribed manner, so Dillard recognizes the twirling fall of the maple key as "blown" (268). To be blown or to be pitched suggests, of course, that certain aspects of life cannot be changed; one has no choice in the general condition. But both Dillard and Hopkins find a similar ecstasy in what remains for one whose path is preordained: in the fall downward, in the circumscribed path, one might choose to twirl, to delight in the fall itself, to accept the limitations and to use free will in directing the beauty of the fall. In its fall the maple key is torn and splintered, according to Dillard, but will "burgeon into flame," a sign of epiphanic light (*Pilgrim* 268). Since both Hopkins and Dillard recognize their limitations, they are able to work intently at what is left to them—close and holy examination of an environment studded with blue eggs and maple keys.

Robert Bridges, Hopkins's confidant and literary correspondent, is a case in point of one who gave up religious structures and wrote poetry contemporaneously with Hopkins. Bridges is the friend who kept and first published Hopkins's poetry long after the poet's death. He appears to have recognized Hopkins's genius and been somewhat envious of what he himself could not compose, revealing in a letter to Hopkins's mother a year after the poet's death why he had suppressed Hopkins's work: "I should prefer the postponement of the poems til a memoir is written, *or* I have got my own method of prosody recognised separately from Gerard's. They are the same, and he has the greater claim than I do to the origination of it" (quoted in Ellsberg 6). F. R. Leavis points out that Hopkins is "really difficult" and "every word in one of his important poems is doing a great deal more work than almost any word in a poem of Robert Bridges" (164–65). Possibly Bridges would have written his poetry no matter what structures he avoided; but in Hopkins's case, it appears genius was germinated by a "greenhouse" seclusion. In the "yoke" of the church Hopkins became an original poet. Like Dillard, he needed an "anchor-hold" to keep him "steadied in the current." "Down is a good place to go," Dillard writes, "where the mind is single" (*Teaching* 15), a clear reference to living single-mindedly like a weasel, but she speaks of her own life, and suggests the life of her "brother-priest" when she writes:

> Could two live that way? Could two live under the wild rose, and
> explore by the pond, so that the smooth mind of each is as
> everywhere present to the other, and as received and as
> unchallenged, as falling snow?

We could, you know. We can live any way we want. People take vows of poverty, chastity, and obedience—even of silence—by choice. The thing is to stalk your calling in a certain skilled and supple way, to locate the most tender and live spot and plug into that pulse. A weasel doesn't "attack" anything; a weasel lives as he's meant to, yielding at every moment to the perfect freedom of single necessity. (*Teaching* 16)

Hopkins and Dillard have found not only freedom in limiting themselves to a "single necessity," but have created in their seclusion new landscapes built from the mind through language, rather than metaphoric replicas of a physical space which lay about them.

Creating the Landscape

Dillard narrates an incident about one of her own students, a graduate student who has written a long "bits and pieces" poem containing disparate fragments; a future critic "presumably could point out each occasion on which lines alluded to Christianity on one hand and NASA on the other" ("Purification" 299). For Dillard these parts did not cohere. She studied it, searched for its underlying form, but found none. "Art can borrow neither significance, power, nor beauty from the world. Art must make its own," she exclaims ("Purification" 299). Dillard's point is clear. The internal structure of a poem, or any work of art, is just that, internal. It cannot rely on symbols which only reflect the external world; it makes its own world through balances and tensions created with language. Hopkins also sees his language-world as real, a self-sufficient and living landscape. W. A. M. Peters writes that for Hopkins "a word was just as much an individual as any other thing; it had a self as every other object, and consequently just as he strove to catch the inscape of a flower or a tree or a cloud, he similarly did not rest until he knew the word as self" (141–42). E. R. August writes that to Hopkins "words are like other creatures: they have inscapes beautiful in themselves. . . . The numerous philological notes in the journals record word inscapes" (24–25). Hopkins's sense that words have "selves" can be connected, according to Ellsberg, with the relationship between the Eucharist and its transformation into the body and blood of Christ. She submits that Hopkins's tendency to make the word "real" comes from his belief in transubstantiation:

The revival of the power and significance of emblems, allegories, and symbols can be related to the revival of sacramental doctrine associated with the Oxford Movement. To state the terms of this revival briefly, before the Reformation religious language itself—for example, the words of the consecration at mass, "This is my body"—had power to transform what it referred to. The growth of science in the seventeenth and eighteenth centuries, an increasingly empirical approach to language, and the Protestant concept of the sacraments gradually sapped this power. Just as the Oxford Movement represented, in part, an effort to restore supernatural interpretation to the sacraments, the Pre-Raphaelite poets entertained the conscious goal of restoring "sacramental" content to the language of poetry. But as Humphry House points out, it was arguably Hopkins and not the so-called aesthetes who developed the aim of the Pre-Raphaelites. (Ellsberg 56–57)

Ellsberg's theory suggests that Hopkins's belief in the poetic word as something real, something more than symbol, comes from his Catholic belief in the reality of the bread and wine transformed into the body of Christ. She says that Protestantism introduced the symbol, or the word separated from what it represents, while Catholicism integrated word and subject, a notion not far removed from contemporary linguistic assertions. J. Hillis Miller has even gone so far as to state that the "history of modern literature is in part the history of the splitting apart of this communion," that is, the words of the Mass in their participation in the transformation of the Eucharist (3). Further, the "realness" of words is best manifested at the moment of epiphany, when few words are of great moment, the words themselves not symbolizing but becoming the moment. Patricia Ball has commented on this word-reality, noting that Hopkins "is acutely conscious of the close relation between verbal denotation and his sense of a universe in being. . . . Words bring about an incarnation" (112). For him the poem, she continues, "stands as a 'thing which is'. Not only is it capable of impressing on the mind the inscapes of the world, but in itself it possesses an inherent vitality of design which confers upon it its own distinctive being. It sustains an inscape to be perceived like any other. What it says cannot be separated from what it is" (113). Hopkins writes, "To be and to know or Being and thought are the same. The truth in thought is Being, stress, and each word is one way of acknowledging Being and each sentence by its copula is (or its equivalent) the utterance and assertion of it" (*Journals* 129). Here Hopkins attempts to eliminate the gap that appears between a word or "thought" and the concept it represents or "Being." He will not allow the word, or the essence of his poetic language, to be a simulacrum; thus he insists the word has its own life, an organicism, or "vitality," as Ball calls it, which bears the same importance as a man, a bird, or a flower.

The methods by which Hopkins tried to make each word "be" are numerous. First, the poet actually tried to avoid metaphor. He was convinced that the word had its own essence which reverberated through the sound of the word, or when he coined words, through the combination of sound and sense. Ellsberg observes that she "cannot think of any poem in which Hopkins used a direct symbol, and this was because the particularity of an object, its selfhood, must be significant as it stood. A falcon, for example, was not something other than itself" (85). The word must be itself as nature's particulars must be themselves, for "selving" is holiness; this is particularly significant for language, which for Hopkins did not symbolize but was—the word itself coming to bear holiness, rather than imitate holiness. Many critics have alluded to "The Windhover" as an analogy of Christ, the bird in its "buckling" dive representing Christ's beauty through incarnation. But Ellsberg writes that, although the poem was dedicated to "Christ our Lord," there is "no reason to conclude that the bird was a symbol, direct or indirect, of the crucified or risen Christ. Nature was for Hopkins, as Plotinus put it, 'the poetry of God.' Down to the least separable part, the individuality of phenomena must inhere in poetry, as in nature" (85).

When metaphor is removed from language other devices must substitute, although Hopkins might flinch at this hint of artificiality in language. Hopkins "demanded new words and new metrical forms to embody its power in language" (Nichols 168), creating a new world out of language, where the vehicle of language becomes as important as, if not more important than, the content. The vehicle of language, however, does not assume this increased emphasis because the content is outdated or hackneyed, although in one sense Hopkins asserts the "old" message by virtue of accepting the Jesuit order; language, in Hopkins's work, becomes important because it forms a new world, or thought process, like the mangrove tree makes it own soil, picking up its own significances. James Milroy has made an excellent study of Hopkins's original language giving examples of coined or unusual usages in the Hopkins lexicon, noting that many "are not standard English words ('pash,' 'mammock,' 'slogger'), but more often words which are standard in form are used in senses which are not the normal standard ones" (Milroy 154). Other words have developed a peculiar or specific Hopkinsian usage, and often words are used in "two or more parts-of-speech classes ('catch,' 'coil,' 'comb,' 'ruck')" (Milroy 154). Examples of coined words appear in "Spring and Fall" ("Though worlds of wanwood leafmeal lie") and "Inversnaid." In the latter, "twindles" is a portmanteau word the poet coined, combining "twitches" and "dwindles," suggesting the froth stirred up by rushing water. "Flitches of fern" is another which suggests the "movement of fern as it twitches, flinches and switches back after being flicked or brushed aside by a passer-by" (Milward

78–80). The portmanteau word, which according to Milward lies "somewhere between compounding and echoism" (175), is one technique Hopkins uses to compress language into its own life. In addition to these word variations and coinages, Hopkins used a Welsh technique called "cynghanedd," which involves "piling on, listing alliteration, [and] consonant-chiming," allowing the words to become more than a sound pattern, a reproduction of the reality they describe (Ellsberg 61). Hopkins was determined to wrench out of each word its full being; when each word was fresh and individual, it lived.

These word techniques are accompanied in Hopkins with a semantic message which is allowed to remain open-ended, a technique which points to the nature of epiphany. Hopkins, straining to find the heart or self of the word, avoids metaphor in a line of poetry and then does not tie loose ends together. He allows the word to speak for itself, forcing the reader into the process of making the discovery of the word's "self." Dillard suggests this open-endedness when she writes of moments "on which a great many pressures bear down. The mind returns to them; their meaning is never resolved" ("Four Bits" 69).

The brilliant image of the "windhover" illustrates Hopkins's desire to let the language speak for itself. The bird is described as "daylight's dauphin, dapple-dawn-drawn Falcon," the air lifting it as it hovers: "in his riding / Of the rolling level underneath him steady air, and striding / High there, how he rung upon the rein of a wimpling wing / In his ecstasy!" (2–5). The "brute beauty and valour and act" of the bird announces the epiphanic fall as it "buckles," the fire glinting off its wing. The bird is "a billion / Times told lovelier, more dangerous" in the act of falling, as other elements when fallen, or gashed—like ploughed fields and dying embers—reflect and show a more brilliant light in the cut or fall. In like manner, when Dillard's finch rips open the thistle to strew the downy seed, the "fall" becomes the action of beauty:

> It jerked, floated, rolled, veered, swayed. . . . It shuddered onto the tips of growing grasses, where it poised, light, still wracked by errant quivers. I was holding my breath. . . . Her fragile legs braced to her task on the vertical, thorny stem. . . . I was weightless; my bones were taut skins blown with buoyant gas; it seemed that if I inhaled too deeply, my shoulders and head would waft off. Alleluia. (*Pilgrim* 216–17)

But Hopkins leaves this image open since he does not set up a metaphor for the falcon. "God now is not manifested in experience itself, as was always the case in traditional revelation," Nichols writes, referring to

"The Windhover" (175). Nichols goes on to say that a theophanic interpretation is added onto the epiphany in many poems but first the experience speaks for itself:

> the "dearest freshness deep down things," whether bird, stars, or poplars, retains the open-ended quality of the modern epiphany. . . . Hopkins demonstrates, both before and after his ecclesiastical vows, that the power of unmediated experience can overcome all his attempts at interpretation. (175)

But it can be asserted that Hopkins keeps his mystery and open-endedness by radically disjointed grammatical structures even in the interpretive sections Nichols calls theophanic. Nichols says that "Hopkins's epiphanies become theophanies when the image produced by the mind is transformed further into a trope of a dogma that demands assent. Such an assent ends not in mystery but in a final, self-validating assertion of understanding. . ." (174). Here Nichols illustrates with "The Lantern out of Doors," which begins with the narrator watching a lantern moving at night, to which he asks, "And who goes there? / I think; where from and bound, I wonder, where, / With, all down darkness wide, his wading light?" (1–4). The poem continues with the idea that after men leave the vision of the narrator they are out of mind—"out of sight is out of mind"; but in the last stanza the poet attaches what Nichols would call a theophanic interpretation: "Christ minds: Christ's interest, what to avow or amend / There, eyes them, heart wants, care haunts, foot follows kind, / Their ransom, their rescue, and first, fast, last friend" (11–14). But it should be considered that at the same time Hopkins "closes" the meaning, as Nichols would assert, he "opens" the structure of language with his inversions, odd uses of verbs, and ellipsis of grammatical structures. This openness in language is Hopkins's revolutionary technique to keep the poem unconfined, organic, and alive to its own internal meanings.

Dillard and Hopkins are both attempting to keep their material fresh and moving within its own setting, with as little symbolic reference to an outside world as possible. In the process of making the language real, they both seem to project what could be construed as a kind of staginess or artificiality. But this artificiality is, in fact, the desire in both writers to be as real in language as possible. Both come to language, understanding that it is a thing in itself, rather than a representative of things, and desiring to wring out of words their essences. Dillard alludes to this staginess directly as in *Holy the Firm* when she calls artists "pyrotechnic fools" who manipulate the language to make up a universe (50) or when she describes Bible characters as "Sunday school watercolor figures, who are so purely themselves in tattered robes" (56). Dillard often highlights objects or persons in her narrative as if they were sculptures or paintings. The surreal atmosphere of "An Expedition to the Pole" and the image in *Pilgrim* of camels, magi, and Amelia Earhart floating in Tinker Creek together add to the sense that Dillard's images are building materials rather than language. She sets up scenes as if she is preparing a stage with properties:

> I seem to see a road; I seem to be on a road, walking. I seem
> to walk on a blacktop road that runs over a hill. The hill creates
> itself, a powerful suggestion. It creates itself, thickening with
> apparently solid earth and waving plants, with houses and browsing
> cattle, unrolling wherever my eyes go, as though my focus were a
> brush painting in a world. I cannot escape the illusion. The
> colorful thought persists, this world, a dream forced into my ear
> sent round my body on ropes of hot blood. (*Holy* 28)

Although Dillard is purporting to deal with actual objects in the real world here, her presentation of these objects, even the repetition of phrases, adds to the artificial quality of the scene. In the essay "Teaching a Stone to Talk" she writes, "We can stage our own act on the planet. . . ." (72), and in "A Field of Silence" she writes of the "distant woman and her wheelbarrow" as "flat and detached, like mechanized and pink-painted properties for a stage" (*Teaching* 136).

Hopkins, in his own attempt to rid language of its sentimental and metaphoric qualities, also manages words as things rather than symbols. In "Hurrahing in Harvest" he attempts to achieve more than a description of clouds when he compounds words and toys with syntax: "up above, what wind-walks! what lovely behaviour / Of silk-sack clouds! has wilder, wilful-wavier / Meal-drift moulded ever and melted across the skies?" (2–4). His repetition of "w," suggesting a smooth, winding movement of the clouds, and his inversion and separation of verb parts ("has," "moulded ever," "melted") in his description of cloud fragments are attempts to present the heavens in their "barbarous. . .beauty," rather than counterfeit clouds (1). In the second stanza he uses one-syllable words to echo the narrator's stepping and praising: "I walk, I lift up, I lift up heart, eyes, / Down all that glory in the heavens to glean our Saviour" (5–6). The blunt and simple repetition of "I" and a verb and another repetition of "lift" suggest an athletic stride out to the hills. He walks; his actions take precedence over thought; his eye turns upward; and in praising "our Saviour," his lips ring with the rolling sound of "r." Certainly, Hopkins is forced into metaphoric uses of language, as that is the nature of language, but he strains against these comparisons.

In "Harry Ploughman" Hopkins disassembles language almost to the point of nonsensicality in his desire to avoid simply "copying" a young man at a plough.[10] The poet insists that the figure be presented to the reader whole, intact, the ploughman and the words organically interchanging, each having an inscape that releases its instress. In letters to Robert Bridges, Hopkins wrote that this poem is "a direct picture of a ploughman, without afterthought" and "I want Harry Ploughman to be a vivid figure before the mind's eye; if he is not that the sonnet fails" (*Letters* 262, 265). The first eight lines of the poem reveal Hopkins's intensity:

> Hard as hurdle arms, with a broth of goldish flue
> Breathed round; the rack of ribs; the scooped flank; lank
> Rope-over thigh; kneebank; and barrelled shank—
>   Head and foot, shoulder and shank—
> By a grey eye's heed steered well, one crew, fall to;
> Stand at stress. Each limb's barrowy-brawned thew
> That onewhere curded, onewhere sucked or sank—
>   Soared or sank—,
> Though as a beechbole firm, finds his, as at a rollcall, rank
> And features, in flesh, what deed he each must do—
>   His sinew-service where do.

The unusual phrase "broth of goldish flue / Breathed round" suggests downy hair on the boy's arm but Hopkins's usage of "broth" is so rare it defies identification. Noting the configuration of the ploughman's muscles and flesh, Hopkins presents technical description reminiscent of a page in a medical textbook. Muscles appear under the flesh like "Rope-over thigh"; the flank is concave and the calf is convex like a barrel. When Harry begins to move with his plow, Hopkins moves the words in the swing of the labor—a simple, straining force: "He leans to it, Harry bends, look. Back, elbow, and liquid waist / In him, all quail to the wallowing o' the plough" (12–13). Hopkins's odd use of "look" without an "s" jars the grammatical sense in that "look" cannot, by hints of punctuation or proper usage, be assigned absolutely to the ploughman's looking about or a command to the reader to "look."

In the final lines, Hopkins blends the idea of the boy's blonde curls and the "curl" of the ploughed ditch:

>   'S cheek crimsons; curls
> Wag or crossbridle, windloft or windlaced—
>   See his wind-lilylocks-laced—;
> Churlsgrace too, child of Amansstrength, how it hangs or hurls
> These—broad in bluff hide his frowning feet lashed! raced

> With, along them, cragiron under and flame-furls—
> With-a-wet-sheen-shot furls. (13–19)

The boy's blonde hair ("lilylocks") is tossed by the wind, and Hopkins apparently tries to echo the wind's action by intertwining the locks with the wind in the compound "Wind-lilylocks-laced." "Harry Ploughman" exemplifies Hopkins's poetic techniques; here he brings together coined words, inversions, echoing sounds of real-world objects, and what he must have believed was a straightforward presentation of a young man. In these details, Hopkins hoped to put forth the figure without language interference. Paradoxically, the more he contorted the poem's language to make it real, the more he produced an artificiality in the poem's presentation. He obviously recognized the pasteboard quality of "Harry Ploughman" when he wrote to Bridges that it "is very highly studied . . . . perhaps it will strike you as intolerably violent and artificial" (*Letters* 263). Later, Hopkins wrote to Richard Watson Dixon that the poem was a work of "infinite, of over great contrivance," and he feared that it produced the "annulling in the end of the right effect" (*Correspondence* 153). In his search for the world's inscape, which is the effect he desired, Hopkins condensed the essences of words and found that his resulting language landscape could seem contrived.

Like Hopkins, Dillard at times condenses her language almost to the point of unintelligibility, producing passages whose main tone is artifice. In *Holy the Firm* her language bears the burden of philosophy, religion, and intense artistic elaboration. Here she enjoins a small living god of the day with the earth's globe that sizzles as if it is part of a child's chemistry set. The narrator's perspective metaphysically moves and telescopes in size, creating a Hopkinsesque tone with extremely condensed and unusual metaphoric leaps:

> The god of today is rampant and drenched. His arms spread, bearing moist pastures; his fingers spread, fingering the shore. He is time's live skin; he burgeons up from day like any tree. His legs spread crossing the heavens, flicking hugely, and flashing and arcing around the earth toward night.
>
> This is the one world, bound to itself and exultant. It fizzes up in trees, trees heaving up streams of salt to their leaves. This is the one air, bitten by grackles; time is alone and in and out of mind. The god of today is a boy, pagan and fernfoot. His power is enthusiasm; his innocence is mystery. He sockets into everything that is, and that right holy. Loud as music, filling the grasses and skies, his day spreads rising at home in the hundred senses.

> He rises, new and surrounding; he *is* everything that is, wholly
> here and emptied—flung, and flowing, sowing, unseen, and
> flown. (30–31)

The number of ideas crowded into the first several sentences assails the
senses like Hopkins's cryptic description of Harry Ploughman. The passage of twenty-four hours, a non-physical entity, is described as physically flourishing and wet. Again, the physical god that makes up time
holds up wet landscapes with fingers that somehow create the fringey
contour of land and sea. Immediately this god is reduced to just the surface or skin of time, and, in an abrupt turn of image, rises out of time
like the growth of a tree. Later in this passage the god is small, bearing
leaf feet, and is somehow able to join like a "socket" into matter. Dillard
calls upon all senses to work simultaneously in these images; sound
("Loud as music") is united with sight ("filling the grasses and skies,"
which forces the reader to sweep metaphysically from earth to heaven),
and kinetic energy ("his day spreads rising at home"). All are encountered through senses which are hyperbolically mysterious as they are increased to "a hundred." Like Hopkins, Dillard insists upon making the
words work almost to the point of nonsensicality, thus creating images
that are object-like. Condensations and skewed grammar generate these
objects on the page because they discourage a link with reasonable landscapes in time; therefore, they become surrealistic properties, doing
their work in another sphere, the staged landscape of language. In this
way, the language makes its own significance, power, and beauty rather
than borrowing it from the concrete world.

The stage-property, artificial character of Hopkins's and Dillard's
work is increased by precise language (again, that which tries to avoid
metaphor), a kind of energy which works toward tightening the language so that it "springs" to its climactic final lines, these lines usually
marking an epiphanic moment, and paradoxically strained statements.
Many critics have noted Dillard's precise language: "at their best, Dillard's sentences have a clean, penetrating edge" (Swan 115); Dillard describes the world "with such precision, and so lovingly" (Grumbach 32);
the questions Dillard poses are not new, but the "poetic and very precise
language" are original (Phillips 94). Hopkins seems to strive for that
same precision, as a Ruskin advocate of accurate observation; Milward
cites as an example the poet's reference to the windhover as "the thing"
("the achieve of, the mastery of the thing"): "To some this may seem a
weak word, as being too general; but to Hopkins it is strong precisely in
its generality or universality, emphasizing the concrete actuality or
(what he calls in 'Duns Scotus's Oxford' 'realty' of the event)" (50–51).

The "gear and tackle and trim" in "Pied Beauty" also exemplifies the plain, precise language Hopkins chose to represent the simple "trades" of nature (6).

Hopkins and Dillard use an energy-bent, speed-gathering momentum in their poetic and/or prose lines. "Sprung rhythm" is Hopkins's coinage for this poetic momentum which he mentions in a letter: "in the winter of '75 . . . I had long had haunting my ear the echo of a new rhythm which I now realized on paper. To speak shortly, it consists in scanning by accents or stresses alone" (*Correspondence* 14). In another letter he writes that

> it is the nearest to the rhythm of prose, that is the native and natural rhythm of speech, the least forced, the most rhetorical and emphatic of all possible rhythms, combining, as it seems to me, opposite and, one would have thought, incompatible excellences, markedness of rhythm—that is rhythm's self—and naturalness of expression. (*Letters* 46)

In a last letter to Robert Bridges, Hopkins writes a poetic reply that illustrates not only Hopkins's use of the technique but also a defense of it; this appears to be a response to what must have been a censory letter from Bridges: "O then if in my lagging lines you miss / The roll, the rise, the carol, the creation, / My winter world, that scarcely breathes that bliss / Now, yields you, with some sights, our explanation" (*Poetical Works* 11–14). The increased sense of drama in speed, anticipation, and sound, the "roll, the rise, the carol, the creation," reveals Hopkins's common trajectory of poetic language and subject. Dillard's language consistently moves along the same trajectory: the "fernfooted" god "rises, new and surrounding; he *is* everything that is, wholly here and emptied—flung, and flowing, sowing, unseen, and flown." These writers give a pulsating charge of energy through their rhythms, a rhythm, which like their nonmetaphoric precision, tries to be true to the nature of a thing; it tries to be "rhythm's self" and "natural expression" in Hopkins and a language which is neither prose nor poetry in Dillard. For the Victorian Hopkins this rhythm represented the "opposite and antidote to the enervated, predictable . . . entropic meters of 'Parnassian' verse" (Ellsberg 59).

Both writers move with increased speed toward the epiphany; the motion increases with an explosion at the final lines, ecstatic; Wordsworth places his objects within language at equal distances from one another, creating the sense that one object of language is not more important than another within the literary epiphany. The objects' powers are equally distributed (girl, pitcher, beacon, etc.) and seem to

radiate from an epiphanic center. But Dillard's objects seem to be gradu-
ated as they move toward climax, a forward movement like Hopkins's.
The motion of sprung rhythm echoes the tightening of Dillard's circle
epiphany; an idea tightens with speed, with repetition, utilizing few transitions, and springs into epiphany.

The tightening of language within areas of literature which appear to
be artificial or object-like is called "heightening of language" by James
Milroy, who says that Hopkins's use of the technique may be observed
on three levels: "the phonetic, the lexical and the syntactic," levels
which Hopkins "often exploits . . . in the same figure" (113). This exploi-
tation, a technique which presses so much meaning into one image, is a
primary reason for Dillard's and Hopkins's similar "sound," but another
reason is their use of contradictory or paradoxical language. Margaret
Loewen Reimer believes Dillard's power "arises from her strength to
maintain the contradictions within a single vision" (190) as she keeps
the dialectic of vision operating with a paradoxical statement: "We
know now for sure, Dillard writes in *Pilgrim,* that there is no knowing"
(207). Even the setting of Tinker Creek is a contradiction because it contains both beauty and terror. The paradoxical language of Hopkins and
Dillard keeps the image both open and artificial. Dillard discusses the artificiality of modernist lyric poetry, which she says has "a taste for deep
metaphysics and a taste for the art of shallow surfaces" ("Purification"
293). The shallow surface refers to the artificial quality which has been
discussed here, a shallowness which for these two writers is a desire for
holy matters solid on the page. Deep metaphysics are best expressed
through an object poem or essay because these genres tend to eradicate
simulacrums. Archibald MacLeish states it clearly in "Ars Poetica" when
he writes that "A poem should not mean / But be."

Various technical similarities in Hopkins and Dillard which allow the
language to "be" rather than to "mean" have been discussed thus far.
One way in which these writers vary, however, points up their alliance
with their own centuries. This variance may be illustrated with an analogy that views language as having two tiers of operation: first, an upper
tier, which involves the grammatical, linguistic functions of language;
second, a lower tier or understructure that administers the logical, syllo-
gistic or otherwise accepted content of language. Together these two
tiers or operations make up the "meaning" of a literary piece.

In building their language-scapes, Dillard and Hopkins emphasize different tiers of language. Both are aware that they must radically change
the language to wring out of it a new "being"; therefore they set out to
twist, invert, objectify and subvert what has been accepted language
practice. Hopkins applies his changes to the upper or grammatical areas,

and Dillard works primarily on the second level. Even with these differing emphases their language remains strikingly similar. The discussion thus far has emphasized Hopkins's inversions, compressions, and coinages, but it should be added now that these radical changes in language work to make a grammatical ellipsis for the reader. Hopkins, in skewing the language, hopes to pull the reader down into the inscape of his poetry. This forces the reader into a "leap" of understanding, to make grammatical connections which Hopkins has left out, a pressure which causes the reader to undergo with the poet the epiphanic moment. Robert Langbaum has suggested this with his "Criterion of Fragmentation or the Epiphanic Leap" (see page 65). Dillard, however, creates the ellipsis in the understructure of her language. She has noted in her discussion of modernists and contemporary modernists that the latter have smoothed the rough edges, the "jagged surfaces, completing sentences, clarifying transitions, and generally composing a fictive surface, an occasion, which serves to bind the poem's parts on the page as surely as they are bound intellectually beneath the surface" ("Purification" 297). Like other contemporary modernists, Dillard has smoothed out her surfaces, allowing the upper tier of grammar and syntax to move without abrupt changes. But her lower tier allows ellipsis; transitions of logic are removed, frequently forcing the reader into tying together whole ideas rather than grammatical structures. Her understructure skips like a pebble in a stream over helpful transitional thoughts causing both an increase in ideational tempo and a large amount of space for interpretation. Dillard's ellipsis of understructure works for the same final meaning as Hopkins's ellipsis of surface material; they both desire to pull the reader down into the language-scape, to make it real right there on the page in the moment of reading; they desire their language to "be." When the language becomes the "thing," when it "is" rather than "means," it is a moment centering on praise of the spirit.

This concept of language tiers finds some validation in Dillard's own comments on language and how it works. "Skin" and "topology" are the central motifs in *An American Childhood*, which deals with surfacing to intense consciousness and, in some respects, surfacing to the upper tier of language. At one point Dillard describes the techniques of joke-telling she learned from her parents:

> He [Dillard's father] had to go off alone and rouse himself to an exalted, superhuman pitch in order to pace the hot coals of its dazzling verbal surface. (53)
> As we children got older, our parents discussed with us every technical, theoretical, and moral aspect of the art. We tinkered

with a joke's narrative structure: "Maybe you should begin with the Indians." We polished the wording. . . . (50)

While Dillard's ellipsis is primarily in the lower tier or understructure of the language and Hopkins's is in the upper, their works remain nonetheless similar in subject matter, vocabulary, and tone. "That Nature is a Heraclitean Fire" begins with clouds jostling about, glittering in the sun's light. Man's "footprint" eventually is eradicated from the earth by the "bright wind" that dries the earth. Finally, even "Man" himself, nothing more than a "firedint," is "blacked out" by "Million-fueled, nature's bonfire" but is finally saved by the Resurrection as an "immortal diamond." Dillard's language in this passage from *Holy the Firm* provides much of the same tone and meaning. The exalting language introduces the idea that the burned Julie Norwich should be a nun:

> Hoopla! All that I see arches, and light arches around it. The air churns out forces and lashes the marveling land. A hundred times through the fields and along the deep roads I've cried Holy. I see a hundred insects moving across the air, rising and falling. Chipped notes of birdsong descend from the trees, tuneful and broken; the notes pile about me like leaves. Why do these molded clouds make themselves, overhead innocently changing, trailing their flat blue shadows up and down everything, and passing, and gone? Ladies and gentlemen! You are given insects, and birdsong, and a replenishing series of clouds. The air is buoyant and wholly transparent, scoured by grasses. The earth stuck through it is noisome, lighted, and salt. Who shall ascend into the hill of the Lord? or who shall stand in his holy place? "Whom shall I send," heard the first Isaiah, "and who will go for us?" And poor Isaiah, who happened to be standing there—and there was no one else—burst out, "Here am I; send me."
> There is Julie Norwich. Julie Norwich is salted with fire. She is preserved like a salted fillet from all evil, baptized at birth into time and now into eternity, into the bladelike arms of God. (72–73)

Both writers are discussing "preservation by holy fire"; they are using images of tossed-clouds reflecting on earth's objects, even to the point of choosing the same vocabulary (compare Hopkins's "long lashes lace" and "wherever an elm arches" with Dillard's "air churns out and lashes the marveling land" and "All that I see arches, and light arches around it"), but Hopkins jars the "upperstructure" with inversion and ellipsis ("Down roughcast, down dazzling whitewash, wherever an elm arches") while Dillard, maintaining a smooth grammatical flow, leaves an ellipsis of logic in sentences such as "The earth stuck through it is noisome,

lighted, and salt," followed by a leap to a biblical allusion, "Who shall ascend into the hill of the Lord?" The ecstasy and praise and, in fact, the
meaning of such passages becomes apparent through the very fragmentation that creates the epiphanic leap, but in different areas of the language. Hopkins recognized the two-tiered operation of the poet's
language when he wrote to a friend in 1883 that certain works of literature have

> two strains of thought running together and like counterpointed;
> the overthought that which everybody, editors, see . . . and which
> might for instance be abridged or paraphrased in square marginal
> blocks as in some books carefully written; the other, the
> underthought, conveyed chiefly in the choice of metaphors etc
> used and often only half realized by the poet himself. . . . an
> undercurrent of thought governing the choice of images used.
> (*Further Letters* 252–53)

Hopkins's "overthought" and "underthought" advance the analogy of
tiered language, "overthought" aligned with the "upper tier" which
might be translated into editorial summaries, and the "underthought"
aligned with a "lower tier" which chooses metaphors and arranges language according to the writer's deep logic. He understood that these operations were intrinsically bound to one another and no transliteration
would be unambiguous.

Dillard and Hopkins work within their own tiers of language, but often they edge toward one another's level; when this occurs their voices
are almost homophonic, not to mention the similar distribution of their
proclivities such as artifice, ecstasy, and theology. But in their choices of
what to "leave out," each writer prefers ellipsis on a separate level.
Richard Pearce addresses the concept of ellipsis when he writes that
modern art "is distinguished by its acceptance of, or insistence on,
holes—discontinuities, disruptions, dislocations, leaps in perspective, ab-
sences. . . . Indeed much in modern literature derives its power from
the holes that our scholarly training impels us to fill in" (79). These
holes occur on the surface of the language for Hopkins and below the
surface for Dillard.

There are frequent instances in the work of Dillard and Hopkins
when the two tiers of language intersect, moments when the upper
structure of language joins the logic of language to strike a literary juncture which becomes luminous. It is a literary moment which Dillard has
described in *Living by Fiction:*

> one does not *choose* a prose, or a handling of paint, as a fitting
> tool for a given task, the way one chooses a $5/16$ wrench to loosen

a ⁵/₁₆ bolt. Rather—and rather creepily—the prose "secretes" the book. The narrative is a side effect of the prose, as our vision is a side effect of our seeing. Prose is a kind of cognitive tool which secretes its objects—as though a set of tools were to create the very engines it could enter, as though a wielded wrench, like a waved soap bubble wand, were to emit a trail of fitted bolts in its wake. (124)

This moment should not be viewed as one in which any nonsensical approach to language can achieve a literary piece, but should reconfirm the concept that the structure of language is powerful enough to create its own validity, that it is at least as powerful as content and at the moment of juncture could possibly be appreciated simply for its beauty and sound alone. It is, as Arthur Schopenhauer suggests, a "free moment of genius...without shell and kernel" (Beja 31). This should not be confused with the notion of art for art's sake, or that the "music" of language is enough to suffice for "meaning" in life. This is exactly what Dillard and Hopkins eschew. For them there is the deepest meaning in the universe, linked with nature and gods, but this meaning can make itself visible in the complete and holy artifice of language. Further, that moment when artifice meets logic, the upper tier of language joining the movement of the understructure is the epiphanic moment itself. Scheick has approached this idea of juncture in Dillard, seeing it occur both in her language and her apprehension of nature:

> In Dillard's work this underlying continuity is suggested by her narrative fringe—moments when surface details in her account are brought to the edge of visibility, where momentarily they lose their revealed and verbalized temporal surface opacity (their "thingness," their conventional meaning) and seem—to author and reader—to become translucent; in *Holy the Firm,* as in nature for Dillard, this translucency suggests a concealed and unverbalizable, eternal depth, where an artlike continuity and design can be faintly detected. (55)

In Scheick's view Dillard's illuminations are translucent because suddenly both author and reader can see into the murky depths of a pool where lie the aspects of holiness or "eternity," which can never be fully verbalized. Dillard and Hopkins at these moments do come close to the unverbalizable nature of eternity, as close as one can approach in language, an approach that is a product of language as much as what lies behind language; for Hopkins and Dillard, perhaps, language in epiphany *is* pure spirit. Hopkins believed a word had inscape, a being or life of its own, and Dillard's work "doesn't simply explain meaning, but through its use of language, internal tensions and rhythms, becomes meaning" (Major 363).

Margaret Ellsberg sees Hopkins in terms of what Dillard calls the "wrench emitting the bolts," or what could be called the vehicle and content of language. She notes that Hopkins criticized both Swinburne and Wordsworth for somehow missing the mark. Swinburne gave the "negative lesson," Hopkins believed, that "words only [without spiritual content] are only words," while Wordsworth, whom Hopkins considered to write often with "uninspired poetic diction," lacked the vehicle of language:

> In Hopkins it is this wholeness, this sacramental interpenetration of accidents and substance, that eventually saved him from erring on the side of either matter or spirit. In Hopkins, intensity of rhetoric and intensity of spiritual insight combine to produce one of the most complex, difficult collections of verse in the English language. (Ellsberg 24)

Further, the subject of a poem "seemed to determine the rhetorical form it would take, according to the 'inscape'—the deep unity—of what he perceived" (Ellsberg 53). This deep unity, emphasizing as it does the inscape of language, "has left him open to a range of criticism. Some critics have accused him of 'mannerism,' though ironically, his poetic practice was nothing if not an effort *against* mannerism, preciousness, and escapism" (Ellsberg 53). What appears to be manneristic in Dillard and Hopkins is their attempt to equally distribute power between the vehicle and content of language. Both recognize in language a life emanating from words themselves; Hopkins sees the inscape of a word and calls it holy, while Dillard often characterizes a word as a self-perpetuating entity that is able to discover knowledge. At these times, when an energetic word seeks out knowledge, Dillard's language vehicle seems to pull ahead of her language content, the word itself impowered with a mysterious radar. She expresses this concept in *The Writing Life* with an analogy of a bee: "To find a honey tree, first catch a bee" (12). Dillard implies that this honey bee is like the first "caught" word of a writer. This single word, like the bee, will lead the artist forward to the next bee and then the next, until "Bee after bee will lead toward the honey tree" (12). When the final bee flies into the tree, or the final word has propelled itself onto the page, the writer ultimately perceives the idea that was until then unknown. In an extension of this analogy, the bee has not only led the seeker to the honey, but has also created the honey, just as the word has created the poem or essay.

In an explication of "To What Serves Mortal Beauty," Florence Riddle suggests that Hopkins accepts the essence of form as an end in itself, an indication that he too will allow the vehicle to lead the content. The form or structure of this poem is its meaning, or in Hopkins's lexicon, its inscape. The argument of the sonnet on one level is that mortal beauty exists as an analogy for spiritual beauty, a repetition of platonic or Christian dualism. Beauty has its function in linking humankind with God, as in the case of Pope Gregory, who noticed the Anglo boys being sold in a Roman marketplace and remarked, "Non Angli, sed angeli"; thereafter, Gregory sent missionaries to convert the Angles to Christianity.

> To what serves mortal beauty—dangerous; does set danc-
> Ing blood—the O-seal-that-so face, prouder flung the form
> Than Purcell tune lets tread to? See, it does this: keeps warm
> Men's wits to the things that are; what good means—where a glance
> Master more may than gaze, gaze out of countenance.
> Those lovely lads once, wet-fresh windfalls of war's storm,
> How then should Gregory, a father, have gleaned else from swarm-
> Ed Rome? But God to a nation dealt that day's dear chance.

Riddle maintains that Hopkins contradicted the explicit or surface statement that mortal beauty is symbolic of a more important spiritual life. This is revealed in the nature of the sonnet itself:

> On the surface lies the idea that the virtue of mortal beauty is its teaching the nature of the good by analogy; that the physical is the emblem of the spiritual; that physical beauty is not to be appreciated for itself but for its symbolic value to the spirit. However, the poem's texture of metaphor, syntax, and sound suggests insistently that the spiritual value of mortal beauty is emergent from it and inseparable from it. (70)

Riddle concludes her explication by stating that "Hopkins's aesthetics tell us that mortal beauty is an end in itself, that pattern is the essence of poetry" (85). But to amend Riddle, I suggest that Hopkins believed that within mortal beauty lies the essence of God. Mortal beauty that dwells in humankind and/or poetry is not the "emblem" of spirit, but the embodiment of spirit, made visible through its inscape. Hopkins and Dillard can never be successfully "paraphrased in square marginal blocks" because their language bears a holiness which cannot be extricated from logic. The overthought and the underthought are more than the word as an arbitrary symbol for the real meaning below the surface of language; the word has its own life, or being, which is inseparably entwined with its meaning. The message of a poem to less insightful readers may be summarized or paraphrased; but a secondary and more important meaning or undercurrent of thought lies below the surface of the physical word on the page. This, for Hopkins and Dillard, is neither metaphor nor symbol, but an essence of language which lies tangled within the syntax, grammar, and sound of the words themselves.

Colloquialism and Praise

The language landscapes of Dillard and Hopkins are distinguished by their use of colloquialisms that enter into the ecstatic vocabulary of praise. Both writers make a juncture of the apparently insignificant and the highly significant, usually focusing on the nature of God or the universe. These colloquialisms appear in three areas: the narrator's epithets and addresses to a divinity; the narrator's keen interest in common or domestic, or even objects and attitudes of popular culture; and the narrator's tone, which projects to the reader that language and the created universe are games, albeit, at times awe-inspiring games, which are played with terror and beauty. Nichols observes,

> In all traditional religious inspiration certain experiences are interpreted as external influences of the divine on the mundane. In the literary epiphany ushered in by the Romantics, this traditional order is reversed; the ordinary is rendered remarkable by an imaginative transformation of experience. The visible reveals *something* invisible, but the status of the invisible component is left unstated. Its mystery becomes part of the value of the experience. (21)

Dillard and Hopkins take the literary epiphany into another sphere as they not only reveal that the ordinary is remarkable but also, the obverse: that divine power is ordinary, that is, God is treated in colloquial terms. God appears in the work of these writers variously as a partner, a working-class pal, a gentleman farmer, and a petty tyrant who tricks the world with outlandish behaviors. Colloquial accoutrements, "tackle and gear," fill the epiphanic worlds of Hopkins and Dillard. The use of current phrases and slang also creates the sense of a child's game in progress, further strengthening the impression that the divine is ordinary indeed. When language jests about an all-powerful supreme being who can illuminate or bullishly dominate a weak humanity, and when these moments are further supplied, often metaphysically with commonplace properties, the effect is startling and paradoxical.

Both writers pursue colloquialisms for another reason: to make language more particular and real, providing a freshness that will once again turn the language into a landscape the reader can enter emotionally rather than metaphorically. Ellsberg notes that Hopkins uses a "contrary language, to express the pointedness and particularity of his perceptions" (75); one way to achieve this contrariety or counterpointing was his use of the colloquial. In similar fashion, Muriel Haynes notes that Dillard "slides in and out of the colloquial and every day to the reverential and the celebratory" (35), a technique which is also a hallmark of Hopkins, who addresses the subject of his tone when he writes to Bridges that "the poetical language of an age should be the current language heightened, to any degree heightened and unlike itself, but not (I mean normally: passing freaks and graces are another thing) an obsolete one" (*Letters* 89). In another letter written years later Hopkins remarks, "I hold that by archaism a thing is sicklied o'er as by blight. Some little flavours, but much spoils, and always for the same reason—it destroys earnest: we do not speak that way. . ." (218). Hopkins, in using the phrase "current language," refers to a spoken rather than a literary language, and Milroy suggests these components of the poet's spoken language: it is monosyllabic, everyday speech of Anglo-Saxon (Germanic) origin, and it is "at its most perfect in the mouths of country people" (74). It is often "the vocabulary of rural crafts and trades" (Milroy 80).

Hopkins used much language, or variants of language, based on country life. But as Milroy notes,

> he does not necessarily use them as they are used in their original dialect. In prose and poetry alike, his overwhelming desire is to select the word that most perfectly captures the present inscape. Country words will obviously be valuable for this, but Hopkins is always influenced by the belief that sound and sense are related. (97)

Further, Hopkins uses Anglo-Saxon words because they

> contract much more complex, subtle and far-reaching networks of relationship within the language than do Classical borrowings, and that is so whether the relationships are grammatical, semantic or phonaesthetic. Such words can be said to have more "meaning" in the sense that they have more associations, and one word from the set (e.g. "stalwart," from the "stand," "stall," "stallion," "stead," "steady" set) suggests the "meaning" of one or more of the others and partakes of some of their "meanings" by association. (Milroy 156)

When language is current the reader faces fewer barriers to the material itself. Both Hopkins and Dillard desire to tear away esoteric obstructions so that the reader can be immediately involved with words; current language, even slang, tends to penetrate emotionally rather than intellectually.

Hopkins's style, in both his poetry and prose, is colloquial, common in rhythm, vocabulary, syntax, and voice. This point, for which many critics and readers have vilified Hopkins, is also what makes the poet's work original. As Milroy writes:

> In dealing with *current language* and its *heightening*, . . . we must recognize that Hopkins's attitude to these is bound up with his general attitudes to language and his rejection of what we have called the "standard model." He sought a basis for his diction in the language that he heard spoken around him and his interest in ordinary speech was greater than that of most poets of his time, carefully cultivated as it had been over a period of years. (31)

Milroy suggests that Hopkins's use of current language grew from his interest in etymological studies of the mid-nineteenth century. Based on notes about etymology and philology which Hopkins kept in his 1863–64 diary, Milroy concludes that the poet assumed, among other things, "that linguistic change occurred by means of figurative transfers of meaning" and championed "the onomatopoetic theory of language origins" (69). These assumptions would account, in part, for Hopkins's unusual and daring poetic diction, although Milroy also concedes that Hopkins has an innate sense of "suggestiveness in sound" which goes beyond onomatopoeia and etymological origins (66). But the link between mid-century language scholarship and Hopkins's etymological notes does not account for much of what might be deemed eccentric and colloquial usage in his poetry. Hopkins desired to freshen and particularize all that seemed distant and unapproachable; he had to draw God close to himself as he did the particularities of leaves and eggs. To achieve this closeness, God had to be seen as man, working domestically and diurnally within the language-scape.

Bidney writes that Wordsworth blends natural and supernatural, and at the "point of juncture the epiphany occurs" ("Radiant Geometry" 114). With this in mind, it could be said that the epiphanic point of juncture for Hopkins and Dillard occurs at the intersection of the colloquial (often scientific) and the spiritual. Their "natural" worlds are made to appear much more work-a-day rustic than Wordsworth's.

The use of colloquial language also renders a sense of strength in the work of Hopkins and Dillard. Both avoid pious and sentimental language that could sap the strength of epiphany. The audacity of their approach to spiritual matters creates similar tensions in their work. Hopkins addresses God as "sir," demanding to know why "sinners' ways prosper," and commanding that God "send my roots rain" ("Thou art indeed just, Lord, if I contend" 2–3, 14). Christ is characterized, like

Hopkins, as "Jack, joke, poor potsherd, patch, matchwood" in "That Nature is a Heraclitean Fire." There is a sense of bold courage bordering on profanity in Hopkins's language as he cries, "let joy size / At God knows when to God knows what" ("My own heart" 12) and "That night, that year / Of now done darkness I wretch lay wrestling with (my God!) my God" ("Carrion Comfort" 13–14). Dillard domesticates her praise with similar figures when she writes, "the creator loves pizzazz" (*Pilgrim* 137), "God is one 'G' " (*Pilgrim* 89), and "there is almost manic exuberance about a creator who turns them out, creature after creature" (*Pilgrim* 233–34). Speaking of the priest who at the altar slings the sacrificed "wave breast" at God, Dillard rages with the priest, "Now look what you made me do. . . . We are people, we are permitted to have dealings with the creator and we must speak up for the creation. God *look* at what you've done to this creature, look at the sorrow, the cruelty, the long damned waste!" (*Pilgrim* 264). In addition, God is characterized as a "spendthrift genius" who churns out the intricate particulars of life, and as a creator who "is apt to create *anything*. He'll stop at nothing (*Pilgrim* 127, 134).

Colloquial language appears everywhere in Dillard, from the moon's surface, described as the "soft frayed. . . heel of a sock" (*Pilgrim* 38), to the act of writing, proffered as a game of chance where the writer should "spend it all, shoot it, play it, lose it" (*The Writing Life* 78). Dillard writes that "a sense of the real exults me" (*Pilgrim* 242), an exalted reality which Hopkins also finds in "all trades, their gear and tackle and trim" ("Pied Beauty" 6). When Dillard can create a scene on an icefloe in which a "woman is sitting on the telephone book and banging out the Sanctus on the keys" (she later breaks into "The Sound of Music") while Sir John Franklin's polar crew "rough-houses" with a "rascally acolyte" and a farmer's wife "keeps her eyes on her painted toenails" (*Teaching* 51–52), she is simply extending, with twentieth-century accoutrements, Hopkins's need for commonplace particulars, particulars which are themselves holy and irregular. Dillard propounds, however, indicating that even the irregular and unbeautiful have spiritual needs and grace as they pursue the Absolute, "how can any of us tone it down?. . . We are nearing the Pole" (*Teaching* 52).

Dillard's use of slang phrases or pop-culture references matches Hopkins's need to approximate real, rural speech in his poetry. She calls the body "the mind's sidekick" and combines a philosophic imperative with a hackneyed expression when she tells the reader that life should be spent boldly with a full spirit: "We are making hay when we should be making whoopee; we are raising tomatoes when we should be raising Cain, or Lazarus" (*Pilgrim* 268). Considering that a century's difference in common usages separates Hopkins from Dillard, a like affinity for the everyday appears in his phrasing, as in "shook foil" and "ooze of oil / Crushed" of "God's Grandeur," or the "stipple upon trout" and the "fickle, freckled" strangeness of "original" or domestic things of "Pied Beauty." When Dillard juxtaposes the trite phrase "threw out the baby with the straw" with a theological argument about the need to combine spiritual values with scientific discovery, she is not revealing a dearth of vocabulary, but a passionate desire to colloquialize "referent" subjects into reality. She weaves this colloquialism into the fabric of the narration; and when "little" words meet "big" subjects, in the language of an artist such as Dillard or Hopkins, the result is an unsettling, brilliant literary moment.

When Dillard asks in *Living by Fiction* who will "interpret the raw universe in terms of meaning," she is positing an artist like herself or Hopkins, for it is certain they have both attempted to take the raw materials of life, both language and landscape, to find meaning. They have tried to popularize difficult ideas to make these ideas more real. Dillard has written theological-gag analogies such as this from *Holy the Firm*:

> The joke of the world is less like a banana peel than a rake, the old rake in the grass, the one you step on, foot to forehead. It all comes together. In a twinkling. You have to admire the gag for its symmetry, accomplishing all with one right angle, the same right angle which accomplishes all philosophy. One step on the rake and it's mind under matter once again. You wake up with a piece of tree in your skull. (42)

There is a grim and yet tantalizing tangibility to a theological argument couched as a gag or the equally dismal children's line, "Ashes, ashes, all fall down," which Dillard sings sardonically in part 2 of *Holy the Firm*, suggesting the tragedy of Julie Norwich's burning (43). For Dillard, "shadows define the real" (*Pilgrim* 62); for Hopkins, the world is filled with a "barbarous beauty" ("Hurrahing in Harvest" 1). They both cry to God asking him to account for outlandish, maniacal behaviors and praise him for his appearance in common objects; they cry in a contemporary speech which they believe will break through any language barriers. Using similar ecstatic language in their work, Hopkins and Dillard make God particular only to find reason in the end to praise him. Hopkins writes, "He fathers-forth whose beauty is past change: / Praise him" ("Pied Beauty" 10–11), and Dillard concurs, "And like Billy Bray I go my way, and my left foot says 'Glory,' and my right foot says 'Amen': in and out of Shadow Creek, upstream and down, exultant, in a daze, dancing, to the twin silver trumpets of praise" (*Pilgrim* 271).

Many other similarities exist in the epiphanic work of Dillard and Hopkins: the prominence of terror and beauty; the frequent metaphysical flights above earth's globe; the recurrence of egg, arc, and circle motifs; the preponderance of ecstatic expletives; and the use of biblical allusions and rhythms. Further, an interesting study could be built around the way these writers explicate their epiphanies or the manner in which the narrator-poet places himself within the epiphany. Hopkins, for example, often does not seem to be present in his epiphany; the moment belongs to outside forces, a result of Ruskinian observation, and yet the epiphany is ecstatic. Dillard the narrator is present in illumination, but she maintains a cool distancing with language, a conscious effort to keep the surface artificial. Both Dillard and Hopkins are prone to spiritual explication of the moment, and yet both achieve Wordsworthian open-ended epiphanies. Despite this difference, however, an uncanny relationship exists between this poet-priest and artist-nun, writers who created weedy and jeweled landscapes for epiphany and studded those landscapes with technically brilliant language, landscapes that could be traversed by Giacometti's sculpture *Man Walking,* Dillard's childhood passion:

> artists laid down the vision in the form of beauty bare—Man Walking—radiant and fierce, inexplicable....
> It all got noticed: the horse's shoulders pumping; sunlight warping the air over a hot field; the way leaves turn color, brightly, cell by cell, and even the splitting, half-resigned and half-astonished feeling you have when you notice you are walking on earth for a while now—set down for a spell—in this particular time for no particular reason, here. (*American Childhood* 213)

6

Feints at the Unknown

Epiphany On and Off the Page

All literary epiphanists are concerned with the inadequacy of language to achieve epiphany and yet are in constant pursuit of a language that can create the illumination on the page which they have experienced in the real world. "Language can give no sense of this sort of speed" (*Teaching* 100), Dillard writes of her moment during the eclipse of the sun. She asserts that certain experiences are lost in the recording because "we have no words" for them; we have only "two little tools, grammar and lexicon: a decorated sand bucket and a matching shovel" to "do all the world's work" (*Teaching* 99). But with these tools Dillard has certainly spent her literary life searching for a way to record her luminous moments. Even her denial that the experience can be recorded is one more way to make the epiphany real in the structure of her literary work.

Dillard once connected the real-life experience of epiphany and the literary epiphany when she commented in an interview that "the terror that you feel during an eclipse is similar to the terror—that dreadful irrational state—that you put yourself in while you're writing sometimes. It's the terror that you won't be able to come out of it" ("Drawing the Curtains" 35). This suggests at least two areas of epiphanic occurrence: the moment of epiphany in nature, as perceived by the creative artist, and the moment of epiphany as recreated, in Dillard's case, by the written word. The latter may be subdivided into two aspects, the epiphany transposed to the page and an epiphanic, inspired reaction in the writer as a result of the composition. To this can be added the response the literary epiphany creates in the reader—the reader's epiphany.

David Ferry, writing of Wordsworth's approach to poetry, says that the poet gives way to a mystical view which tends toward the destruction "of all articulation. It is an experience of the unutterable, the immediate experience of *that* for *which there is no image*" (33). The paradox of epiphany is that the unutterable must be uttered to become the literary epiphany, a literary product which can only be encountered through art. Words must become transmitters of more than information and fact; they must do more than imitate the artist's encounter in nature. The modern literary epiphany must, indeed, be a charged moment that is perpetually available to the reader as a living moment. Walter Pater writes that "art comes to you proposing frankly to give nothing but the highest quality to your moments as they pass, and simply for those moments' sake" (224). It is the passion of the epiphanist to find the way to the highest quality in the moment; paradoxically, the epiphanist finds that the literary epiphany must be concerned with what is left out in language just as much as what remains in order to steer the reader through the epiphanic experience.

A Symbol-less World

The absence of symbol lies at the heart of the literary epiphany. It works in this way: the artist appears to place emphasis on objects in the scene as the epiphany commences; but in fact the artist places paramount importance on the center of the moment, which has no objects, only the nonvisual entity of time, and the only way time can be considered is by the human conception of motion, (i.e., is time still, or passing, or past or present?) The objects of the scene are never hardened into symbols in epiphany; these objects are, instead, the boundaries of the moment. They become a circle of objects which radiate tensions, or vibrations, between themselves; the invisible internal section or center of the moment is vibrating, and because it is moving, it also avoids a transposition to symbols, which are more static with many exterior interpretations laid upon them. This nonsymbolic center becomes the important area. Thus, neither the physical objects of epiphany nor the moving center of epiphany is symbolic and should never be recalled as symbol. However, this very nonsymbolic essence of epiphany is what makes it belong to language so entirely, and, also, what makes it so much a part of the reader's experience. The epiphany occurs in the motion of language each time it is read. The motion cannot happen unless it is activated by language; the act of reading sets up the motion in the object-less center of epiphany, the act of reading occurring *in* time and subject to time's permutations. The epiphany's power cannot be delivered by meaning attached to specific objects the artist chooses to describe, but is activated by the space (of time) which lies about or between these objects. Readers set off the moment at each reading, for they formulate a new composite thought from interaction between the objects, rather than from the objects themselves. This also accounts for the individuality of epiphanies; they are never representative of other epiphanic moments; they must be read as individual entities, each creating its own tensions, which become, in fact, the reader's during the act of reading.

As discussed in the preceding chapter, Dillard often uses explicit references to the stage-like qualities of her epiphanic objects. But this tendency to create "stagish" epiphanic objects should not be identified with creating symbols. The moment is staged in language; Dillard recognizes that she is using an artificial device (language), but she keeps the stage open for motion, the objects acting only as properties that allow the mind to rove between objects.

Dillard in describing the intricacy of a fringed world creates a metaphor that aptly illustrates the notion of the space between the physical objects in epiphany. Rhetorically, she asks readers, or herself, to think like sculptors, sculptors who have all the universe as their material. But physical material and space are reversed; the sculptor's cast is all that is physically present in the universe and the finished sculpture is the shape of the air which remains after the cast has been taken away:

> Mentally reverse positive and negative space, as in the plaster cast
> of the pine, and imagine emptiness as a sort of person, a
> boundless person consisting of an elastic, unformed clay. . . . The
> clay man completely surrounds the holes in him, which are
> galaxies and solar systems. The holes in him part, expand, shrink,
> veer, circle, spin. . . . Through the fabric of this form the clay man
> shuttles unerringly, and through the other feather-holes, and the
> goose, the pine forest, the planet, and so on. (*Pilgrim* 131)

The clay man is representative of the important space that lies between the objects of epiphany. The objects are there to form the space, which seethes with activity during the incursion of the spirit.

The space between must be perceived and/or constructed by the epiphanist as movement of time, a point discussed in chapter 3. All epiphany deals with the interception of diachronic time; therefore, *something* must happen to time's flow to set off the epiphany. As a result, time is always the subject and is always altered in epiphany. Time's alteration can only be perceived by its effects on visible objects (sometimes on the epiphanist's psyche, but a psychic alteration which is still defined and made operable by change occurring on physical objects within the moment). Because time must be set against an appropriate foil to reveal itself, the objects which appear in epiphany, that is, those things with which time is to be contrasted, are made to appear artificial. For if the objectless center of epiphany is the vital portion of epiphany, everything else that participates in the moment must be of a lesser importance. Hence, worldly objects become almost stilted, often artificial, part of a staged border around the epiphanic center.

Wordsworth's girl with the pitcher, the beacon, and the pool are "painted"; Wordsworth actually uses vocabulary that connotes artifice: "I should need / *Colours* and *words* that are unknown to man / To *paint* the visionary dreariness" (emphasis added); these artificial properties surround the nonvisible altering of time. The same artificiality marks Dillard's "Field of Silence" with the "distant woman and her wheelbarrow" which are "flat and detached, like mechanized and pink-painted properties for a stage." These properties define the boundaries but are not symbols for the epiphanist. Therefore, it can be said that all of the critical attention that has been given to Wordsworth's objects in his spots of time, in an attempt to find equivalent values (the girl as Wordsworth's dead mother, for instance), is attention wrongly placed. The objectless space between the girl, the beacon, and the pool is where the attention should be placed, and this space can only be understood through observing the poet's perception of time. The heart of epiphany can only be observed obliquely, as it glances off the bordering objects of the moment. But just as the physical objects or the staged properties of epiphany should not be seen as symbolic or metaphoric, so the objectless center should not be considered as symbol. The symbol is too static a device for the extreme organic quality an epiphanist must achieve.

Dillard discusses at length in *Living by Fiction* the idea of an art object that does not metaphorically represent an idea, calling this entity a "nonallegorical symbol"; the closed symbol that makes a firm connection between itself and an exterior entity, on the other hand, is an "allegorical symbol" (164–65). Dillard, then, would consider the object that becomes part of the epiphanic enclosure to be a type of nonallegorical symbol. She writes that these nonallegorical symbols

> are not precise. It is when these symbols break their allegorical boundaries, their commitment to reference, that they start stepping out on us. The laxity of their bonds permits them to enter unsuspected relationships. They become suggestive. These artistic symbols do not represent things in the great world directly. . . . Instead, these symbols, like art objects themselves, are semi-enclosed worlds of meaning the essence of whose referential substance we may approximate, but whose boundaries and total possibilities for significance we can never locate precisely or exhaust. (165)

Dillard, addressing the concept of an art object as suggestive rather than allegoric, is commenting indirectly on the nature of the epiphanic object. Left open-ended to the reader its "total possibilities for significance" are never exhausted. At the same time that this unsuggestive, common object is offered up by the epiphanist, it is reflected upon by a force manifested in the changing elements. Readers are left to expand their own knowledge by groping intuitively, finding their own meanings for a flaming cedar tree, or a woman in pink, or a girl with a pitcher. This groping for understanding becomes an expanded "true" knowledge for Dillard and is, in fact, all we can ever know as human beings. "Feints at the unknown" (166), an acceptance of intuition and mystery in Dillard, become the soil for the next launching into a more distant unknown territory. Dillard calls this nonallegorical symbol a "rocket ship," for "it opens new and hitherto inaccessible regions" (167). Her nonallegorical symbol "does not only refer; it acts" (169), a repetition of MacLeish's dictum that a "poem should not mean / But be." The epiphany, which can be considered the purest form of the "nonallegorical symbol," reduces the object to total insignificance as object (hence, its paste-board, artificial, stagish quality) and places all significance on what lies outside the object. The epiphanic device must, however, allow the artificial object to reflect a spiritual power, for spirituality cannot be apprehended by any other method than reflection.

An essential of the romantic epiphany is simplicity; that is, the focused objects of the moment are simple and real in nature. Robert Langbaum recognizes this when he notes that "imagination operates best through a plain style that allows intensification to take place" on "realistic material that requires transformation" (336). This transformation during epiphany changes simple objects to artificial properties at the borders of the moment. Beja's Criteria of Incongruity and Insignificance, also indicators of the objects within the literary epiphany, can be further identified here as the stage properties of epiphanies; but they are not so much insignificant or incongruous as they are artificial and devitalized, objects set up as foils and boundaries for the space between.

For an illumination to qualify as a literary epiphany, the center of the epiphany must be organic each time it is read; this, of course, must happen in the reader's mental processes. Since epiphany is happening through language, the language cannot be static, dated, or even anticipated. If the reader anticipates or already knows the words that are determinate indicators of specified meanings, then the moment does not "happen" and therefore cannot be considered an epiphany. But if the language is left open, if spaces are left between word meanings, the moment can occur.[11] The effect of holes or discontinuities in epiphany forces readers to search out their own meanings, to dive down into their own psyche for connections to fill out the epiphany. This diving creates on each reading the sensation of epiphanic pleasure, a startling reorganization of thought in the space between language, a space which is a paradigm for the space between objects in the physical setting of epiphany. Both the space between language and the space between objects are open, free areas for perpetual reorganization, first suggested by the writer and then reactivated by the reader. These spaces are at the very heart of the literary epiphany and should be viewed in direct contrast to symbol and metaphor.

Joseph Frank recognizes that temporality in modern poetry has been superseded by a "space-logic that insists that the meaning must be "perceived simultaneously" rather than with a time-sequence logic (12). Thus, the reader of modern poetry must read an entire piece before connections can be made between the disjointed word-groups; when the piece has been fully taken in, the various meanings can be simultaneously understood. This movement simply stated is one which reflects the movement of epiphany—the dynamic does not move forward in a line, but circles around itself and is seen as a unit all at once, or simultaneously, as Frank puts it. Not all modern poetry is epiphanic, but its general tendency is toward epiphany. In Dillard's epiphanies, as in Wordsworth's, the suspension of understanding causes further intensification of Frank's "space-logic." Rather than the moment finally being uncovered and understood at a completed reading, as Frank suggests for modern poetry, a point at which the disjointed word-groups can be related to one another, the epiphany insists on perpetual suspension, the word references bearing little or no connection between themselves. If the references within Dillard's "field of silence"—the distant woman, the wheelbarrow, and the dog that lopes "up the distant driveway, fluid and cartoonlike, toward the pink woman"—were to relate to one another, to somehow create secondary meanings and relationships, the epiphanic power of the moment would be lost. But these objects are part of an "unhinged. . .world" (*Teaching* 136), objects which are reflecting the power of the emptiness or space between and/or around them. What allows the moment to continue as reader-epiphany is the very fact that they cannot be connected. These objects must be dealt with each time the reader comes back to the literary epiphany, the reader allowing the objects to remain separated, suspended, doing their work as boundaries of the unseen epiphanic power that moves between. For this reason, Wordsworth leaves his "naked pool," the girl with the pitcher, and the beacon to reflect the power which vibrates between them. What is more, he does not choose to give one of these objects precedence over another because they are never intended to be viewed as important for their outside meanings. They contain the spot of time for Wordsworth, as do the naked wall, the single sheep, and the whistling hawthorne of another spot, this one his waiting for the horses. Similarly, Eliot's epiphanic objects are suspended, the roses, the empty alley, the drained pool, and the laughter of children are never drawn together as objects that interrelate or reflect on one another. When an object like Dillard's cedar tree seems to be significantly highlighted by light or flame or other elemental actions, the object must still be viewed as object, an object which is simply reflecting the spiritual power ranging about. The cedar tree and the mourning doves, as we have seen, are "charged and transfigured" by a tremendous power emanating from a door that has opened from eternity. The objects themselves, particulars in time, are the only means by which the epiphanist can observe this power. Even Hopkins, who appears to center on a particular thing so intently, is still dealing with the space between, as in the flight of the windhover, which is seen not as a bird for the beauty of the bird, but as a bird that has circled "forth on swing / As a skate's heel sweeps smooth on a bow-bend" and "Rebuffed the big wind" to reflect a fire that in turn makes it "a billion / Times told lovelier." The motion of the bird in its space is the key to its epiphanic beauty, and Hopkins has maintained his epiphanic space by using grammatical ellipsis.

Frank further comments on the space when he calls language in modern poetry "reflexive" (13); it must reflect back on its own structures and language to have meaning. He continues:

> The meaning-relationship is completed only by the simultaneous perception in space of word-groups that have no comprehensible relation to each other when read consecutively in time. Instead of the instinctive and immediate reference of words and word-groups to the objects or events they symbolize and the construction of meaning from the sequence of these references, modern poetry asks its readers to suspend the process of individual reference temporarily until the entire pattern of internal references can be apprehended as a unity. (Frank 13)

The literary epiphany can be likened to a living mammoth unloosed from the ice each time it is read; Wordsworth's epiphanies are alive and moving a century beyond the poet's time because they live in the tensions of the reader's mind each time they are read. Wordsworth was able to unleash this moment because of what he left out, not because of what he included. Further, Wordsworth and all other epiphanists include elemental substances (fire, wind, earth, air) as a visceral poetic response to that moment; these substances allow the literary epiphany to act beyond its composition and, in effect, to live forever in the space between.

Epiphanic Action: Three Levels

The epiphany should be seen as an occurrence at three levels: the natural epiphany, the artistic epiphany, and the reader's epiphany. The natural epiphany is the event that happens in the real world, on a natural landscape, and is much touted by the writer as an event so illuminating that it must be set down in language. What happens in the real world and in the mind of the artist has already been discussed at length; those concepts will not be repeated here except to say that the landscape and its properties appear to change in some dramatic way as the epiphanist encounters the moment.

The flash and fire of such moments have obviously occurred in some real way; however, there is evidence, particularly in Dillard's comments, that what is truly epiphanic in these moments does not occur until the moment of composition. This idea can, no doubt, be related to Wordsworth's "emotion recollected in tranquillity," but in many respects goes beyond this Wordsworthian dictum. The natural epiphany is described in such dramatic terms and accompanied by such elemental changes that it seems to dismiss the notion of tranquility at any level. Dillard writes about the cedar tree epiphany that "The flood of fire abated, but I'm still spending the power....I was still ringing. I had been my whole life a bell, and never knew it until at that moment I was lifted and struck" (*Pilgrim* 33–34). She attempts to make the reader know the moment occurred *in* nature, that it is a real moment, more real, in fact, than words can ever depict. But there appears to be a moment of mental composition, a "verbalization," as Dillard calls it, which makes the epiphany jell into form. And it is this form, this hardening through language, which, paradoxically, makes the epiphany an epiphany. This composition of epiphany can be considered to be the artistic epiphany.

A contradiction appears when one considers that Dillard believes that self-consciousness takes away the ability to participate in the epiphanic moment, for self-consciousness certainly must be present in the artist for the creation of the literary epiphany; an artist cannot compose without some degree of self-consciousness. The visionary moments fade when consciousness begins "to edit the experience," James Martin Aton writes (93). And yet Dillard has written that "interior verbalization is helpful to enforce the memory of whatever it is that is taking place" (*Pilgrim* 81).

It follows that language itself must take on spiritual abilities to transmit the epiphany to the page. In Dillard's world, in fact, the epiphany on the page appears to be more real and vital than the epiphany in nature. The art-form becomes more sacred than the natural moment.

Ashton Nichols notes that Joyce used the term "epiphany" to signify two events: the "moment of revelation, in which an object (often a person) or an experience reveals itself" and the "verbal strategy by which numerous details in a poem or story are coalesced into a sudden disclosure of meaning" (10). Alluding to the same idea, Robert Langbaum believes that all romantic artists "dissolve the distinction between life and art. The epiphany occurs in the author's life, and the author expends art to make it occur in the reader's life" (337). This extension, of course, can only be accomplished through conscious artistry, a fundamental paradox of the literary epiphany.

These moments are kept alive by verbalization; and this verbalization occurs in the work of the writer the first time, but in the mind of the reader on all subsequent occasions. Dillard writes that "Seeing is of course very much a matter of verbalization" (*Pilgrim* 30) which suggests that the moment of the cedar tree did not really happen until it happened on paper. Dillard continues with a reference to Ruskin:

> It is, as Ruskin says, "not merely unnoticed, but in the full, clear sense of the word, unseen." My eyes alone can't solve analogy tests using figures, the ones which show, with increasing elaborations, a big square, then a small square in a big square, then a big triangle, and expect me to find a small triangle in a big triangle. I have to say the words, describe what I'm seeing. (32)

Mary Davidson McConahay suggests that Dillard, like Thoreau experiencing his moment on Mount Katahdin, can take language to transform the "paradox of the grotesque" into affirmation (113–14). Dillard's ability to see steadily "is the same as the ability to order," according to McConahay (114). This ordering is achieved through language, where the epiphany can be said to occur. Pursuing this language-epiphany connection, Patricia Ward notes that Dillard is dealing with the "process of her own consciousness as she moves between observation and poetic vision" (974). Writing makes the natural epiphany more clear.

Maurice Natanson discusses the "power of language to epiphanize transcendent meanings through its own instrumentality" (144):

> The moment, then, is revealed in language because its very character is constituted of language: the image of the real *is* the real or as much of it as man can grasp, and language draws us into the vortex of full expression. The points in language when such

perfection of meaning and image, or word and reality, is achieved are epiphanies; they are, we may say, *privileged moments* of consciousness. (149)

Natanson is attempting to define the epiphany with much of the same vocabulary others have used, referring to the merging of two levels of language in "perfection of meaning and image" and noting that the moment becomes the real as opposed to simply imaging the real. Beja concludes his work on the modern novel and epiphany by stating the essential feature of epiphany, that it is an organic and psychological experience created in language by the artist who "attempts not merely to record epiphanies but to produce or reproduce them." In producing the epiphany, Beja continues, writers realize that "they've got to use words when they talk to us. But they have tried through those words to bring about the effect not so much of communication as of revelation. The ultimate goal is always greatness" (232).

Lying at the furthest extreme from the initial or natural event is the reader epiphany, which should be considered not only the most significant of the three levels mentioned above, but also the greatest contribution to revelatory, mystic, visionary, and illuminary literature in general. "In art, epiphany is something that happens to the reader," Langbaum asserts (337). Aton discusses Thoreau's belief that reading is the other side of writing or could be construed as the metaphor for writing itself (23). This is particularly true for the writing and reading of the literary epiphany, as the reading of epiphany is an active engagement with language which goes far beyond the traditional involvement of writer and reader. Beja also recognizes that the reader undergoes the epiphany rather than stands outside of the literary moment. He notes that modern novelists feel that "the work of art attains its greatest power when the artist does not merely record, but produces in his audience a sense of new and sudden vision" (19).

Langbaum has offered some explanation on how the reader actually experiences epiphany. He suggests with his Criterion of Fragmentation or the Epiphanic Leap that "the text never quite equals the epiphany," and notes that this fragmentation in modernist literature "blocks grammatical or logical organization in order to enforce psychological organization" (341). The fragments of which Langbaum speaks are usually presented in the form of artificial objects, which have been discussed previously; a literal space is developed by the epiphanist in the landscape and language of the illuminated moment. Langbaum's leap can also be more accurately portrayed as a dive to the deeper portions of the reader's psyche followed by an emergence (or surfacing) with the conclusions or reactions of the reader, conclusions which he has drawn himself, thus making the epiphanic reading a personal and significant experience. For the reader to undergo the literary epiphany the author cannot give too much information. Langbaum recognizes this when he comments about the reader's involvement in transforming the words of the literary epiphany. The writer cannot supply instructions for feeding the moment: "For if realistic notation is to become art, the reader must be relied on to transform the details into visionary significance—a visionary significance that cannot be stated as a meaning" (Langbaum 338). Using "Simon Lee" as an example of a poem where "nothing happens," Langbaum says that "the author does not 'tell' the reader the story, but plays upon him as though he were a musical instrument—making him move through a series of associations that will produce the epiphany in 'him'" (345). Nichols concurs with this concept when he writes, "Any reader of a literary epiphany becomes a potential participant in the experience" (12).

The reader's epiphany is created out of the reader's need to conceptualize the material that has been eliminated in literature. Forced into the primary process by making loose connections among scattered words, the reader undergoes an illumination. There is, indeed, an identifiable strain in epiphany to escape the word entirely and become palpable; that is, the literary epiphany strains to engage the "signified" (the inexpressible concept which lies behind the language) rather than the signifier (language). In this manner the primary areas of the psyche are tapped. According to Ferdinand de Saussure, language is a " 'system of signs that express ideas,' a network of elements that signify only in relation to each other" (Silverman 6). Saussure's formulation can be linked with Freud's early construction of the psyche: the unconscious and the preconscious. Kaja Silverman discusses at length Freud's topography and its connection with language in *The Subject of Semiotics* (see chapter 2). The unconscious, which corresponds to Saussure's area of the signified, is the seat of primary human activity. The preconscious blocks and makes ready for language the material from the unconscious; this blocking and processing from unconscious and preconscious makes language occur. This Freudian theory implies that the unconscious is perpetually blocked from full realization by the delimiting activity of the preconscious. The signifier is never able completely or accurately to present the signified.

Simon O. Lesser suggests that the more readers are forced to call up their imagination or conceptualizing powers the more powerful becomes the literary work (Iser 45). The less information supplied, the greater the effect on readers. A work of art becomes more powerful when it deals in cipher, "for the more open and direct" the work of art, the less effect it "will have upon the recipient" (Iser 45). The literary epiphany, becoming more loosely fitted together with the absence of metaphor and transition, requires readers to disentangle the language. This lack of direct material in epiphany causes the psyche, particularly the unconscious to perform rigorously in making connections. The act of deciphering moves the readers deeper into the primary process and closer to pure conceptualization of the subject. This need to move to pure conceptualization and away from that which only "signs" the concept is also that which makes the epiphanist avoid metaphor and erect staged objects. A metaphor would in effect be a sign of a sign, one step further away from the primal event the epiphanist seeks to call up. When too much information is given the powerful primal effect is diffused. The literary epiphany brings together epiphanic objects whose "meanings" can be tapped into only with the assistance of primary conceptualization. It must be understood quickly, its objects encountered simultaneously.

Surface and Understructure

Dillard makes the point that both "plot" and "vision" are important in a work of art. For Dillard plot is the "narrative surface" and vision the "understructure" of a piece. She emphasizes the necessity for coherent surface narrative, strung together with smooth grammar, because the writer is "talking to people, after all. You're not just whizzing around in your own head for your own amusement" ("Drawing the Curtains" 33). Dillard is identifying what has been alluded to in chapter 5 as the two tiers of language usage, but she is using the terms somewhat differently here. Her narrative surface, combining a smooth grammar and coherent narrative—although often a very thin layer of narrative in Dillard's work—refers to the upper tier of language. Her understructure or vision refers to the meaning of the work as it is used in chapter 5.

Dillard's luminous prose is very much a surface work, imitating in some respects modernist poetry, which becomes a collage of "manipulable bits, like tesserae, from which the poet constructed that complex, reflexive, internally coherent plan for beauty" ("Purification" 293). But Dillard has smoothed out the surface of her prose grammatically with little evidence of grammatical or syntactical scattering, a characteristic which takes her further away from the modernists and later into the twentieth century. With a deceptively smooth and artificial surface she places the burden of her metaphysics on the understructure of her work, a combination which she notes when she writes that "a taste for deep metaphysics and taste for the art of shallow surfaces often go together" ("Purification" 293).

Poetry in general moves swiftly, and, with the application of little detail, forces the mind to plumb the depths of the unconscious or preconscious, picking up ideas which lie deep in the psyche, ideas which when jostled in our depths make us respond to eternal or primitive questions. Traditional prose or fiction supplies more detail, consequently becoming the "literature of depth and engagement," a literature more concerned with humankind or "reality," as are the works of Tolstoy and Hardy ("Purification" 294). The surface-understructure paradigm can be seen to act in this way: realistic details, usually present in the domain of fiction and traditional prose, are used to sculpt a representation of the real world of human activity; this literature's surface is textured and, like a relief map, becomes a facsimile of the perceived world. On the other hand, unusual, artificial, sometimes jeweled and glittering pieces of information make up the smooth surface of a modern and/or contemporary poem; the function of this artificial surface is to raise questions which lie beyond the realm of human activity, so that this type of work deals with the "relationship between time and eternity" ("Purification" 293).

Scheick discusses this moment as it occurs in Dillard's language: "These moments of translucency reveal the liminal edge of the particular (the temporal, the opaque surface) where it touches the universal (the eternal, the transparent depth)" (53). When Dillard achieves this moment in language the surface and the understructure appear to merge, the surface, although it remains generally undisturbed, becoming somewhat ruffled with repetition, shortened sentences, shouts of praise. The understructure concurrently becomes more elliptical, an ellipsis achieved through metaphysical leaps and paradoxical juxtapositions, including conflations of time periods, combinations of colloquial and elaborate diction, and infusions of chaotic motion which is acting in elements such as fire or water. The extended epiphany where Dillard carries communion wine in *Holy the Firm* illustrates this merging of upper and understructure. Already highly artificial in tone, the scene's surrealism increases as the event progresses with the Dillard persona walking through a painted landscape with the communion wine, "Christ with a cork," bearing down on the arc of her ribs (64). Here the Dillardian ingredients for epiphany begin to show themselves: the bold, colloquial language describing God in a bottle and the presence of part of the holy circle in her ribs. Her environment begins to change, signifying the realignment of the surface narrative and the understructure:

The landscape begins to respond as a current upwells. It is starting to clack with itself, though nothing moves in space and there's no wind. It is starting to utter its infinite particulars, each overlapping and lone, like a hundred hills of hounds all giving tongue. The hedgerows are blackberry brambles, white snowberries, red rose hips, gaunt and clattering broom. Their leafless stems are starting to live visibly deep in their centers, as hidden as banked fires live, and as clearly as recognition, mute, shines forth from eyes. (64–65)

An energy that has no apparent source begins to rise out of the moment and to jostle objects on the surface. Like T. S. Eliot's roses in "Burnt Norton" which had the look of "flowers that are looked at" (29), the foliage moves although "nothing moves in space and there's no wind." The landscape is reacting to an eternal force that emits its own power; this motionless environment contains a swelling kinetic force, or, again reminiscent of Eliot, it is "still and moving" ("Burnt Norton" 73).

The bare twiggy brambles of November stir "deep in their centers," and Dillard suggests this hidden energy is like "banked fires," a link with the necessary elements of light and fire that reflect epiphany. The moment becomes increasingly translucent, light no longer refracts from surfaces, which are now being penetrated, but shines into and through objects on the land: apples are "wet and transparent"; cattle are "cell by cell" becoming "translucent"; the wine bottle sheds "light in slats" through the narrator's rib cage and "fills the buttressed vaults of my ribs with light pooled and buoyant" (65). As the epiphany progresses, light shines through all persons and objects in the landscape, the moment culminating in the baptism of Christ. The transparency of surface barriers becomes even more evident in this surrealistic presentation of Christ rising out of the water:

He lifts from the water. Water beads on his shoulders. I see the water in balls as heavy as planets, a billion beads of water as weighty as worlds, and he lifts them up on his back as he rises. He stands wet in the water. Each one bead is transparent, and each has a world, or the same world, light and alive and apparent inside the drop: it is all there ever could be, moving at once, past and future, and all the people. I can look into any sphere and see people stream past me, and cool my eyes with colors and the sight of the world in spectacle perishing ever, and ever renewed. I do; I deepen into a drop and see all that time contains, all the faces and deeps of the worlds and all the earth's contents, every landscape and room, everything living or made or fashioned, all past and future stars, and especially faces, faces like the cells of everything, faces pouring past me talking, and going, and gone. And I am gone. (67)

In this scene, light transpires through all things, all barriers are broken, and worlds metaphysically expand and contain all objects of earth. Christ has arisen from a translucent element, where he was "coiled and white under the water," and this same element explodes into billions of worlds, each a transparent drop beading from Christ's body. The greatest intensity occurs, however, when the narrator enters one drop and in this single bead of water perceives all time, "all the earth's contents," people, landscapes, and rooms; she, now translucent, becomes a portion of a greater translucency.

Dillard suggests broken surfaces of physicality *and* language; light penetrates the objects of her narrative while a kind of psychological "light" breaks through the ellipses in her language. The surface of her smooth prose breaks into poetic particles with repeated phrases in simple language: notice the repetition of "water" and the preponderance of one-syllable words in "He lifts from the water. Water beads on his shoulders. I see the water in balls." The phrase "Perishing ever, and ever renewed" is biblically poetic in nature, and her short punctuating clauses "I do" and "And I am gone" break up the surface narrative. At the same time as this top tier of narration is disrupted, the understructure of meaning becomes more elliptical, sketchy, and metaphysical. Tiny beads of water expand into planets and the narrator decreases in size to enter a single drop. But most significant of all, this moment culminates in the fusing of the surface and the understructure with the narrative and its meaning, its techniques and its content, woven into the epiphanic circle of no time:

> For outside it is bright. The surface of things outside the drops has fused. Christ himself and the others, and the brown warm wind, and hair, sky, the beach, the shattered water—all this has fused. It is the one glare of holiness; it is bare and unspeakable. There is no speech nor language; there is nothing, no one thing, nor motion, nor time. There is only this everything. (67–68)

The two tiers of language are jarred and disassembled by Dillard's approach, but at the same time they are reassembled or "fused" into a perfect epiphanic circle. Earlier in the narrative, the narrator characterizes her own disjointed movement within a fractured setting where "Pieces of the sky are falling down": "I myself am falling down, slowly, or slowly lifting up" (66). This movement indicates her own lack of direction; the motion begins to turn in upon itself. It cannot in the end be vertical or horizontal but must arc and then circle. As she describes herself in the final action of this epiphany, Dillard is within the moment, at the center of time, and the circle draws around her, tightening into a "surface" of

Christ and earth. God has literally enclosed her, and the light that was shining through translucent barriers, now in a fiery "glare of holiness," holds her in an event that has neither time nor language.

William J. Scheick comments on Dillard's elliptical narrative when he says,

> However much the reader might prefer this fulfillment of a conventional expectation of a narrative, he or she will not find sufficient continuity at the surface level of *Holy the Firm*; the absence of this continuity at the linear, temporal narrative level urges the reader to find it elsewhere in Dillard's book. (55)

The critic observes here that all of the book's narrative is disrupted, and it is true that *Holy the Firm* could be viewed as one extended epiphany, since the language is epiphanic throughout; but Dillard's discontinuous surface narrative becomes even more disrupted at specifically heightened epiphanic moments. It is interesting to note that while Scheick labels them differently, he nonetheless recognizes the two tiers in Dillard's prose-poetry which on most occasions run separately but are seen to be merging at translucent moments. It is a moment when everything that has been turning in language, grammar and logic, suddenly locks into perfect alignment, achieving the literary epiphany. Dillard writes that "Our layered consciousness is a tiered track for an unmatched assortment of concentrically wound reels. Each one plays out for all of life its dazzle and blur of translucent shadow-pictures; each one hums at every moment its own secret melody in its own unique key. We tune in and out" (*Pilgrim* 84). It could be said that at the moment of epiphany, that which occurs in the literal world and that which occurs in language, all of the tiered tracks are suddenly aligned, the moment is "singing" in one key, and the artist's and reader's vision is momentarily cleared. This alignment within the moment is Dillard's focus in "Total Eclipse" when she writes that "The lenses of telescopes and cameras can no more cover the breadth and scale of the visual array than language can cover the breadth and simultaneity of internal experience" (*Teaching* 95). Although here Dillard denies, in effect, that language can achieve this effect her work is evidence that the translucent moment is her literary grail.

Dillard discusses her manipulation of surface and understructure in language when she writes about her early problems in writing a "long poem" that had a "solid intellectual structure" but leaped on the surface "from mountain peak to mountain peak" ("Drawing the Curtains" 32). She recognized after its composition that "it needed to have a coherent narrative *surface* as well" ("Drawing the Curtains" 32). Dillard suggests that her narrative (rather than sentence structure) becomes sequential and smooth in her later prose, but her prose, very like poetry, remains disjointed and oddly juxtaposed.

Dillard, in discussing contemporary modernist art in *Living by Fiction*, says, "the work of art is above all a chunk in the hand. It is a self-lighted opacity, not a window and not a mirror. It is a painted sphere,not a crystal ball" (47–48). Although she is speaking of fiction here, this opacity is apparent in Dillard's prose-poetry, illustrated by a passage from *Holy the Firm*:

> I elaborate the illusion instead; I rough in a middle ground. I stitch
> the transparent curtain solid with bright phantom mountains, with
> thick clouds gliding just so over their shadows on green water,
> with blank, impenetrable sky. The dream fills in, like wind
> widening over a bay. Quickly I look to the flat dream's rim for a
> glimpse of that old deep. . . and, just as quickly, the blue slaps
> shut, the colors wrap everything out. (29)

Here she writes with the perspective of an artist in the plastic arts, emphasizing the illusion created by artistic materials, highlighting the surface of the visible world and the blank, impenetrable surface that confronts the individual who might be watching for something more meaningful, "for a glimpse of that old deep." Dillard composes with a contemporary modernist's opacity, utilizing her pyrotechnical skills to create beautiful artificial surfaces furnished with artificial properties, until she reaches the moment of epiphany. For as a neoromantic she must somehow plunge through the surface, even for a millisecond of meaning. The epiphany breaks through every artificial barrier which has been erected or smoothed out by the contemporary modernist. The moment is irrational, beyond the structuring power of the artist, and is made to appear even more revelatory because it is occurring in the center of a blatantly artist-made and artificial landscape. When Dillard writes that the contemporary modernist piece is opaque and that it does not allow vision *through* to a spiritual or redeemable facet of art, as in a window, or vision *reflected* from something innately spiritual in art's form, as in a mirror, she is setting up an aesthetic she intends to penetrate. For in her epiphany she does see through a window for a fleeting moment, or she watches in a blaze of light, always claiming that this light is beyond her literary power to express or her accumulated knowledge to understand. She asserts that she sees into the heart of God. In this way, Dillard's "painted sphere" of language does, in the literary epiphany, become a "crystal ball," like the expanded world in a bead of water.

Dillard believes that art is, like a Genesis creation, "the whole ball of wax, coherent, hollowed out from chaos and held" ("Some Notes on the Uncertainty Principle" 50). Art is difficult; it is more than idea and better than argument ("Some Notes" 50). Aton says that Dillard sees "god as artist" (96). "The poet-seer who achieves the correspondence between these disparate objects and occurrences fully participates in god's creation"; the artist's participation in a creative act is the "true way one can know god" (Aton 96). On many occasions Dillard has hinted that language itself might be all there is, that these signifiers might be the result of the brain's need to order what lies about us even as there is the horrible possibility that the ordering itself is "a grotesque trick of tissue" (*Living* 181). Perhaps there is no beauty, no order except that which we perceive, that perception having grown out of its own random soil, like the mangrove tree: "In the fabrication of these things we are skilled," Dillard speculates, "because the skill feeds and preserves us, as the specially adapted tissues of benthic fishes or of dragonflies feed and preserve them. Our brains secrete bright ideas and forms of order; armored scale insects secrete wax from their backs" (*Living* 182). If this scenario is true, then language and any art piece, is, in fact, the only god, a simulacrum, an entity created out of the human need for significance, which arises from truly insignificant and accidental drifts of time. Language may be the silly god itself. But, Dillard writes, "Let us cover this archaeological pit for the nonce and build a high tower" (*Living* 182). The tower is a lofty hope that there is some power behind our language which we can emulate. Did we build the high tower of language through our own evolving brain tissue, or have we discovered a "reason and harmony in the universe" as we signify with language (*Living* 182)? There is every evidence in Dillard's work that she believes there is an order behind language which grows out of an entity beyond the human brain. But, paradoxically, language must be seen as something to escape when all has been made right in eternity.

T. S. Eliot pursues a similar thought process in *Four Quartets*, in which he uses a language motif he concludes in "Little Gidding," emphasizing that when all of earth's timeless moments suddenly merge with eternity, when the "fire and the rose are one," language will be able to express what it could never express in a spiritually incomplete and earthly state. Only in the timeless or epiphanic moments of Eliot's work does language even begin to enter the realm where the artist is able to communicate the full holiness of art. He has tried "to learn to use words" but "every attempt / Is a wholly new start, and a different kind of failure"; each time he has begun to use words the "venture / Is a new beginning, a raid on the inarticulate / With shabby equipment always deteriorating / In the general mess of imprecision of feeling" ("East Coker" 174–75, 178–81). This language for Eliot is the inadequate signifier attempting to communicate the conceptual signified but always falling short of its goal because the nature of language is to delimit. However, within the boundaries of the literary epiphany language is able to hint at eternity via a momentary breakthrough with words into a state of perfection that is both still and moving. The literary epiphany comes closest to the complete moment when, in Eliot's words, the "beginning" and the "end" become one:

> And every phrase
> And sentence that is right (where every word is at home,
> Taking its place to support the others,
> The word neither diffident nor ostentatious,
> An easy commerce of the old and the new,
> The common word exact without vulgarity,
> The formal word precise but not pedantic,
> The complete consort dancing together)
> Every phrase and every sentence is an end and a beginning,
> Every poem an epitaph.
> ("Little Gidding" 216–25)

This sense that language at the moment of epiphany—whether it is perpetual epiphany outside of time or the hint of eternal epiphany that occurs within earthly time—will communicate fully what eternity and spirit is, is a sense which guides the epiphanist. Language is the way to mold or encapsulate the concept of holiness; therefore, language, as the best purveyor of concept and idea, itself becomes holy, the "complete consort dancing together."

Language in epiphany is burdened with more responsibility than it can normally bear. Dillard is always seeking to make it mean more, do more; one way by which she achieves this empowerment is to look beyond language at vision. Her metaphor for this use of language is offered in this way: "Aim for the chopping block. If you aim for the wood, you will have nothing. Aim past the wood, aim through the wood: aim for the chopping block" ("Wish I Had Pie" 84). She looks to the vision, and though the surface of her writing is predominantly opaque, she is attentive to the moment when this opacity will clear to the vision for which she has aimed. Dillard believes that this language-composition moment, when she hits the vision beyond the words, serves as a holy act bordering on the eternal:

> The page, the page, that eternal blankness, the blankness of
> eternity which you cover slowly, affirming time's scrawl as a right
> and your daring as necessity; the page which you cover slowly,
> ruining it, but asserting your freedom and power to act,
> acknowledging that you ruin everything you touch but touching it

anyway, because acting is better than being here in mere opacity; the page which you cover slowly with the crabbed thread of your gut, the page in the purity of its possibilities, the page of your death against which you pit such flawed excellences as you can muster with all your life's strength; that page will teach you to write. ("Wish I Had Pie" 83–84)

Language has the "purity of possibility" but its "opacity" is difficult to penetrate. Dillard, however, will use all of her artistic strength to tap into the mysteries she sees. The page is like the blankness of eternity, in which a powerful force created form out of chaos; on this page Dillard takes "time's scrawl" and forces it into timelessness. Time, epiphany's essential ingredient, is compared to language; time is scrawling its mark on eternity, just as language is attempting to defy language by signifying the unsignifiable.

Dillard writes that "Many excellent poets writing today believe in the ordering and even redemptive quality of art" ("Purification" 296). It is evident that she can be counted among that number. Although she speaks obliquely of Christianity and the epiphanies she finds in and through nature, the real epiphany is that magnificent, concentrated, vibrating form which appears in print. The literary epiphany, however, should be seen as language and nonlanguage; it should be considered as a device used to escape language, which is primarily supported by the space between words. But while we are set down here for a while, the artificial and glittering word is our nearest brush with holiness. For a moment, in Annie Dillard's epiphanic art, the Word is God.

Notes

1. All subsequent citations for William Wordsworth's *The Prelude* will be from the 1805 version of *The Prelude 1799, 1805, 1850: Authoritative Texts, Context and Reception, Recent Critical Essays*. Book and line numbers will be indicated.

2. Subsequent citations for Wordsworth's poetry other than *The Prelude* will be from *The Poetical Works of William Wordsworth*. Poetry line numbers will be given.

3. Colette Gaudin has collected and translated Bachelard's ideas in *On Poetic Imagination and Reverie: Selections from the Works of Gaston Bachelard*.

4. Note Eliot's famous early statement about his identity as "classicist in literature, royalist in politics, and anglo-catholic in religion" (ix) in *For Lancelot Andrews: Essays on Style and Order*.

5. This "illusion" will be seen later to be more than illusion, as the epiphanic process is a real fluctuation in the reader's epiphany.

6. Hopkins was born July 28, 1844, in Stratford, Essex, and died June 8, 1889, in Dublin, Ireland. Dillard was born April 30, 1945, in Pittsburgh, Pennsylvania.

7. All of Hopkins's poems will be cited from *The Poetical Works of Gerard Manley Hopkins*. Poetic lines will be indicated. Hopkins's peculiar metrical markings have been omitted for this study, but for an excellent discussion of these marks and their variations in Hopkins's manuscripts, see MacKenzie's "Introduction," lii–lix.

8. Notice the unusual word presentation (e.g., "multiply," "possible") as Dillard tries to echo in language her desire to be "present" at the exact moment of observation.

9. Recall Muir's attempt to epiphanize his mountain climbing; see chapter 2 of this study.

10. MacKenzie's text gives this poem with Hopkins's undeleted alternative phrases. In order to make our reading more accessible in an already difficult poem, I have used the phrase that appears first in the line.

11. Recall Pearce's comment about the nature of modern literature deriving its "power" from the "holes" or "discontinuities" that we as readers are forced to "fill in"; see chapter 5 of this study.

Works Cited

Abrams, M. H. *The Mirror and the Lamp: Romantic Theory and the Critical Tradition*. New York: Norton, 1953.

———. "Structure and Style in the Greater Romantic Lyric." *From Sensibility to Romanticism: Essays Presented to Frederick A. Pottle*. Ed. Frederick W. Hilles and Harold Bloom. New York: Oxford UP, 1965. 527–60.

Ammons, A. R. "Conserving the Magnitude of Uselessness." *Norton Anthology of Modern Poetry*. Ed. Richard Ellman and Robert O'Clair. 2nd ed. New York: Norton, 1988. 1171–72.

Aton, James Martin. " 'Sons and Daughters of Thoreau:' The Spiritual Quest in Three Contemporary Nature Writers." Diss. Ohio U, 1981.

August, E. R. "Word Inscapes: A Study of the Poetic Vocabulary of Gerard Manley Hopkins." Diss. U of Pittsburgh, 1964.

Bachelard, Gaston. *On Poetic Imagination and Reverie: Selections from the Works of Gaston Bachelard*. Trans. Colette Gaudin. New York: Bobbs-Merrill, 1971.

Ball, Patricia M. *The Science of Aspects: The Changing Role of Fact in the Work of Coleridge, Ruskin and Hopkins*. London: Athlone, 1971.

Bate, Walter Jackson. *From Classic to Romantic: Premises of Taste in Eighteenth-Century England*. New York: Harper, 1946.

Beja, Morris. *Epiphany in the Modern Novel*. Seattle: U of Washington P, 1971.

Bidney, Martin. "Radiant Geometry in Wordsworthian Epiphanies." *Wordsworth Circle* 16 (1985): 114–20.

———. "The Structure of Epiphanic Imagery in Ten Coleridge Lyrics." *Studies in Romanticism* 22.1 (1983): 29–40.

Blake, William. "Auguries of Innocence." *English Romantic Poetry and Prose*. Ed. Russell Noyes. New York: Oxford UP, 1956. 222–24.

Bornstein, George. *Transformations of Romanticism in Yeats, Eliot, and Stevens*. Chicago: U of Chicago P, 1976.

Bunyan, John. *Grace and Death Abounding and The Life and Death of Mr. Badman*. Everyman's Library 815. New York: Dutton, 1928.

Cohen, Michael P. *The Pathless Way: John Muir and American Wilderness*. Madison: U of Wisconsin P, 1984.

Coleridge, Samuel Taylor. *Biographia Literaria, or Biographical Sketches of My Literary Life and Opinions.* 2 vols. Ed. James Engell and W. Jackson Bate. *The Collected Works of Samuel Taylor Coleridge* Vol. 7. Bollingen Series 75. Princeton: Princeton UP, 1983.

———. *Collected Letters of Samuel Taylor Coleridge.* Ed. Earl Leslie Griggs. 6 vols. Oxford: Clarendon, 1956–71.

———. *The Complete Poetical Works of Samuel Taylor Coleridge.* Vol. 1. Ed. Ernest Hartley Coleridge. 2 vols. Oxford: Clarendon, 1912.

Dillard, Annie. *An American Childhood.* New York: Harper, 1987.

———. "Drawing the Curtains: An Interview with Annie Dillard." By Karla M. Hammond. *Bennington Review* 10 (1981): 30–38.

———. *Encounter with Chinese Writers.* Middletown, CT: Wesleyan UP, 1984.

———. Foreword. *Wind on the Sand: The Hidden Life of an Anchoress.* By Pinions. New York: Paulist, 1981.

———. "Four Bits." *Ploughshares* 10.2–3 (1984): 68–73.

———. *Holy the Firm.* New York: Harper, 1977.

———. Letter to William Reyer. n.d. [1978?].

———. "The Living." *Harper's Magazine* Nov. 1978: 45–64.

———. *Living by Fiction.* New York: Harper, 1982.

———. "A Note on Process." *Christian Science Monitor* Apr. 30, 1979: 25.

———. *Pilgrim at Tinker Creek.* New York: Harper's Magazine, 1974.

———. "The Purification of Poetry Right Out of the Ballpark." *Parnassus* 11 (1983–84): 287–301.

———. "Singing with the Fundamentalists." *Yale Review* 74 (1985): 312–20.

———. "Some Notes on the Uncertainty Principle." *New Lazarus Review* 1 (1978): 49.

———. *Teaching a Stone to Talk: Expeditions and Encounters.* New York: Harper, 1982.

———. "Wish I Had Pie." *Black Warrior Review* 8.2 (1982): 75–84.

Dunn, Robert Paul. "The Artist as Nun: Theme, Tone, and Vision in the Writings of Annie Dillard." *Studia Mystica* 1.4 (1978): 17–31.

Elder, John C. "John Muir and the Literature of Wilderness." *Massachusetts Review* 22 (1981): 375–86.

Eliot, T. S. *For Lancelot Andrews: Essays on Style and Order.* London: Faber and Gwyer, 1928.

———. *Four Quartets.* New York: Harcourt, 1943.

Ellsberg, Margaret R. *Created to Praise: The Language of Gerard Manley Hopkins.* New York: Oxford UP, 1987.

Emerson, Ralph Waldo. *Nature, Addresses, and Lectures.* Vol. 1 of *The Collected Works of Ralph Waldo Emerson.* Cambridge: Belknap, 1971.

Ferry, David. *The Limits of Mortality: An Essay on Wordsworth's Major Poems.* Middletown, CT: Wesleyan UP, 1959.

Fox, Stephen. *John Muir and His Legacy: The American Conservation Movement.* Boston: Little, Brown, 1981.

Frank, Joseph. *The Widening Gyre: Crisis and Mastery in Modern Literature.* New Brunswick, NJ: Rutgers UP, 1963.

Gardner, Helen. "The Landscapes of Eliot's Poetry." *Critical Quarterly* 10 (1968): 313–30.

Grumbach, Doris. Rev. of *Pilgrim at Tinker Creek*, by Annie Dillard. *New Republic* Apr. 6, 1974: 32–33.

Hargrove, Nancy. *Landscape as Symbol in the Poetry of T. S. Eliot*. Jackson: UP of Mississippi, 1978.

Haynes, Muriel. "We Are All Nibblers . . ." Rev. of *Pilgrim at Tinker Creek*, by Annie Dillard. *MS*. Aug. 1974: 38–39.

Hoffman, Eva. "Solitude." Rev. of *Pilgrim at Tinker Creek*, by Annie Dillard. *Commentary* Oct. 1974: 87–91.

Holloway, John. "The Epiphany-Poem in the Romantic Period." *Le Romantisme Anglo-Américain: Mélànges offerts a Louis Bonnerot*. Ed. Roger Asselineau et al. Paris: Didier, 1971. 55–68.

Holman, C. Hugh, and William Harmon, eds. "Sublime." *A Handbook to Literature*. 5th ed. New York: Macmillan, 1986. 489.

Hopkins, Gerard Manley. *The Correspondence of Gerard Manley Hopkins and Richard Watson Dixon*. Ed. Claude Colleer Abbott. London: Oxford UP, 1935.

——. *Further Letters of Gerard Manley Hopkins Including His Correspondence with Coventry Patmore*. Ed. Claude Colleer Abbott. 2nd ed. London: Oxford UP, 1956.

——. *The Journals and Papers of Gerard Manley Hopkins*. Ed. Humphry House. London: Oxford UP, 1959.

——. *The Letters of Gerard Manley Hopkins to Robert Bridges*. Ed. Claude Colleer Abbott. London: Oxford UP, 1935.

——. *The Poetical Works of Gerard Manley Hopkins*. Ed. Norman H. MacKenzie. Oxford: Clarendon, 1990.

Iser, Wolfgang. *The Act of Reading: A Theory of Aesthetic Responses*. Baltimore: Johns Hopkins UP, 1978.

Keats, John. *John Keats*. Ed. Elizabeth Cook. The Oxford Authors. Oxford: Oxford UP, 1990.

——. *Letters of John Keats*. Ed. Robert Gittings. Oxford: Oxford UP, 1970.

Kitchen, Paddy. *Gerard Manley Hopkins*. New York: Atheneum, 1979.

Krauth, Laurie. "Diving into Life with Annie Dillard." *The Blade* (Toledo, OH). Feb. 14, 1988, F:1–2.

Langbaum, Robert. "The Epiphanic Mode in Wordsworth and Modern Literature." *New Literary History* 14 (1983): 335–58.

Leavis, F. R. *New Bearings in English Poetry: A Study of the Contemporary Situation*. New York: George W. Steward, 1950.

Leopold, Aldo. *A Sand County Almanac and Sketches Here and There*. Oxford: Oxford UP, 1949.

Lindenberger, Herbert. *On Wordsworth's Prelude*. Princeton: Princeton UP, 1963.

Lopez, Barry Holstun. *Of Wolves and Men*. New York: Scribner's, 1978.

McConahay, Mary Davidson. " 'Into the Bladelike Arms of God': The Quest for Meaning through Symbolic Language in Thoreau and Annie Dillard." *Denver Quarterly* 20.2 (1985): 103–16.

McIlroy, Gary. "Ordinary Noons: A Comparative Literary and Cultural Study of *Walden* and *Pilgrim at Tinker Creek.*" Diss. U of Detroit, 1984.

MacKenzie, Norman H. *A Reader's Guide to Gerard Manley Hopkins*. Ithaca: Cornell UP, 1981.

Major, Mike. "Annie Dillard: Pilgrim of the Absolute." *America* May 6, 1978: 363–64.

Massey, Irving. *The Uncreating Word*. Bloomington: Indiana UP, 1970.

Miller, David S. "The Silence of Nature." *Sewanee Review* 92 (1984): 160–67.

Miller, J. Hillis. *The Disappearance of God*. Cambridge: Harvard UP, 1975.

Milroy, James. *The Language of Gerard Manley Hopkins*. London: Andre Deutsch, 1977.

Milward, Peter, S.J. *Landscape and Inscape*. Grand Rapids, MI: Eerdmans, 1975.

Moynihan, William T. "Character and Action in *Four Quartets.*" *T. S. Eliot*. Ed. Linda Wagner. New York: McGraw-Hill, 1974. 73–104.

Muir, John. *John of the Mountains: The Unpublished Journals of John Muir*. Ed. Linnied Marsh Wolfe. Boston: Houghton, 1938.

——. *The Mountains of California*. 1894. Berkeley: Ten Speed, n.d.

——. *My First Summer in the Sierra*. Foreword and A Note on the Text by Frederick Turner. Sierra Club Books. San Francisco: Yolla Bolly, 1988.

Natanson, Maurice A. "Privileged Moment: A Study in the Rhetoric of Thomas Wolfe." *Quarterly Journal of Speech* 43 (1957): 144.

Nichols, Ashton. *The Poetics of Epiphany: Nineteenth-Century Origins of the Modern Literary Moment*. Tuscaloosa: U of Alabama P, 1987.

Nigro, August. Lecture. "Thomas Hardy and T. S. Eliot: Landscape and Literature." Manchester College, Oxford, England, Aug. 10, 1988.

Pater, Walter. *The Renaissance*. Cleveland: World, 1961.

Pearce, Richard. "Voices, Stories, (W)holes: The Politics of Narration." *New Alliances in Joyce Studies: "When It's Aped to Foul a Delfian."* Ed. Bonnie Kime Scott. Newark: U of Delaware P, 1988.

Perrin, Noel. "Her Inexhaustible Mind." Rev. of *An American Childhood*, by Annie Dillard. *New York Times Book Review* Sept. 27, 1987: 7.

Peters, W. A. M., S.J. *Gerard Manley Hopkins: A Critical Essay towards the Understanding of His Poetry*. London: Oxford UP, 1948.

Phillips, Robert. Rev. of *Holy the Firm*, by Annie Dillard. *Commonweal* Feb. 3, 1978: 94.

Pick, John. Introduction. *A Hopkins Reader*. By Gerard Manley Hopkins. New York: Oxford UP, 1953. xi–xxvii.

Pope, Alexander. *Poetical Works*. Ed. Herbert Davis. London: Oxford UP, 1966.

Reimer, Margaret Loewen. "The Dialectical Vision of Annie Dillard's *Pilgrim at Tinker Creek.*" *Critique: Studies in Modern Fiction* 24 (1983): 182–91.

Riddle, Florence K. "Form as Meaning in Hopkins's Sonnet on Mortal Beauty." *Romanticism, Modernism, Postmodernism*. Ed. Harry R. Garvin. Lewisburg, PA: Bucknell UP, 1980. 69–87.

Scheick, William J. "Annie Dillard: Narrative Fringe." *Contemporary American Woman Writers: Narrative Strategies*. Ed. Catherine Rainwater and William J. Scheick. Lexington: UP of Kentucky, 1985. 51–67.

Silverman, Kaja. *The Subject of Semiotics.* New York: Oxford UP, 1983.

Smith, R. J. Rev. of *Teaching a Stone to Talk: Expeditions and Encounters,* by Annie Dillard. *Southern Humanities Review* 19 (1985): 94–95.

Stevens, Wallace. *The Collected Poems of Wallace Stevens.* New York: Knopf, 1964.

——. *Opus Posthumous.* New York: Knopf, 1957.

Swan, Annalyn. "Godspells." Rev. of *Holy the Firm,* by Annie Dillard. *Time* Oct. 10, 1977: 113–15.

Thoreau, Henry David. *Collected Poems of Henry Thoreau.* Ed. Carl Bode. Baltimore: Johns Hopkins UP, 1964.

——. *The Maine Woods.* Ed. Joseph J. Moldenhauer. Princeton: Princeton UP, 1974.

——. *Walden.* Ed. J. Lyndon Shanley. Princeton: Princeton UP, 1971.

Vaughan, Henry. "The World." *The Complete Poetry of Henry Vaughan.* Ed. French Fogle. The Stuart Editions. New York: New York UP, 1965. 231–33.

Ward, Patricia. "Annie Dillard's Way of Seeing." Rev. of *Pilgrim at Tinker Creek* and *Holy the Firm,* by Annie Dillard. *Christianity Today* 22 (1978): 974–75.

Welty, Eudora. "Meditation on Seeing." Rev. of *Pilgrim at Tinker Creek,* by Annie Dillard. *New York Times Book Review* Mar. 24, 1974: 5.

Wordsworth, William. *The Poetical Works of William Wordsworth.* 5 vols. Ed. E. de Selincourt and Helen Darbishire. Oxford: Clarendon, 1940–49.

——. "Preface" to *Lyrical Ballads. The Prose Works of William Wordsworth.* 3 vols. Ed. W. J. B. Owen and Jane Worthington Smyser. Oxford: Clarendon, 1974. 1:118–59.

——. *The Prelude 1799, 1805, 1850: Authoritative Texts, Context and Reception, Recent Critical Essays.* Ed. Jonathan Wordsworth, M. H. Abrams, and Stephen Gill. New York: Norton, 1979.

Wymard, Eleanor B. "A New Existential Voice." Rev. of *Pilgrim at Tinker Creek,* by Annie Dillard. *Commonweal* Oct. 24, 1975: 495–96.

Yeats, William Butler. *The Poems.* Vol 1 of *The Collected Works of William Butler Yeats.* Ed. Richard J. Finneran. Rev. ed. New York: Macmillan, 1989.

Index

Alphabetization is letter by letter. Titles of works not otherwise identified are by Dillard.

The Space Between
was composed in 11 ½-point Perpetua leaded ½ point
by Point West, Inc.;
printed by sheet-fed offset
on 55-pound Glatfelter Natural acid-free stock,
Smyth sewn and bound over binders boards
in ICG Arrestox B-grade cloth
and wrapped with dust jackets printed in two colors
by Braun-Brumfield, Inc.;
designed by Will Underwood;
and published by
THE KENT STATE UNIVERSITY PRESS
Kent, Ohio 44242